The Americanization of Brazil

AMERICA IN THE MODERN WORLD
STUDIES IN INTERNATIONAL HISTORY

Warren F. Kimball
Series Editor
Professor of History, Rutgers University

Volumes Published

Lawrence Spinelli, *Dry Diplomacy: The United States, Great Britain, and Prohibition* (1989). ISBN 0-8420-2298-8

Richard V. Salisbury, *Anti-Imperialism and International Competition in Central America, 1920–1929* (1989). ISBN 0-8420-2304-6

Gerald K. Haines, *The Americanization of Brazil: A Study of U.S. Cold War Diplomacy in the Third World, 1945–1954* (1989)
ISBN 0-8420-2339-9

Harry Harding and Yuan Ming, eds., *Sino-American Relations, 1945–1955: A Joint Reassessment of a Critical Decade* (1989)
ISBN 0-8420-2333-X

The Americanization of Brazil

A Study of U.S. Cold War Diplomacy in the Third World, 1945-1954

Gerald K. Haines

A Scholarly Resources Imprint
WILMINGTON, DELAWARE

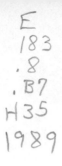

The paper used in this publication meets the minimum requirements of the American National Standard for permanence of paper for printed library materials, Z39.48, 1984.

Scholarly Resources Inc.
104 Greenhill Avenue
Wilmington, DE 19805-1897

Library of Congress Cataloging-in-Publication Data

Haines, Gerald K., 1943-
    The Americanization of Brazil: a study of U.S. cold war
diplomacy in the Third World, 1945–1954 / Gerald K. Haines.
        p. cm. — (America in the modern world; v. 3)
    Bibliography: p.
    Includes index.
    ISBN 0-8420-2339-9 (alk paper)
    1. United States — Foreign relations—Brazil. 2. Brazil—Foreign
relations—United States. 3. United States—Foreign economic
relations—Brazil. 4. Brazil—Foreign economic relations—United
States. I. Title II. Series
E183.8.B7H35 1989
327.73081—dc20   89-32065
                                                                         CIP

To Robert L. Haines,

My brother, my friend, and my trusted adviser

About the Author

Gerald K. Haines, who received his Ph.D. from the University of Wisconsin, Madison, is senior historian for the Central Intelligence Agency. Among his other work is *A Reference Guide to Department of State Special Files* (1985), winner of the Thomas Jefferson Award given in 1987 by the Society for History in the Federal Government.

Contents

Introduction

Following World War II the United States assumed, out of self-interest, responsibility for the welfare of the world capitalist system. American leaders tried to reshape the world to fit U.S. needs and standards. They perceived American security and continuing prosperity as being dependent upon the establishment of a peaceful, stable world and the maintenance of a strong international economy with free access to markets and raw materials.[1] Viewing the Soviet Union as a major threat to the achievement of this kind of world, U.S. officials came to a bipolar definition of the postwar world. From Washington's perspective, the world was reduced to two hostile and competing blocs. The United States, as leader of the capitalist world, was trying to further world peace, political democracy, and an open world trading system. The Soviet Union, leader of the Communist world, was trying to divide and disrupt the world and to impose its totalitarian system on all. During the early postwar period the United States used its enormous political and economic powers to develop and pursue a policy designed to contain Communist expansion and preserve as much of the world as possible for capitalist development.[2] This book is a study of that effort as it related to Brazil.

Although both the Harry S. Truman and the Dwight D. Eisenhower administrations concentrated most of their foreign policy efforts on Europe and Asia, they did not neglect Latin America, especially Brazil, the largest country in South America. Throughout Latin America, but especially in Brazil, U.S. policymakers worked to preserve and expand U.S. influence. They strove to maintain the area as an important market for U.S. surplus industrial production and private investments, to exploit its vast reserves of raw materials, and to keep international communism out. In short, they desired a closed hemispheric system in an open world.[3]

The Truman and Eisenhower administrations pursued essentially the same policies with regard to Brazil. They opposed economic nationalism and state control of economic life, sought a favorable climate for U.S. business and private investment, encouraged U.S. access to raw materials (especially oil and other strategic minerals), resisted "excessive industrial development," and defined world peace and prosperity in American terms and as the rejection of Communist ideology.[4] Policymakers in both administrations assumed that a reformed capitalist system would best protect and promote human liberties and enhance the economic well-being of North and South Americans alike. They firmly believed it was the mission of the United States to shape and direct Latin America's development. At the same time, both administrations attempted to avoid committing major U.S. government financing to development projects. Only when faced with direct foreign economic competition or no reasonable alternative did decision makers in the Truman and Eisenhower administrations provide direct U.S. government loans for modernization.[5] The question of providing finances for development was intertwined in all American-Brazilian negotiations regarding economic development and affected all aspects of the two countries' relations.

While Washington attempted to maintain a U.S.-dominated hemisphere, Brazilian planners embarked on a postwar economic development policy designed to make Brazil a modern, independent, industrialized nation.[6] By promoting rapid industrialization, Brazilian officials hoped to emerge from an underdeveloped semicolonial nation into a world power. Seeing themselves as pragmatists unencumbered by rigid commitment to ideas or principles, they were determined to industrialize.[7]

Brazilian leaders viewed development and especially industrial development as the hallmark of a modern economy. They desired the material standard of living of the wealthy nations of North America and Western Europe. They came close to thinking that the economic development of Brazil was the panacea that would attain all their social objectives. It would make Brazil economically independent and gain world power status for the country.[8] Development was a national goal, yet there was no consensus on the means toward this end. Some believed in a nationalist ideology that encouraged central control of the country's production and growth of the public sector to reinforce the state's predominant position. Others advocated classic economic liberalism: free trade and the development of industry without government intervention.[9]

Despite differences in style, the governments of Getúlio D. Vargas, Eurico Gaspar Dutra, and João Café Filho were all basically governments of compromise, favorably inclined toward industrialization, strong ties to the United States, and a commitment to free enterprise capitalism. Pledged to a capitalist mode of development, these governments followed similar policies. They promoted Brazil's endogenous and autonomous development in a private enterprise system under the direction of a national entrepreneurial group, and they used the state as an agency for planning, coordinating, and supplementing this effort. They increasingly viewed Brazil's relations with other states in terms of economic advantages and disadvantages.[10] Most of all, they desired U.S. government loans to help finance their development plans. They correctly saw the United States as the only power with the resources to aid their modernization efforts. Their views often came into conflict with American foreign policy goals.

This book examines the early postwar years of Brazilian development and details American efforts to control, influence, and mold Brazil's progress toward modernization. It focuses not only on American attempts to promote democracy and anticommunism in Brazil but also on Washington's endeavors to foster private enterprise, avoid direct U.S. government financing of development projects, exploit strategic resources, and promote American business practices, both in industry and in agriculture. It also examines American undertakings in cultural and social areas as integral parts of the campaign to make Brazil over in the American image, eliminate foreign competition, and integrate Brazil into an American-dominated world capitalist system.

Although I have attempted to incorporate Brazilian attitudes on internal development, economic expansion, and the role of the United States, the emphasis here is on American policy and its implementation. This work is primarily a study of American attitudes, policies, and actions. My principal interest is in explaining Washington's response to Brazilian development within the context of overall U.S. foreign policy objectives from 1945 to 1954. Consequently, this book does not pretend to be a comprehensive history of U.S.-Brazilian relations, nor does it pretend to offer the final word on the actions and motivations of other major actors: the British, Soviets, French, Germans, Japanese, or the Brazilians themselves.

The period from 1945 to 1954 was selected primarily because it was an era of major change and transition for American foreign policy, as well as a period of enormous political and economic change in Brazil. It was an era dominated by Getúlio Vargas and a time when the traditional Brazilian ruling elites were undergoing vast changes as nationalist and populist concepts emerged and the military increasingly regarded itself as the ultimate arbiter of the system. It was also a time of major changes in the Brazilian economy and of the initial emergence of Brazilian industry and Brazil as a modern society. During this period American policymakers in both Truman and Eisenhower administrations made their first attempts to deal with emerging Third

World nationalism and the Third World's political and economic problems.

Other considerations in selecting this period for study was the ready availability of primary source materials and the wide variety of secondary literature on the Truman and Eisenhower administrations as well as on Vargas. Moreover, viewed from the perspective of the present, the years from 1945 to 1954 were vital in the shaping of the American response to Third World development and to the emergence of Brazil as a new industrial nation. It is an important period for understanding subsequent policy development in both the United States and Brazil.

As for organization, the study is presented topically rather than in a strict chronology in order to focus in detail on the major aspects of U.S. policy as they applied to Brazil. This technique at times gives the reader a sense of repetitiveness, but this is outweighed by its thoroughness and precision, and it provides a sense of the pervasiveness of the American effort in Brazil.

What emerges from this study is a consistent and continuing effort on the part of American policymakers to channel and direct Brazilian development activities into areas beneficial to the United States and to preserve U.S. power and influence in the region by eliminating foreign, particularly Communist, influence and by promoting American methods and practices as well as culture.[11]

Despite setbacks, even failures, and Brazilian reluctance to accept totally American guidance and counsel, America's Brazilian policies were enormously successful. From 1945 to 1954, Brazil followed the United States' lead in opposing communism in the hemisphere and generally adhered to American theories and advice concerning developmental policies. Brazilian leaders committed their nation to a capitalistic economy and maintained strong ties to the United States.

Admittedly U.S. policymakers, animated by an all-embracing Cold War ethos, misread the internal dynamics of Brazilian society, especially its emerging nationalism and its consuming drive for industrial development. This led to later political and economic problems. However, even viewed from today, U.S. policy toward Brazil in the early postwar period appears successful. In affecting the direction of Brazilian development, Washington intensified Brazil's financial dependence on the United States, influenced its government's decisions affecting the allocation of resources, and nudged Brazil into the U.S.-dominated world trading system.[12]

Notes

1. Barton J. Bernstein, "Truman and the Cold War," in Barton J. Bernstein, ed., *Politics and Policies of the Truman Administration* (Chicago: Quadrangle Press, 1970), pp. 15–77.

2. Thomas G. Paterson, "Foreign Aid under Wraps: The Point Four Program," *Wisconsin Magazine of History* 56:2 (1972–73): 120; Paterson, "The Quest for Peace and Prosperity: International Trade, Communism, and the Marshall Plan," in Bernstein, ed., *Politics and Policies of the Truman Administration*, pp. 78–112; Bernstein, "Truman and the Cold War," pp. 16–18.

3. David Green, "The Cold War Comes to Latin America," in Bernstein, ed., *Politics and Policies of the Truman Administration*, p. 165. See also Stanley Hilton, "The United States, Brazil, and the Cold War, 1945–1960: End of the Special Relationship," *Journal of American History* 68:3 (December 1981): 599–624. Hilton makes the traditional claim that U.S. policymakers neglected Brazil during this period.

4. Samuel L. Baily, *The United States and the Development of South America*, 1945–1975 (New York: New Viewpoints, 1976), pp. 51, 54–58; John G. Stoessinger, *The Might of Nations: World Politics in Our Times*, rev. ed. (New York: Random House, 1965); Stephen G. Rabe, *Eisenhower and Latin America: The Foreign Policy of Anticommunism* (Chapel Hill: University of North Carolina Press, 1988), pp. 82–83.

5. See, for example, Harrison R. Wagner, *United States Policy toward Latin America* (Stanford: Stanford University Press, 1970); and Gordon Connell-Smith, *The United States and Latin America* (New York: John Wiley, 1974).

6. Development usually denotes the expansion of a society's productive capacity. More broadly construed, and as used in this study, it refers to the whole range of changes in technological, political, social, and cultural practices that accompany and facilitate economic expansion. It is a total process encompassing economic, political, and social transformations resulting in the improvement of the standard of living and the general welfare. It is not a purely economic problem, although the economic aspects predominate. See Luiz Carlos Bresser Pereira, *Development and Crisis in Brazil, 1930–1982*, trans. Marcia Van Dyke (Boulder, CO: Westview Press, 1984), p. 5; and Maria Helena Moreira Alves, *The State and Opposition in Military Brazil* (Austin: University of Texas Press, 1985), pp. 3–4.

7. Frank Bonilla, "A National Ideology for Development: Brazil," in Kalman H. Silvert, ed., *Expectant Peoples: Nationalism and Development* (New York: Random House, 1966).

8. Robert T. Daland, Brazilian Planning: *Development, Politics and Administration* (Chapel Hill: University of North Carolina Press, 1967), p. 74; Nathaniel H. Leff, *Economic Policy Making and Development in Brazil, 1947–1964* (New York: Wiley, 1968), pp. 46–47. See also E. Bradford Burns, *Nationalism in Brazil: A Historical Survey* (New York: Praeger, 1968).

9. See Thomas E. Skidmore, *Politics in Brazil, 1930–1964: An Experiment in Democracy* (New York: Oxford University Press, 1967), for a discussion of these groups.

10. See Hélio Jaguaribe, *Economic and Political Development: A Theoretical Approach and a Brazilian Case Study* (Cambridge: Harvard University Press, 1968), p. 178; Peter Flynn, Brazil: *A Political Analysis* (Boulder, CO: Westview Press, 1979), pp. 141–43; Charles H. Daugherty, "Foreign Policy Decision Making in Brazil: Case Studies in Brazilian Policy towards the Soviet Union, 1945–1961" (Ph.D. diss., Georgetown University, 1974), p. 122; and Pereira, *Development and Crisis in Brazil*, p. 11.

11. See Rabe, *Eisenhower and Latin America*, p. 39. Both administrations sincerely believed that if Brazil simply followed the U.S. example, both nations would benefit.

12. See Hilton, "United States, Brazil, and the Cold War," pp. 599–624; Harry Magdoff, "Imperialism without Colonies," in Roger Owen and Robert Sutcliffe, eds., *Studies in the Theory of Imperialism* (London: Longman, 1977), pp. 144–70; and Diego C. Asencio, "Brazil and the United States: Friendly Competitors," in Julian M. Chacel, Pamela S. Falk, and David V. Fleischer, eds., *Brazil's Economic and Political Future* (Boulder, CO: Westview Press, 1988), pp. 247–51.

Chapter One

Attitudes and Images

The goals and objectives of American policymakers concerning Brazil in the early postwar period can be best understood by placing their attitudes and policies within the overall framework of the great geopolitical changes that occurred after World War II and America's perception of this postwar world. A brief examination of the images and stereotypes that Americans and Brazilians held of themselves, each other, and their respective positions in the world sheds light on U.S. policy toward Brazil and its drive for development.[1]

World War II precipitated the emergence of two great superpowers and the reduction of the major prewar European nations and Japan to secondary roles. By 1945, Europe lay devastated, civil war raged in China, and the preeminent position of Britain and France in much of the underdeveloped world was under attack by rising nationalist forces. In Latin America the net effect of the war was to freeze traditional regimes in power as the United States worked to maintain stability in the region and to enhance its dominance.[2]

The war also, however, produced pressures that made the maintenance of the status quo progressively more difficult. The "revolution of rising expectations" and a vigorous, broad-based, and assertive nationalism swept the world at the very time Washington fixed its attention almost exclusively on the Cold War and the Soviet Union.[3]

For most American policymakers preoccupied with the reconstruction of Europe and Asia, confronted with the disorganization of the international political and economic order, and saddled with new worldwide responsibilities, the Western Hemisphere and its developmental problems took a subordinate place in foreign policy considerations. Placing a tertiary value on events in Latin America, high-level officials in both the Truman and Eisenhower administrations left the area to middle-level and lower-level subordinates. Even when confronted with a major crisis in Latin America, U.S. officials generally saw the problem in terms of the Cold War and confrontation with the Soviet Union. Washington had a great deal of difficulty placing such developmental problems as Brazil was experiencing in a foreign policy increasingly dominated by events in other parts of the world.[4]

The United States emerged from the war stronger than ever in terms of its overall military strength, its worldwide economic power, and its political and cultural prestige. Many Americans envisioned the postwar world as the opening of an "American Century" built upon the forward-looking principles of American internationalism and the sharing of American political institutions, industrial products, and technical skills.[5] American leaders continuously emphasized the role of the United States as the guarantor of a prosperous world peace. As a matter both of national self-interest and of world betterment, the United States would use its power to help develop the resources, the standards of living, and the prosperity of peace-loving countries the world over. In short, American officials projected an image of the United States as the guardian and promoter of the free enterprise system, as the exporter of technology, as the international Good Samaritan, and as the protector against godless communism.[6] Postwar policymakers in both the Truman and Eisenhower administrations espoused the classical liberal belief that human progress could be best served by the free flow of men, goods, and ideas within and among nations.

To most of these policymakers the United States was the epitome of the successful modern state with competitive dynamic capitalism as its touchstone. They looked out on a universe that they believed was predictable and intelligible. Rational solutions were possible, and every problem had a solution. Their world was on the threshold of the ultimate integration of science, technology, and production. It was a world operated by technicians according to the hierarchical model of modern administrative management. There were no natural limits to the increase of scientific knowledge or to technological innovation. The United States represented the possibility of infinite power, subject only to the limitation of finite resources. It was a society based on modernity and progress, a society of "growth and prosperity without end."[7] Only communism threatened the creation of this prosperous peaceful world.

The image projected by Washington during this period was one of a stable participatory democracy with well-functioning political institutions, strong political parties, self-confident chief executives, a judiciary beyond reproach, and a uniquely effective system of separate institutions sharing powers. American policymakers pointed toward a growing, prosperous economy and an efficient society of hard-working people committed to the work ethic. They boasted of a fiscally responsible and prudent system featuring balanced budgets and sound investment policies.[8] These beliefs provided American officials with a rationale for the pursuit of an energetic economic internationalism and for the cultivation of major foreign markets, both politically and commercially. What these policymakers sought was a U.S.-dominated trading and political system.[9] They assumed that America had interests in common with other nations and that U.S. intentions were good, even benevolent.

At the same time that American leaders called for an open world, they looked upon Latin America and the entire Western Hemisphere as falling within the unique sphere of influence of the United States. In accordance with the rhetoric of the Monroe Doctrine and the Good Neighbor policy, they expected the other American republics to follow Washington's lead and help eliminate or expel foreign ideology and economic theory from the hemisphere. If the rest of the international system should fail, the United States should have a secure, stable hemisphere to fall back upon, reasoned military and civilian leaders.[10]

Closely related to the perceptions the American public and its leaders shared of their own society, the rest of the world, and the Western Hemisphere were the images and attitudes they held regarding Brazil and its people. Perhaps, most importantly, the general American public exhibited little interest in Brazil. The sparse newspaper and journal coverage of the country, the small number of college courses offered on Brazil and the Portuguese language, and the almost complete lack of radio programs or films featuring any aspect of Brazilian culture or society all reflected this fact. What images that did filter through to the general public were often crude and condescending and reflected deep-seated preconceptions and stereotypes developed in Hollywood and popular magazines. This was a version of life in the tropics, especially the Amazon and the legendary easygoing Rio de Janeiro, that pictured Brazil as a land of stark contrasts. There were the endless white sandy beaches, the idle rich, and the Copacabana Casino as well as the deep, unexplored, massive jungle inhabited by cannibals.[11] John Gunther wrote, for example, of the overwhelming feeling he had while visiting Brazil that the "untamed wilderness seeps into the cities, oozes into the suburbs and proliferates in the gardens, and crawls into your backyard."[12]

The myth of the fabulous wealth and potential of Brazil also persisted in the American mind. Terms such as the "great promised land" and the "sleeping giant" were common in the scant literature available in the United States on Brazil. Dean G. Acheson, for example, upon his return from a trip through Latin America, described to a congressional committee his tremendous enthusiasm for the future of Brazil. "It was a glorious country with all sorts of possibilities for development. They have none of the problems which exist in other hopeful parts of the world."[13] Others pictured Brazil as a study in superlatives. Gunther envisioned it as a great land and people richly endowed and awaiting development.[14] The noted geographer Preston James projected Brazil as the Latin American country with the greatest possibilities for future growth, and Oliver Holmes in *Foreign Policy Report* described the Brazilians as having something of the same dynamic psychology that had prompted the peoples of the United States to consolidate the resources of their continental domain. They were easygoing, intelligent, receptive to new ideas, and confident in their future.

Both James and Holmes cautioned, however, that the Brazilian character, unlike the American, tended to the opportune, to "the ideal of collecting the fruit without planting the tree."[15] Inherent in much of the literature was a patronizing attitude and a pervasive racial arrogance—explicit or implicit—that relegated the mixed Brazilian nation to a second-class status.[16] For example, Louis Halle of the Department of State Policy Planning Staff, writing under the pseudonym "Y" in *Foreign Affairs*, cautioned that the Latin American countries were "like children." The United States would have to follow a policy of noblesse oblige toward them, for they were not yet ready to exercise for themselves the responsibility of adult nations.[17]

State Department official George F. Kennan also set forth this ambivalent view of Brazilians and Latin Americans in a long memorandum he prepared after a fact-finding trip to Latin America in 1950. Kennan compared the prospect for South America, with its "unhappy and hopeless" background for the conduct of human life, with that of the great North American continent. He depicted the Mississippi serving a "great basin of fertility" in contrast with the Amazon reaching "great fingers into a region singularly hostile to human activity," and contrasted the highly developed United States with the great pathless expanse of central Brazil.[18]

The official attitude of the U.S. government toward Brazil was far more reserved, although not much different in substance. Like the general public, major decision makers in the Truman administration (such as President Truman himself, Secretary of State Dean Acheson, and his close adviser Clark Clifford) showed little direct interest in Brazil or Brazilian affairs. Similarly, President Eisenhower and his secretary of state, John Foster Dulles, were inattentive to Brazilian concerns. Mid-level and low-level officials, especially in the Department of State, were left to make the everyday decisions regarding Brazilian affairs.[19] As spelled out by the Brazilian and Latin American experts in the department, U.S. policy recognized that Brazil was the largest and most populous country in Latin America, was traditionally the closest ally of the United States in the Western Hemisphere, dominated the South Atlantic and was thus strategically located vis-à-vis Africa, and possessed great economic potential. But these officials also cautioned that Brazil was still a backward country with vast underdeveloped regions. It had only a rudimentary transportation system, and a great majority of its population was illiterate and poverty-stricken.[20] Privately, they often spoke of Brazil as the world's largest banana republic and ridiculed its leadership for its "absurd pretensions."[21]

For their part, Brazilian policymakers exhibited the xenophobia with which elites on the Latin American periphery of the Atlantic world typically viewed the industrial powers. They had a deep colonialist inferiority complex. They thought of themselves as racial and intellectual inferiors to the industrialized peoples, without the same capacity for work, initiative, and success.[22] Nevertheless, Brazilian leaders were determined to "modernize," that is, to recreate Brazil in the image of the United States or Western Europe. Like their counterparts elsewhere in the underdeveloped world, Brazilian officials wanted rapid development and social progress. They saw in the United States an unambiguous example of how prodigious growth could be achieved. They tended to copy foreign political institutions and the financial and economic practices of the industrial countries, especially the United States, without considering economic, social, and national differences.[23] Brazilian policymakers committed themselves to Western-style industrial development as a means of establishing their country's economic and political independence, and they identified Brazil's future with industrialization, urbanization, and modernization.[24] Brazilian thought on development was also shaped by a belief that European and North American expansion had resulted in the developed countries' exploitative control over the Third World.

Brazilians in general distrusted American motives, and most perceived that Brazilian interests were kept subservient to U.S. capitalist interests.[25]

Convinced that because of its great size and economic potential Brazil would inevitably become a great power, its leaders expressed their resentment toward any implication of colonial status and insisted upon Brazil's right to a more important position in international affairs. Brazil was, according to this view, an apprentice world power. Brazilian politicians considered their country to be the preeminent nation in South America, and they expected support from the United States in maintaining this preeminence, especially vis-à-vis Argentina.[26] At the same time, these officials and most of the Brazilian public expected the United States to be influential, attributed influence to it, and credited it with far more of a role in the shaping of world events than it actually had.[27]

Just as U.S. citizens had a stereotyped image of Brazilians so, too, did Brazilians perceive Americans. The Brazilian public, unlike its northern counterpart, however, sought out things American. The U.S. presence in Brazil grew as consumption on the U.S. model was actively pursued and American cultural ways invaded Brazilian society. According to most Brazilians, Americans were rich and powerful. They had houses, automobiles, and televisions. Gleaning their knowledge from American films, television, and popular magazines, many Brazilians saw a powerful, suburban-idealized, middle-class white America; ruthless and violent organized crime; and a mythical western-frontier cowboy justice.[28]

These images, attitudes, and stereotypes had a profound effect on U.S. efforts to direct Brazilian affairs. Each side, America as well as Brazil, had a tendency to oversimplify and stereotype the other's motivations and to ignore the completely different frames of reference and cultural backgrounds. Each side wrongly perceived the situation by projecting its own norms and values on the other. American policymakers formulated and projected a policy almost entirely based on images and myths, with no regard for Brazilian sensitivity or cultural differences. A closer examination of the political, economic, and cultural aspects of these policies and objectives will illustrate more clearly the interplay and influence of these images and attitudes on U.S. policy toward Brazil.

Notes

1. For a discussion of the effect of attitudes and images in relations between countries see Akira Iriye, "Culture and Power: International Relations as Intercultural Relations," *Diplomatic History* 3:2 (1979): 115–20.

2. See Baily, *Development of South America*, pp. 51–54; and Edwin Lieuwen and Miguel Jarrin, *Post-World War II Political Development in Latin America* (Study prepared at the request of the Subcommittee on American Republic Affairs of the Senate Foreign Relations Committee, November 19, 1959, Washington, DC: Government Printing Office, 1959).

3. See Robert J. McMahon, "The Eisenhower Administration and Third World Nationalism: A Review Essay, Critique of the Revisionists," *Political Science Quarterly* 101:3 (1986): 453–73. For a general description of the Cold War see John Lewis Gaddis, *Strategies of Containment: A Critical Appraisal of Postwar American National Security Policy* (New York: Oxford University Press, 1982); and J. Samuel Walker, "The Cold War," in Gerald K. Haines and J. Samuel Walker, eds., *American Foreign Relations: A Historiographical Review* (Westport: Greenwood Press, 1981), pp. 187–98.

4. See David Green, *The Containment of Latin America: A History of the Myths and Realities of the Good Neighbor Policy* (Chicago: Quadrangle Press, 1971); Green, "The Cold War Comes to Latin America"; Baily, *Development of South America*; Stanley Hilton, "The United States, Brazil, and the Cold War"; Richard H. Immerman, "Guatemala as Cold War History," *Political Science Quarterly* 94 (Winter 1979–80): 575–99; and Immerman, *The CIA in Guatemala: The Foreign Policy of Intervention* (Austin: University of Texas Press, 1983).

5. See Green, *Containment*, p. 116; and Stephen G. Rabe, *Eisenhower and Latin America*, p. 12. See also Henry Luce, editorial, *Life* 10:61 (February 17, 1941): 3; and W. A. Swanberg, *Luce and His Empire* (New York: Charles Scribner and Sons, 1972), pp. 80–83.

6. Green, *Containment*, pp. 116–17.

7. Thomas E. Skidmore, *Black into White, Race and Nationality in Brazilian Thought* (New York: Oxford University Press, 1974), pp. 124–25; Tom J. Farer, "Reagan Country," *New York Review of Books* 27:20 (December 18, 1980): 9–10.

8. For a comparison with attitudes in the 1980s see Abraham F. Lowenthal, "Manana Land No More," *Washington Post*, January 20, 1981.

9. Green, *Containment*, pp. 19–20.

10. See Baily, *Development of South America*, pp. 65–67; and the testimony of Secretary of War Robert Patterson, Fleet Admiral Chester Nimitz, and General of the Army Dwight D. Eisenhower before the House Foreign Affairs Committee, U.S. Congress, House Foreign Affairs Committee, *Hearings on Inter-American Military Cooperation Act, 1947*, 80th Cong., 1st sess. (Washington, DC: Government Printing Office, 1947), pp. 26–44.

11. See Hollywood's *Flying Down to Rio*, and *The Man from Rio*. A review of the periodical literature available in the United States for the period 1945–1954 revealed only 92 articles on Brazil, compared with over 250 on China for the same period. See *Readers Guide to Periodical Literature, 1945 to 1954*, vols. 14–19 (New York: H. W. Wilson Co., 1945–1955). A review of the *New York Times Index* yielded similar results: 33 articles on Brazil and 121 on China. See *New York Times Index, 1945–1954*, vols. 33–42 (New York: New York Times Co., 1946–1955).

12. John Gunther, *Inside Latin America* (New York: Harper, 1947), pp. 37–71.

13. U.S. Congress, Senate Foreign Relations Committee, *Report of the Secretary of State to the Committee*, 83d Cong., 1st sess. (Washington, DC: Government Printing Office, 1953), 5:26.

14. Gunther, *Inside Latin America*, p. 37.

15. Oliver Holmes, "Brazil: Rising Power in the Americas," *Foreign Policy Reports* 27 (October 15, 1945): 210–19; Preston James, *Latin America* (New York: Odyssey Press, 1946), p. 400; Hubert Herring, *A History of Latin America from the Beginnings to the Present* (New York: Alfred A. Knopf, 1963), pp. 723–24. See also Roy Nash, "God, Coffee and Conversation," *U.N. World* 4 (October 1950): 36.

16. See John F. Santos, "A Psychologist Reflects on Brazil and Brazilians," in Eric N. Baklanoff, ed., *New Perspectives of Brazil* (Nashville: Vanderbilt University Press, 1966), pp. 233–63; and Flynn, *Brazil: A Political Analysis*.

17. See Louis Halle [Y, pseud.], "On a Certain Impatience with Latin America," *Foreign Affairs* 18 (July 1950): 565–79.

18. Memorandum from George F. Kennan (counselor of the State Department) to secretary of state, March 29, 1950, U.S. Department of State, *Papers Relating to the Foreign Relations of the United States, 1950* (Washington, DC: Government Printing Office, 1978), 2:598–607 (hereafter cited as *FRUS* followed by year). For Kennan's account of the background and reception of this report see Kennan, *Memoirs: 1925–1950* (Boston: Little Brown and Company, 1967), pp. 476–84. See also Roger Trask, "George F. Kennan's Report on Latin America," *Diplomatic History* 2:3 (Summer 1978): 307–12.

19. A review of the major manuscript collections at the Harry S. Truman and Dwight D. Eisenhower presidential libraries reveals, not unexpectedly, that major U.S. officials devoted most of their time and effort to Europe, Asia, and the Middle East. See also Beatrice Bishop Berle and Travis Beal Jacobs, eds., *Navigating the Rapids, 1918–1971* (New York: Harcourt Brace Jovanovich, 1973), p. 538.

20. Memorandum by DuWayne Clark, "Objectives of U.S. Policy towards Brazil," July 2, 1948, Decimal File 711.328/7-248, General Records of the Department of State (DS), Record Group 59, Diplomatic Branch, National Archives, Washington, DC (hereafter cited as RG 59, NA).

21. See foreword by Ronald M. Schreider, in Wayne A. Selcher, ed., *Brazil in the International System: The Rise of a Middle Power* (Boulder, CO: Westview Press, 1981), p. xvi.

22. Bresser Pereira, *Development and Crisis in Brazil*, 1930-1983, pp. 12–13.

23. Bresser Pereira, *Development and Crisis in Brazil*, p. 13.

24. Division of Research for the American Republics, Intelligence and Research Report 7433, "Brazil—Recent Developments and Probable Trends," February 20, 1957, RG 59, NA; Daland, *Brazilian Planning*, p. 5.

25. Robert Wesson, *The United States and Brazil: Limits of Influence* (New York, Praeger, 1981), p. 5.

26. R & A Report 7433, "Brazil—Recent Developments and Probable Trends," RG 59, NA.

27. Wesson, *Limits of Influence*, p. 4.

28. See Chapter 9, "Cultural Relations and Projecting a Favorable American Image," for a more detailed account of U.S. influence in this area.

Chapter Two

Nurturing a Political System

Politically, American policy toward Brazil from 1945 to 1954 was cautious yet optimistic. Officials in the Truman administration actively promoted democratic institutions in Brazil and generally approved of the Brazilian turn toward a more open political system. When the Brazilian military forced Getúlio Vargas from office in 1945 and called for elections, Washington viewed the action as a step toward democracy. The victory of Eurico Gaspar Dutra further encouraged American policymakers that, indeed, Brazil had become a democracy. American advisers even helped draft a new Brazilian constitution modeled on the U.S. version. Even the election of Vargas to the presidency in 1950 was seen by Washington as "progress." According to the Americans, he had been democratically elected, and the military would watch his every move to ensure that Brazil remained a democracy.

Increasing world tensions, Cold War attitudes, and a growing disillusionment with the ability of the Brazilians to institute democratic reforms brought a change to American policy and attitudes in the early 1950s. Both the Truman and Eisenhower administrations now mainly sought stability and order in Brazil. A strong anti-Communist Brazil, closely allied with the United States, was more important to Washington than were fostering democracy and nurturing Brazil as a proving ground for democratic institutions.[1]

As spelled out by the experts in the Department of State at the end of World War II, the United States based its relations with Brazil on "mutual confidence, effective cooperation, and close friendship." These experts pictured past policies toward Brazil as highly successful. To them, Brazil traditionally had been the closest ally of the United States in Latin America. Despite its flirtation with fascism during the 1930s, Brazil had sided with the United States against the Nazi menace and had cooperated more fully than any other South American government in the war effort. It had sent an expeditionary force to Italy and had allowed the United States to build and operate air and naval bases within its boundaries for the conduct of military operations in the south Atlantic and Africa. These State Department experts cast Brazil as the keystone in the planning and realization of their policy toward Latin America. Reasoning that Brazil was not only the largest and most populous country in Latin America but also, by the end of the war, the most powerful military and economic nation in the region, a State Department position paper concluded that the United States had to intensify its political relationship through cooperation and consultation on every matter involving the interests of the two countries. The position paper emphasized that it would be difficult, despite Brazil's underdeveloped status, to exaggerate its importance to the United States.[2]

Throughout the early postwar period, American policymakers confidently believed that the Brazilian people, and indeed most of the people of the world, wanted to see the kind of international order envisioned in the Atlantic Charter and the Moscow declarations. That is, they wanted to see a world based on sovereign equality, a world guaranteeing people the right to choose their own forms of government, and a world made increasingly prosperous with the expansion of international trade. Moreover, American policymakers believed that Brazil was moving progressively toward becoming a more democratic society based solidly on American principles. The United States simply had to nurture this process along. The reasoning behind this was somewhat questionable, however, for Brazil had no long democratic tradition, and dominating Brazilian politics during this period was Getúlio Vargas.

Vargas rose to power during the 1930s, a period of international crisis and growing disenchantment with democratic forms. On November 3, 1930, a military junta installed Vargas, the defeated candidate for the presidency, as provisional chief of Brazil and terminated the Old Republic, driving from power the agrarian commercial oligarchy that had dominated Brazil for four centuries.[3]

Vargas promised "political renovation" and solidified the support of the Brazilian military behind his regime by promising to build up the armed forces. Following an armed rebellion from the Left in November 1933, Vargas consolidated his power, promising stability and national unity. Forming a strong, centralized government, he embraced authoritarian corporatism and abandoned liberal democracy.

In 1937, Vargas imposed his Estado Novo. Under this "New State," he dissolved congress and all political parties and ruled as a dictator. He established an authoritarian government internally and, after flirting with the Axis powers, adhered to a pro-Allied foreign policy. Vargas called his Estado Novo "a disciplined democracy,"[4] and he claimed that he "had saved Brazilian democracy from contamination of extreme ideologies" and had protected Brazil from communism.[5] This new political system was a highly personal creation despite the corporatist trappings. Brazil from 1930 to 1945 remained conservative, paternalistic, and dominated by the rule of one man, Getúlio Vargas.[6]

During the war U.S. opinion makers painted a favorable picture of Vargas. John Gunther, for example, stated that although Brazil was a dictatorship it had considerable roots in popular support and, on the whole, was benevolent. Moreover, he added, a strong, stable, friendly Brazil was much more important to the United States than were Brazilian domestic civil liberties.[7] Adolf A. Berle, the U.S. ambassador to Brazil, echoed these sentiments. For Berle, although the Brazilian government was a dictatorship, it had kept all of its international obligations, and there was "nothing remotely resembling a police state, exaggerated espionage or terrorism here." Vargas, Berle reported, was the most popular person in Brazil. People trusted him and liked him. Berle, imbued with the American concepts of good government and democracy, warned, however, that a dictatorship is not a popular form of government and that such a style of government always makes people uneasy and afraid.[8]

With the close of the war, pressures increased both internally and externally for Vargas to ease his dictatorial rule and to call elections. Within Brazil itself there were increasing demands for a more open, participatory system. The overwhelming victory of the democratic Allied powers also influenced Brazilian optimism about democratic reforms.[9]

In the United States, the soon-to-be assistant secretary of state for American republic affairs, Spruille Braden, put forth the view that the interests of the United States required like-minded, friendly, sympathetic neighbors and a high degree of hemispheric solidarity. Since democracy must prevail in Latin America before such conditions can be ensured, he reasoned, it should be U.S. policy to encourage democracy by demonstrating a warm friendship for democratic and reputable governments and to discourage dictatorship and disreputable governments by treating them as something less than friends and equals.[10]

Berle and the American embassy in Brazil seemed to be following this advice when they discreetly let it be known that the United States hoped Brazil might return to the path of constitutional democracy. When Vargas bowed to the pressure and moved to hold elections, Berle became increasingly confident that democracy was returning to Brazil. He wrote that "every Brazilian now has available to himself all of the resources available to any American during a political campaign: he can make a speech, hire a hall, circulate a petition, run a newspaper, post handbills, organize a parade, solicit support, get radio time, form committees, organize a political party, and otherwise make any peaceable bid for the suffrage and support of his countrymen."[11] Berle proposed that the embassy continue its policy of quietly encouraging the progress of Brazil toward democratic government. Vargas was not another Juan D. Perón, Berle explained to President Truman. Although a dictator, under quiet encouragement from the Americans he had made the press free, pledged elections, granted amnesty to all political prisoners, and proposed a new election law.[12]

When Vargas seemed to back away from his program of election reforms, however, Berle spoke out on the issue, siding with those demanding elections. After showing his speech to Vargas and discussing it with Braden, who was returning to the United States from Argentina to become assistant secretary of state, Berle delivered his address at the Hotel Quitandinha in Petrópolis on September 29, 1945. He declared that the American public watched with growing happiness moves taken by the Brazilian government to restore constitutional democracy, notably freedom of the press, freedom of political organization, freedom from political constraint, and the announcement of elections. Berle noted that the American people particularly welcomed President Vargas's declaration that he had no intention other than to preside over peaceful elections and to turn over the government to duly elected candidates.[13] Despite this seemingly mild approach, Vargas and his followers immediately attacked the speech as interference by the United States in Brazilian domestic affairs.[14]

Despite the uproar Berle's speech caused, it was Vargas's internal maneuvering and internal politics, not the United States, that prompted the Brazilian military to force him from office in 1945. Fearing his popular appeal, the military pressured him to resign, installed President of the Supreme Court José Linhares as interim president, and declared that elections would proceed as scheduled.[15] These actions delighted Washington. According to the Brazilian Division of the State Department, October 30 marked the end of a fifteen-year period of virtual one-man rule and the beginning of a new era of constitutional parliamentary government.[16]

Viewing the military as a force for democracy, Ambassador Berle remained optimistic. He believed that developments in Brazil were encouraging, that Brazil was now "firmly established on the road to democratic institutions, and that public opinion had been aroused to the extent that any setback was unlikely."[17] Observing the elections on December 7, 1945, Berle wrote in his diary: "They were as fairly done as a country could do it, certainly in Rio. I have seen plenty of worse elections in the United States. As for the attitude of the Brazilians they were free and they were happy and they liked it."[18] Overlooked were the facts that the electorate in 1945 excluded illiterates and enlisted men (over half of the population) and that Brazil had no strong background in the democratic process.[19] Moreover, the election still was fought between the "ins" and the "outs" of elitist politics. Mass political participation was not yet a reality.[20]

To American officials, however, the victory of Eurico Gaspar Dutra and his party, the Partido Social Democrático (PSD), appeared to continue the democratization of Brazil. The new government would be somewhat conservative, the Americans predicted, so no radical changes should be expected. The Dutra administration, according to the State Department, reflected the desires of the majority of Brazilians and provided political stability.[21]

One of the first tasks of the Dutra regime was the promulgation of a new constitution. American policymakers hoped that it would reflect the "democratic aspirations of the Brazilian people." To the American way of thinking this could best be ensured by the adoption of U.S. style institutions and procedures. The Brazilian constitution of 1946 was, in fact, similar in form to that of the United States. It established a government for the United States of Brazil composed of one federal district, twenty states, and four territories. The states and the federal district each elected three senators to serve for eight years in the upper legislative body. Members of the lower house, the Chamber of Deputies, were elected by proportional representation on the basis of population and served for four years. The president was directly elected for a five-year term and could not succeed himself. The basic rights and freedoms of citizens were guaranteed. The constitution even contained an article that combined the principles of the Sherman Anti-Trust Act and the basic regulations of the Federal Trade Commission.[22]

Unlike the U.S. system, however, under certain circumstances the federal government could intervene in the states, replacing a state's government by a federally appointed intervenor. In case of serious internal disorder or war the federal government also could declare a state of siege under which constitutional guarantees could be suspended. The constitution excluded from the franchise illiterates, enlisted soldiers, and people who could not speak Portuguese. It also recognized the special role of the armed forces not only in defending the country but also in safeguarding the constitutional powers and preserving law and order. In addition, it kept largely intact the whole body of corporatist-inspired social and labor legislation from the Estado Novo.[23]

American officials glossed over these differences, however, calling them "common to most Latin American republics."[24] Even the outlawing of the Communist party and the curtailing of freedom of speech by the Dutra regime failed to dampen American optimism that Brazil was moving toward democracy. U.S. Ambassador William Pawley concluded in 1948 that Brazil had taken the correct path in its return to democracy and could not be considered a police state.[25]

Although by 1949 American experts considered Dutra to be a somewhat weak president because of internal economic problems, they remained cautiously optimistic about Brazil's political future. The Dutra government continued, according to this view, to embody the hopes of Brazilians of all classes who wanted to return to democracy. A Brazilian Affairs Division memorandum concluded that the United States should extend all the assistance it could to Brazil during this critical time if the "reborn faltering democracy is to survive."[26] The United States took little action, however, to brace up Brazilian democracy. China was about to fall to the Communists, and Washington riveted its attention there and on the Soviet Union. Some U.S. officials, despite the growing world crisis, continued to follow the Brazilian situation, and they remained optimistic about the future of Brazil as its leaders prepared for general elections in 1950.

The elections saw the reemergence of Getúlio Vargas as a presidential candidate. Now sixty-seven years old, he identified himself with the new, expanding, industrial and urban Brazil and with the working masses in contrast to the social and political elites. He vigorously attacked the Dutra administration.

In the main, this was election rhetoric, but it made U.S. officials nervous. They viewed the general elections of 1950, with Vargas a declared presidential candidate, as crucial in determining whether Brazil would be able to continue its progress toward democracy or would sink into a welter of conflicting interests out of which order could be brought only by some form of authoritarianism. To the Truman administration officials most concerned with Brazilian affairs,

Brazil was "still feeling its way toward a functioning constitutional democracy." If the fifteen years of Vargas's dictatorship were considered black and the desired democratic representative government white, the tenure of office of President Dutra would appear light gray, according to this view. Picturing democracy as an intricate and delicate institution and the Brazilians as lacking experience in its operation, U.S. officials nevertheless saw Brazil moving slowly and haltingly toward a democratic system. U.S. observers thought that most of the forms of democracy had been established, and many of the iniquitous features of the dictatorship had been, if not eradicated, at least suppressed. What was needed was a period of relative political tranquillity in which these democratic forms could acquire sufficient substance and strength to resist any possible future tendency toward a centralized strongman type of government.[27]

The presidential election of 1950 was a critical test. If Vargas won, the Brazil watchers within the Truman administration constantly asked themselves, would he be content to govern within the constitution? Convinced that the democratic elements of Brazil, especially among the armed forces, would be watching the course of any government headed by Vargas very closely and would resist successfully a possible return to one-man rule, U.S. confidence in the progress of Brazil toward genuine democracy remained firm.[28] Vargas, indeed, did win and took office in 1951. It was the first time in Brazilian history that an incumbent government had lost an election.[29]

Although soon weary of his "developmental nationalism," with its proposals for government control of natural resources and limitations of foreign capital, and his rhetoric of national regeneration through social welfare programs, working-class political activity, and economic nationalism, American officials took comfort in the fact that Vargas had at least been democratically elected.[30] Moreover, despite some reservations, most Department of State policymakers believed that Vargas would be pro-American in his foreign policy and would continue the cooperation and loyalty that he had exhibited during the Second World War. Edward G. Miller, chief of the American Republics Division, for example, believed that, although Vargas would "do his best to extract the maximum from us" and would "drive a hard bargain," in the long run he would continue the ties of old friendship and the spirit of cooperation. Even Vargas's flirtation with Juan Perón of Argentina and talk of a reorientation toward Europe, according to Miller, were only attempts to bring greater pressure on the United States for increased aid and attention. "There was absolutely no doubt as to Vargas's ultimate position when the chips are down," he declared.[31] Echoing previous arguments that the Vargas regime in the 1940s had been authoritarian rather than totalitarian and that Brazil was the keystone to U.S. policy in South America, Miller advocated that the United States continue to support Vargas and to encourage his strong collaboration with the United States.[32]

The gradual accumulation of serious economic problems and increasing political tension in Brazil prompted the Eisenhower administration to initiate a fresh survey of the Brazilian political scene in 1953. A State Department report reflected this new assessment. Although it pictured Vargas's political techniques as unsuitable to either proper policy formulation or efficient administration of a government under a constitutional parliamentary regime, the report left little doubt that Vargas would continue to govern within the limitations established by the constitution. Since his election in 1950 he had not attempted to convert the armed forces into a totalitarian instrument, nor had he seriously embarked upon the task of organizing the Brazilian masses into a cohesive political force that would support a bid for absolute power. Although the possibility existed that Vargas might repeat the pattern of 1937 and attempt to seize arbitrary power, the report concluded, there were solid bases for discounting that contention. Vargas was seventy-one years old, tired, and lacked the drive to construct an authoritarian machine. Moreover, the social forces upon which to base an authoritarian regime did not exist in Brazil, and the armed forces watched his every move.[33]

While discounting any effort by Vargas to return to the strongman-style government, the State Department report also reflected a growing American skepticism about developing a democratic system in Brazil. It dismissed the political parties as ineffective and unable to provide leadership to the nation. It saw organized labor as politically immature and incapable of providing leaders or counsel. According to the report, commercial and industrial interests were divided and confined themselves to sporadic lobbying on issues of self-interest; the press was venal and open to subsidy from domestic or foreign sources, its influence thus greatly diminished; and the governmental bureaucracy had a predisposition to graft and corruption, and its level of competence was, with some notable exceptions, relatively low. Contributing to the overall problem was the political inertia of the population. Brazilians simply would not demand radical changes.[34]

This emerging disillusionment with Brazil's ability to create a democratic society fused with the growing Korean crisis of the early 1950s, the perceptions of a continuously worsening world situation, and the Cold War to alter the confident, almost messianic, attitudes of many American policymakers. In his long memorandum on Latin America, written in 1950, George Kennan seemed to set the stage for this change in attitude. He questioned whether the United States should hold its institutions up as remedies for the governmental problems of other peoples. The difference between democratic and authoritarian forms of government, for Kennan, was everywhere relative, rather than absolute, and the distinctions between the two concepts were vague and elusive against the background of Latin American psychology and tradition. Kennan concluded that

> democratic institutions, as we know them in our country, are not universally native to Latin America. Our best prospect of promoting throughout the New World institutions more similar to our own lies in the power of example, and solely in that power. . . . A faith in the ultimate efficacy of our institutions for ourselves does not logically or necessarily involve a similar faith in their universal applicability. . . . Our national experience is in most respects a unique one.[35]

This change in attitude accompanied a change in policy. Perceiving most of the world as being in a state of crisis, and the Soviet Union as an expansionist, imperialist power bent on spreading Communist revolution everywhere, Washington now mainly sought stability in Brazil. If its leaders brought democracy to the country, that was fine, but what was needed most was a stable administration firmly on the side of the United States in the world struggle against communism.

This change in American attitudes and policy helps to explain the quick acceptance by the Eisenhower administration of the Brazilian military's intervention and Vargas's subsequent suicide in 1954. Vargas's resignation and death climaxed a nineteen-day crisis that began with the attempted assassination of the crusading anti-Vargas editor, Carlos Lacerda, on August 5, 1954, when an air force major also was shot and killed. When the local police dragged their heels in tracking down the assassins, the air force took over the investigation, which soon led straight to the palace guard. There is little reason to believe that Vargas personally had anything to do with the affair, but his longtime bodyguard, Gregorio Fortunato, was certainly involved and Luthero Vargas, the president's son, was implicated.

While the press and the political opposition clamored for Vargas to resign, the leaders of the armed forces held endless meetings to decide what was to be done. When General Zenóbio da Costa, minister of war, finally sided with the opposition, the Vargas regime ended. In the early morning hours of August 24 the generals came to Vargas and told him he must resign the presidency. Vargas then went to his bedroom in the Catete Palace and shot himself. In a typewritten note Vargas attributed the ills of his government and his ouster to the machinations of foreign investors and financial interests who "do not want the worker to be free." In an outburst of anti-Americanism, mobs stoned the U.S. embassy in Rio, attacked the U.S. Information Library in Belo Horizonte, and partly burned the U.S. consulate in Pôrto Alegre upon hearing of Vargas's death and suicide note.[36]

The Eisenhower administration was greatly relieved when Vice President João Café Filho, supported by the armed forces, moved quickly to reestablish order and a "national-front, nonpartisan" government. James Scott Kemper, U.S. ambassador to Brazil, believed that the new government, "being composed of the most responsible elements in the country," would be even more favorably disposed toward the United States than its predecessor. "With the backing of the armed forces and the business community," he wired Washington, "Brazil now has what is potentially a stable and pro-United States administration."[37] Kemper never mentioned the possible damage to Brazilian democratic institutions the military intervention may have caused.[38]

American attitudes and goals with regard to the Brazilian political system had gradually changed during the early postwar period from active promotion of democratic institutions to acceptance of any stable, anti-Communist regime that would support the U.S. position in the world. The Eisenhower administration, like the Truman administration, came to pursue a policy that did not directly promote democracy but rather made anticommunism the central feature of its Latin American policy.[39] While not abandoning the rhetoric about the virtues of the American system and its democratic ideals, Washington acquiesced in the interference by the Brazilian military in domestic affairs and in the Brazilian government's acceptance of undemocratic practices as long as the country remained anti-Communist. At the same time, however, U.S. decision makers continued to adhere to the rather myopic belief that, despite their faults, given time and guidance the Brazilians would adopt American principles of good government.

Notes

1. See Green, "The Cold War Comes to Latin America," pp. 149–54.
2. Memorandum by DuWayne Clark, "Policy Statement for Brazil," June 19, 1948, DS 711.32/7-248, RG 59, NA. See also memorandum by Brazilian Affairs

Division, "Brazilian Political Situation," January 24, 1945, DS 711.32/1-2445, RG 59, NA.

3. Robert M. Levine, *The Vargas Regime* (New York: Columbia University Press, 1970), p. 1.

4. During the 1930s military coups replaced governments in four other Latin American republics: Argentina, Bolivia, Peru, and the Dominican Republic. See Levine, *Vargas*, p. 2. On the Estado Novo see Edgard Carone, *O Estado Novo, 1937–1945* (Rio de Janeiro: Defel, 1976); Affonso Henriques, *Ascensao e Queda de Getúlio Vargas* (The rise and fall of Getúlio Vargas), 3 vols. (Rio de Janeiro: Distribuidora Record, 1966); Stanley Hilton, *Brazil and the Great Powers, 1930–1939: The Politics of Trade Rivalry* (Austin: University of Texas Press, 1975); and José Murilo de Carvalho, "Armed Forces and Politics in Brazil 1930–1945" (Paper presented at the July 14, 1981, colloquium on Latin America by the Woodrow Wilson International Center for Scholars, Washington, DC). See also Department of State, R & A Report 6814, "Probable Developments in Brazil," February 21, 1955, RG 59, NA; Skidmore, *Politics in Brazil*, p. 76; and Frank D. McCann, Jr., *The Brazilian-American Alliance, 1937–1945* (Princeton: Princeton University Press, 1973), pp. 4–6.

5. Memorandum by Division of Brazilian Affairs, "President Vargas' Interview to the Press, March 2, 1945," Records of the Division of American Republics, Brazil, RG 59, NA. Louis Halle of the division wrote on the memorandum "This is 5 pages of gargeous [gorge throat] double talk."

6. See Levine, *Vargas*, pp. 138–58; Jaguaribe, *Economic and Political Development*, pp. 142–43; Bresser Pereira, *Development and Crisis in Brazil*, p. 15; Flynn, *Brazil: A Political Analysis*, pp. 94–96; and Frank D. McCann, "Brazilian Foreign Relations in the Twentieth Century," in Selcher, ed., *Brazil in the International System*, p. 7.

7. Gunther, *Inside Latin America*, p. 48; Clarence H. Haring, "Vargas Returns in Brazil," *Foreign Affairs* 29 (January 1951): 308–14; Herring, *A History of Latin America*, p. 760.

8. Telegram from Adolf Berle to secretary of state, no. 2905, September 18, 1945, DS 832.00/9-1845, RG 59, NA; telegram from Berle to secretary of state, no. 3279, October 30, 1945, DS 832.00/10-3045, RG 59, NA; and Berle dispatch to secretary of state, no. 2692, September 3, 1945, DS 832.00/9-345, RG 59, NA.

9. Flynn, *Brazil: A Political Analysis*, p. 132.

10. Spruille Braden, dispatch 9103, April 5, 1945, DS 711.00/4-545, RG 59, NA. For comments concerning this dispatch see memorandum by Division of American Republics, DS 711.00/4-845, RG 59, NA. See also R & A Report 85, "The Development of Democratic Principles and Procedures in the Inter-American System," October 1948, RG 59, NA. Braden became assistant secretary of state for American republic affairs in August 1945.

11. Berle, dispatch to secretary of state, no. 2692, September 3, 1945, DS 832.00/9-345, RG 59, NA.

12. Berle to Truman, September 4, 1945, and draft of Truman's reply attached, September 13, 1945, DS 832.00/9-345, RG 59, NA. Truman states that "it seems to me that things are going along as well as anyone would want. Vargas certainly has been our friend."

13. For a copy of Berle's speech see DS 32.00/10-1645, RG 59, NA. See also telegram from Berle to secretary of state, no. 2905, September 18, 1945,

DS 832/9-1845, RG 59, NA; and instructions from James F. Byrnes to Berle, November 7, 1945, DS 832.00/11-745, RG 59, NA.

14. Memorandum from Daniel Braddock to Ellis Briggs, "Conciliation of Ex-President Vargas," DS 711.32/11-1446, RG 59, NA. See also Sumner Welles's speech attacking Berle attached to memorandum from John Gordon Mein to Braden, January 19, 1946, DS 711.32/1-2946, RG 59, NA. Vargas later claimed that although Berle had shown him the speech, he could not understand Berle's "badly mumbled Portuguese." Berle, in effect, did support Vargas's opponents with the speech. See Flynn, *Brazil: A Political Analysis*, p. 120.

15. Flynn, *Brazil: A Political Analysis*, p. 134.

16. R & A Report 3562, February 29, 1946, RG 59, NA. In 1945 dictatorships also fell in Cuba, Guatemala, Venezuela, and Peru. See Wesson, *Limits of Influence*, p. 19.

17. Memorandum from Berle to Philip O. Chalmers [n.d.], Records of the American Republic Affairs Division, Brazil, RG 59, NA.

18. Berle, *Navigating the Rapids*, p. 562.

19. John W. F. Dulles, "The Contribution of Getúlio Vargas to the Modernization of Brazil," in Baklanoff, ed., *The Shaping of Modern Brazil* (Baton Rouge: Louisiana State University Press, 1969), p. 36; Dulles, "Post-Dictatorship Brazil, 1945–1964," in Baklanoff, ed., *New Perspectives of Brazil*, p. 3.

20. Skidmore, *Politics in Brazil*, p. 64.

21. Memorandum from Mein to Chalmers, "Election of General Dutra to the Presidency of Brazil," DS 832.00/12-1345, RG 59, NA. For the Brazilian view of the Dutra administration see José Cáo, *Dutra* (São Paulo: Instituto Progresso Editorial, S/A 1949); Eurico Gaspar Dutra, *O govêrno Dutra: Algumas realizacões, diretrizes doutrinárias um periodo de paz* (The Dutra government: Lessons learned, leadership principles in a period of peace) (Rio de Janeiro: Editôra Civilizacão Brasileira, 1956); and Mauro Renault Leite and Novelli Junior, *Morechae Eurico Gaspar Dutra, O deves da verdade* (Morechae Eurico Gaspar Dutra, his duty to the truth) (Rio de Janeiro: Nova Fronteira, S/A, 1983).

22. See Jordan M. Young, *The Brazilian Revolution of 1930 and the Aftermath* (New Brunswick: Rutgers University Press, 1967), p. 99; and the Pan American Union, *The Constitution of the United States of Brazil, 1946* (Washington, DC: Pan American Union, 1963).

23. Jorge Sa Almeida, "The Political Influence of the Brazilian Middle Class, 1930–1964" (M.A. thesis, Georgetown University, 1965), p. 53; Flynn, *Brazil: A Political Analysis*, p. 158; Hélio Silva and Maria Cecília Ribass Carneiro, *Eurico Gaspar Dutra, a Espada Sob a Lei, 1946–1951* (Eurico Gaspar Dutra, the sword under the law, 1946–1951) (São Paulo: Grupo de Communicacão Tres, 1983), pp. 39–54.

24. William Pawley, dispatch to secretary of state, "Review of the First Years of the Dutra Administration," December 7, 1948, DS 832.00/12-748, RG 59, NA.

25. Berle, dispatch, February 26, 1946, DS 832.00/2-2646, RG 59, NA.

26. Memorandum by Braddock, "Comments on Brazilian Political Situation," January 9, 1947, Records of the Division of American Republic Affairs, Brazil, RG 59, NA.

27. Erwin P. Keeler (chief, Political Section, Brazilian embassy) to Department of State, September 20, 1950, DS 732.00/9-2050, RG 59, NA.

28. Ibid.

29. Dutra was unable to succeed himself under the constitution. See Sa Almeida, "The Political Influence of the Brazilian Middle Class," p. 55. See also Department of State, R & A Report 6814, "Probable Developments in Brazil," February 21, 1955, RG 59, NA.

30. Green, *Containment*, p. 207; McCann, *Brazilian-American Alliance*, p. 315; Edwin Lieuwen and Miguel Jarrin, *Post-World War II Political Development in Latin America* (Washington, DC: Government Printing Office, 1959).

31. Edward G. Miller to Herschel V. Johnson, January 9, 1951, Records of the assistant secretary of state for inter-American affairs (Edward Miller) 1949–1953, Lot File 53D26, RG 59, NA. Perón wanted to bring the Brazilian government into his proposed ABC Union to resist U.S. influence and to build a third force in the Western Hemisphere. See Sa Almeida, "The Political Influence of the Brazilian Middle Class," p. 59. State Department officials were deeply concerned over Perón's influence in Brazil. See Flynn, *Brazil: A Political Analysis*, p. 130; and Braden's attack on Perón's "neurotic nationalism" printed in U.S. Department of State, *Private Enterprise in the Development of the Americas* (Inter-American Series No. 32, Washington, DC: Government Printing Office, 1947).

32. Miller to secretary of state, DS 732.11/12-2751, RG 59, NA. John M. Cabot repeated the proposal again on February 9, 1954, in order to give evidence of high U.S. regard for Brazil. Memorandum from Cabot to secretary of state, February 9, 1954, DS 732.11/2-954, RG 59, NA.

33. Walter N. Walmsley, Jr., minister counselor, dispatch to Department of State, May 12, 1953, DS 732.00/5-1253, RG 59, NA.

34. Walmsley, "The Political Situation of the Vargas Administration and Its Effects on U.S.-Brazilian Relations," May 12, 1953, DS 732.00/5-1253, RG 59, NA.

35. Memorandum by George F. Kennan, *FRUS, 1950* 2:615–17.

36. James Scott Kemper to Department of State, "Preliminary Estimate of the New National Administration and Its Immediate Problems," September 3, 1954, DS 732.00/9-354, RG 59, NA. See also memorandum by G. R. Monsen, ARA:OSA, "Brazil," September 1, 1954, DS 732.00/9-154, RG 59, NA; and Richard Bourne, *Getúlio Vargas of Brazil, 1883–1954* (London: Charles Knight, 1974), p. 195.

37. Ibid. On the administration of João Café Filho, see Café Filho, *Do sindicato ao catete: Memórias políticas e confissões humanas* (From the labor movement to the Catete Palace: Political memories and human confessions) (Rio de Janeiro: Livraria José Olympia Editôra, S/A, 1966).

38. Skidmore, *Politics in Brazil*, pp. 8–10. The military coup of 1964 and the overthrow of President João Goulart brought to an end the era of Brazilian democratic politics that began in an age of optimism in 1945. By the mid-1950s many Latin Americans claimed that the Eisenhower administration actually preferred dictatorships or military strongmen to reformist, democratic regimes. See Stephen Rabe, *Eisenhower and Latin America*, p. 3; Romulo Betancourt, *Venezuela: Oil and Politics*, trans. Everett Bauman (Boston: Houghton Mifflin, 1979), pp. 359–67; Jose Figueres, "The Problems of Democracy in Latin America," *Journal of International Affairs* 9 (May 1955): 11–21; and Eduardo Santos, "Latin American Realities," *Foreign Affairs* 34 (January 1956): 245–57.

39. See Rabe, *Eisenhower and Latin America*, pp. 38–39.

Chapter Three

Opposing Communism

As a concomitant of its hardening Cold War position in the post-war era, the United States committed itself to an increasingly vigorous anti-Communist line in Brazil and in the entire hemisphere.[1] Both the Truman and Eisenhower administrations attempted to make Brazil into a bulwark against Communist expansion in the Western Hemisphere and perceived Brazil as a key component in their efforts to create a solid front against Communist encroachment. Misreading and misunderstanding the emerging forces of nationalism, and often confusing it with communism, American officials during this early postwar period saw growing nationalism in Brazil as posing a formidable threat to U.S. political objectives and to the creation of a stable, prosperous, anti-Communist hemisphere.[2]

While Washington strove to create a united hemisphere against communism, it unwittingly undermined Brazil's special relationship with the United States. By courting Argentina and treating all American republics equally, U.S. officials offended Brazilian leaders and weakened the traditional bilateral ties between their nations. Nevertheless, Brazilian officials basically followed a strongly pro-U.S. foreign policy and allied themselves closely with American interests during this formative postwar period.

The two countries' perspectives on communism were somewhat different. The primary political problem for Brazil was not a possible Soviet invasion or Communist domination of the hemisphere, but rather internal subversion and domestic instability. The political battle there was predominantly a struggle for access to power rather than for ideology. Brazilian leaders worried more about indirect action by the

Communists and its effect on Brazilian development than the global struggle between the United States and the Soviet Union.[3]

The emergence among U.S. policymakers, both in the Truman and in the Eisenhower administration, of a Cold War mentality opposed to communism in any form affected Washington's position with regard to Brazil and its efforts to influence and guide Brazilian policy. Officials in both administrations firmly believed that the Soviets were intent on exporting social revolution everywhere and that the Western Hemisphere was one of their major targets. Behind this stance were the twin assumptions of American benevolence and Soviet malevolence.[4] A review of U.S. policy concerning Brazil strikingly illustrates these concepts.

Ironically, Brazil had had no formal relations with the Soviet Union since the Bolshevik Revolution of 1917. When Secretary of State Edward R. Stettinius stopped off in Brazil on his return from the Yalta Conference in 1945, he urged Getúlio Vargas, as a gesture toward improving East-West cooperation, to establish formal relations with the Soviet Union. Vargas agreed. There was a generally sympathetic attitude among most Brazilians toward the Soviet Union at this time because of its Allied status. As part of his liberalization policy, therefore, Vargas offered to recognize the Soviet Union, and the two countries exchanged ambassadors.[5]

Vargas also legalized the Communist party of Brazil, the Partido Communista Brasileiro (PCB), and released Luís Carlos Prestes, its almost legendary leader, from jail in May 1945 as part of his plan to remove restrictions on political activities. Ironically, Prestes's first public act on being released from jail was an appearance on the balcony of the American embassy in Rio de Janeiro with U.S. Ambassador Adolf Berle. It was at a ceremony honoring the memory of Franklin D. Roosevelt, who had died the week before.[6] This amicable relationship was short-lived. Prestes and the PCB almost immediately began to verbally attack the United States, and they actively supported the Soviet Union and its satellites.[7]

One of the major factors that delighted the Truman administration with the election of President Eurico Gaspar Dutra in December 1945 was his strong opposition to the Soviet Union and communism. Dutra placed gambling, prostitution, relations with the Soviet Union, and communism on the same plane and opposed all of them vigorously.[8] Furthermore, the Dutra administration perceived the PCB to be a serious danger to Brazilian stability and growth and viewed the Soviet diplomatic mission as a major source of funds and support for local Communists.[9]

In the 1947 general election, seventeen congressmen, one senator (Luís Carlos Prestes), and forty-six assemblymen in fifteen states won office on the PCB ticket. The party won over 500,000 votes, about 10 percent of the total votes cast.[10] The Dutra administration was not the only one concerned about this strong showing. The Truman administration was also alarmed. As early as February 1946, Ambassador Berle claimed that the Soviet policy in Brazil was approximating early Nazi German policy. "Horribly, cynically, and terribly," he wrote the department, "they exploit any center of thought or action which may make trouble for the United States."[11]

Despite increasing concern about the activities of Prestes and his followers, the Department of State could find no conclusive proof or even substantial evidence that the Communists in Brazil followed orders from Moscow. In fact, an Intelligence and Research Report concluded that the official activities of the Soviet embassy and other Soviet official bodies, such as economic missions in Brazil, had not differed markedly from those of other nations. Despite numerous allegations that the USSR mission in Rio de Janeiro was a fountainhead of Soviet propaganda, no real proof could be found that they had done more than attempt to create goodwill toward the USSR and to stimulate commercial relations between the Soviet Union and Brazil. The report concluded, however, that the Soviet Union might conceivably find it to its advantage in the future to fish in troubled inter-American waters in order to focus U.S. attention on its problems closer to home.[12]

Outraged when Soviet Ambassador Jacob Suritz publicly embarrassed his regime during a wave of labor strikes, Dutra moved to outlaw the Party. Using the 1946 constitution, which made unlawful "the organization, registration, or functioning of any political party or association whose program or action was contrary to the democratic regime," Dutra pressed for action against the Communist party.[13] The PCB retaliated by claiming that it was a democratic party, committed to working through the system.[14]

Despite PCB protests, the Supreme Electoral Tribunal outlawed the PCB in May 1947 on the grounds that the Party was an organization in the service of Russia and did not support the democratic form of government as required by the Brazilian constitution. Shortly thereafter came legislation canceling the mandates of all Communist party legislators, thus depriving the Party of all legislative representation. In effect, the Dutra government suppressed the PCB in the name of democracy. The American embassy, not surprisingly, did not levy even a mild protest,[15] but the Soviet Union did. Joseph Stalin reacted to Dutra's ban by recalling Suritz to Moscow.

Several weeks earlier, Brazilian officials had approached U.S. Ambassador William Pawley about a possible break in relations. Pawley, although sympathetic, refused to become involved. Following the publication of a personal attack on President Dutra by a Soviet newspaper, the *Literary Gazette*, the Brazilians took action. On October 7, Dutra in a telegram to Oswaldo Aranha, his ambassador to the United Nations, instructed him not to vote in favor of a Soviet bloc country at the United Nations under any circumstances, and within days Brazil broke official relations. Although somewhat surprised by the move, Pawley and Washington supported the Brazilian position. The United States became the protecting power for Brazil in Moscow.[16] The Soviets quickly blamed the United States for the break in relations, as did the now-illegal PCB.[17] It was the first break in relations between a Western country and the Soviet Union since the war.[18]

The Dutra administration did not operate in a vacuum. It adhered to a strictly pro-U.S. foreign policy. Furthermore, most officials in the Dutra administration acted on the belief that close cooperation with the United States was beneficial for Brazil, and they followed the Truman administration position in opposing communism.[19] Foreign Minister Raúl Fernándes, for example, viewed communism as an inferior way of life and saw Communist expansion as a serious threat to his country. The only sane policy for Brazil, according to Fernándes, was for it to ally itself closely with the United States. Other Brazilian leaders such as Oswaldo Aranha, Eugênio Gudin, and General Colberri do Couto e Silva echoed Fernándes's views. They accepted the conflict between East and West, and the concept of Soviet aggression. It was imperative, according to these leaders, for Brazil to place itself firmly in the Western camp.[20]

As a gesture of friendship and to support these Brazilian leaders, President Harry S. Truman had visited Brazil in September 1947. While there, he reaffirmed his interest in Brazil and his commitment to oppose communism in the hemisphere.[21] Truman gave Dutra a Tennessee walking horse in honor of former Secretary of State Cordell Hull.[22] The two countries seemed close in their opposition to communism.

Although it did not actively encourage Dutra's break with the Soviets and did not publicly support the illegalization of the PCB, the Truman administration was not displeased by these actions. State Department officials were convinced, despite the lack of concrete evidence,[23] that the Soviet Union was bringing in numerous agents and stirring up trouble not only in Brazil but in the rest of Latin America as well. Moreover, these officials perceived the PCB as the strongest Communist party in all of Latin America. It was the only Communist party in South America to have attempted a violent revolution (1935).[24]

While the Truman administration quietly approved of and supported the anti-Communist moves of the Brazilians, it also sought to bolster its inter-American anti-Communist programs. In 1947, for example, it revived the Inter-American Committee on Political Defense, a committee set up during World War II to exchange information on subversive groups, primarily Nazis and Fascists. U.S. officials now urged the committee to concentrate its efforts on the surveillance of Soviet and Communist bloc nations' activities. At the same time, Washington cultivated the friendship of such leading anti-Communist figures on the committee as General Pedro A. Góes Monteiro, the Brazilian member and an influential leader in his nation's military.[25]

In addition to such multinational efforts, U.S. policymakers continued to keep a keen eye on developments in Brazil. Reporting in 1948, the Brazilian Affairs Division estimated that the strength of the Brazilian Communist party had been considerably diminished by Dutra's withdrawal of its legal status. It put Party strength at 80,000 to 120,000, with a very small "hard core." The division thought the Brazilian government had a tendency to exaggerate the Communist threat, but it pointed out that from Brazil's perspective it was eminently desirable to take restrictive precautions rather than to allow the Party to reach a stage of maturity where it might be able to disrupt political and economic stability in the country. Nevertheless, the report summarized that the problem of communism in Brazil was of real importance and that it should not be ignored since a large segment of the Brazilian people existed on a very low standard of living, which conditions offered fertile ground for Communist propaganda.[26]

Once again, George Kennan seemed to set the tone for American policy when he declared: "Our relationship to Latin America occupies a vitally important place in our effort to achieve, within the noncommunist world, a rebuttal of the Russian challenge to our right to exist as a great and leading world power."[27] Kennan pictured the Communists as fanatical, disciplined, and industrious, bent on the destruction of American influence in the Western Hemisphere. While the United States, with its vigorous, healthy body politic, could cope with the "virus of communism" without permitting it to grow to dangerous proportions, Kennan doubted that the societies of Latin America, where traditions of popular government were weak, could withstand the intensity of the Communist attack. He believed that harsh government repression might be the only answer to communism in Latin America.[28]

Despite Kennan's call to pursue the Cold War on all fronts in Latin America, the Truman administration took very little action. American officials proclaimed their support for Resolution 32 of the Final Act of Bogotá of 1948, which declared the political activities of international communism or any totalitarian doctrine incompatible with the concept of American freedom. They continued to call for the full exchange of information concerning Communist activities in the hemisphere but opposed blanket decrees "outlawing the Communist Party from the hemisphere" and merely urged independent legislation patterned on U.S. laws such as the Smith Act and Internal Security Act of 1950. Department officials believed that any real effort to encourage Brazil and the other Latin American states to eliminate Communist influence would have little effect. "They would miss the real communists and put their political opponents in jail."[29]

Seeming to agree with the American advice, the Vargas government in 1950 again moved against the Communists, passing a law providing for the dismissal of officers of the armed forces if they were found guilty of belonging to or supporting the activities of the Communist party. Citing the constitution, which prohibited both class prejudice and propagandizing violent processes to subvert the political and social order, Vargas also banned the celebration of the Communist-dominated Continental Congress for Peace scheduled for March 1952.[30] In 1953, upon the urging of the Vargas administration, the Brazilian congress passed the National Security Law, patterned after the U.S. Internal Security Act. The Communists clamored for Vargas's overthrow.[31]

Despite Vargas's actions and the Communist attacks on his administration, officials in the Eisenhower administration remained skeptical of the sincerity of his anti-Communist intentions. William Wieland, the U.S. public affairs officer in Rio, for example, cautioned that "the party had made tremendous strides in infiltrating almost every vital feature of Brazilian life" and warned that the Vargas regime had taken "only the most ineffectual steps toward driving them out."[32] The American embassy in Rio also warned Washington that, since the inauguration of the Vargas administration, there had been a gradual reorganization of the anti-Communist section of the Federal Political

Police (DOPS) that had had the effect of "weakening the most effective anticommunist civil arm of the government."

The embassy also reported that Vargas had reduced the secret funds of the political unit used to finance the infiltration of secret agents into the Communist party. The U.S. legal attaché believed that these actions were aimed primarily at reducing the influence of the police on organized labor activities and that they stemmed directly from the influence of João Goulart, minister of labor and president of the Brazilian Labor party (PTB).[33] Chargé d'Affaires Walter Walmsley also distrusted Goulart and pictured him as a political opportunist "not unwilling to accept communist support." For Walmsley, Goulart furthered Communist aims by trying to establish a climate of class struggle and, more directly, by allowing Communists to obtain positions of labor leadership and by pandering to ultranationalists and left-wing Socialists.[34]

Despite United States distrust, Vargas continued officially to support the Eisenhower administration's position against Communists in the hemisphere. For example, at the Tenth Inter-American Conference held in Caracas, Venezuela, in March 1954, when Secretary of State John Foster Dulles focused on the Communist issue, especially in Guatemala, most Latin American countries wavered in their support for the secretary's position. Brazil voted solidly with the United States.[35]

American policymakers, not unlike their Brazilian counterparts, in general had a difficult time distinguishing nationalists from Communists and were more likely than not to simply lump the two together and condemn them both. They saw revolutionary nationalism as synonymous with anti-Americanism. Playing upon fears of foreign domination and economic colonialism, this movement, as perceived by Washington, undermined U.S. policy and aided the Communists. Analyzing the Brazilian nationalist movement, a State Department Research and Analysis (R & A) Report described it as being led by intellectuals and university students who had an exaggerated sense of national pride, an urgent need for change, and a fear and resentment of foreign, chiefly American, influence. These individuals tended to translate poorly assimilated economic and political theories from abroad into direct political programs in an effort to find simple solutions to Brazil's problems. In this search for quick solutions, many turned to Marxism, which supplied them with a ready-made vocabulary and a complete program. These radicals lacked an understanding of how capitalism had changed in the United States and

Western Europe in the twentieth century, and they suffered from a collective inferiority complex.[36]

Although they saw Brazilian nationalism as a potential threat to U.S.-Brazilian cooperation, some department officials argued that it was comparatively mild and rational in nature. It was less virulent and xenophobic than that of other Latin American countries, and it was further curbed by a general disapproval of violently antiforeign demonstrations and traditional Brazilian tolerance on all questions of race, creed, and political theories. Nevertheless, it warranted watching.[37]

A few decision makers in the Eisenhower administration, such as Secretary of Defense Charles E. Wilson, took issue with this type of thinking. Wilson believed that the United States had to be careful in its condemnation of nationalism as a force inimical to its interests. He wrote to the Joint Chiefs that "the spirit of nationalism had long flourished in the United States and had played a large part in our development. In many cases it can be a strong force working against communism in the interests of the Free World. We should not simply condemn nationalism per se."[38]

Despite such occasional protests, most American officials continued to link nationalism with communism and to perceive communism in Brazil and elsewhere in Latin America as a tool of the Kremlin used to advance Russian imperialistic designs and to supplant democracy throughout the world with a totalitarian police state system. As seen from Washington, communism was a direct and major threat to the national security of the United States and to that of all the other American republics.

The Eisenhower administration insisted that the security of the hemisphere against the Communist threat must be the major consideration in its dealings with all Latin American nations. It wanted all Latin Americans to understand that the Cold War was the predominant feature of international relations in the postwar world.[39] Brazil and the other Latin American republics, however, were more concerned with their internal socioeconomic problems and internal security needs. They looked to the United States less for leadership against communism than for cooperation in dealing with their economic problems.[40]

The Brazilian elite, almost exclusively preoccupied with domestic problems, expected to exchange its support for U.S. policies in the international field for economic development assistance and a most-favored-nation status with respect to the rest of South America. Resenting Washington's preoccupation with Europe and Asia,

Brazilian officials continually protested their country's neglected status and the American policies that relegated Brazil to the same level as the rest of Latin America. They aspired to a special position in U.S. foreign policy and believed that they had earned such a position through their "undeviating record of friendship for the United States."[41]

Brazil's demand for special treatment posed an almost insoluble dilemma for American policymakers. On the one hand, official public policy was to treat all of the Latin American countries as nearly equal as possible. The structuring of the system centering on the Rio de Janeiro and Bogotá treaties clearly provided for such leveling. On the other hand, American officials were accustomed to thinking of Brazil as a "great and good friend" and "automatically put them on international committees and councils where they could be counted on for their strong support."[42] This dilemma was never resolved, and it constantly resurfaced in U.S.-Brazilian relations, especially with regard to American attitudes toward Argentina.

The Brazilian government wanted close collaboration with the United States at least in part because of its position vis-à-vis Argentina. The traditional rivalry between Portuguese-speaking Brazil and its Spanish-speaking neighbors, especially Argentina, presented special problems for American policymakers.[43]

Although U.S. policy toward Argentina varied from a stiff line to a conciliatory one, Brazilian attitudes remained constant. Brazil wanted to ensure that Argentina did not obtain equal footing. American officials constantly had to reassure the Brazilian government that, despite the fact that it was official policy to treat all nations of Latin America equally, Brazil had a "special friendship" with the United States. The Brazilian Affairs Division in the early postwar period continually pushed for such a declaration, arguing that Brazil had been a loyal ally throughout the war, while Argentina had maintained a neutrality that should not be rewarded.[44]

As policymakers in both the Truman and Eisenhower administrations worked to make the inter-American system into an anti-Soviet unit, however, hemispheric solidarity became their overriding consideration. Argentina was to be welcomed back into the family of American nations on an equal footing.[45] U.S. officials took great pains, nevertheless, to reassure their Brazilian friends that the change in policy with respect to Argentina did not in any way imply any lessening of affection for Brazil. Much like it was consoling a child, Washington assured Brazil that it was still America's principal ally and "special friend" in South America.[46]

Despite receiving little more than rhetorical assurances about Washington's continued concern and friendship for Brazil, the Brazilian government continued to follow a constructive, cooperative policy with the United States in the inter-American system, in the Organization of American States, and in the United Nations. American policymakers were quite pleased. On major East-West political issues the Brazilian delegation to the United Nations "collaborated effectively on all important issues, while at the same time taking care to avoid any appearance of merely following the United States lead." Only Peru voted with the U.S. delegation more frequently than did Brazil on roll calls in which the U.S. and Soviet delegations opposed each other. Brazil voted with the United States on all atomic energy and human rights issues. On UN membership, both the Dutra and Vargas administrations instructed their representatives to vote just for those candidates endorsed by the United States. In fact, even as late as 1971, on the seating of Communist China, only the United States and Brazil cast no votes.[47]

For its part, the United States supported Brazil for membership on the UN Security Council, the International Atomic Energy Commission, and the International Court of Justice.[48] Although Brazil did not secure a permanent seat on the Security Council, due mainly to the opposition of the Soviet Union, it did get elected to a two-year term as a nonpermanent member in 1946. In 1947 the General Assembly elected Oswaldo Aranha president of its second session.[49] Brazil, in general, continued to support closely the United States in the international arena until the 1960s, when the ruling Brazilian military deliberately sought a more neutral international position.

In summary, convinced that communism and the Soviet Union represented a direct threat to the United States, its political system, and its position in the Western Hemisphere, the Truman and Eisenhower administrations advocated a united front against the Communists. What mattered most to American policymakers was to stop the spread of communism and Soviet influence. Brazil was seen as a key to this policy in Latin America. For Brazilian officials, however, the primary concerns were internal stability and domestic development, not international communism. They wanted a "special relationship" with the United States to ensure Brazil's dominance in South America and to promote its economic development. In spite of the contrasting objectives of the two countries, Brazil, in general, supported the United States in the international arena, and American officials continued to perceive Brazil as their major ally in Latin America in the fight against Communist subversion.

Notes

1. See Daland, *Brazilian Planning*, p. 207; and Green, "The Cold War Comes to Latin America," pp. 150–54.
2. See Rabe, *Eisenhower and Latin America*, pp. 2, 30.
3. Daland, *Brazilian Planning*, p. 207.
4. Green, *Containment*, pp. 141, 258; Baily, *Development of South America*, p. 132.
5. The Brazilians considered Moscow a hardship post and the first Brazilian ambassador to Moscow, Mario de Pimental Brandão, continually delayed his departure for the Soviet Union. See Daugherty, "Brazilian Policy towards the Soviet Union," pp. 158, 178–79. See also Flynn, *Brazil: A Political Analysis*, p. 136; and Henriques, *Ascensão e Queda de Getúlio Vargas* (Rise and fall of Getúlio Vargas), 2:342–43.
6. Daugherty, "Brazilian Policy towards the Soviet Union," p. 181; Ronald H. Chilcote, *The Brazilian Communist Party: Conflict and Integration, 1922–1972* (New York: Oxford University Press, 1974).
7. Skidmore, *Politics in Brazil*, pp. 4–5.
8. Daugherty, "Brazilian Policy towards the Soviet Union," p. 153; Cão, *Dutra*.
9. Daugherty, "Brazilian Policy towards the Soviet Union," p. 154; Eurico Gaspar Dutra, *O govêrno Dutra* (The Dutra government), p. 87.
10. Memorandum from Sterling Cottrell to Henry Holland, October 13, 1954, Records of the officer in charge of Brazilian affairs (Sterling J. Cottrell) 1953–1955, Lot File 58D-42, RG 59, NA; Flynn, *Brazil: A Political Analysis*, p. 136.
11. Berle and Jacobs, eds., *Navigating the Rapids*, p. 570.
12. R & A Report 4185, "Soviet Policy and Objectives in the Other American Republics," December 31, 1946, RG 59, NA.
13. Pan American Union, *The Constitution of the United States of Brazil, 1946*.
14. See Dutra, *O govêrno Dutra*, p. 95; and Chilcote, *The Brazilian Communist Party*, p. 53.
15. See memorandum from John C. Dreier to Ellis Briggs, February 7, 1947; telegram from William Pawley to secretary of state, no. 596, May 16, 1947; and David McKey, dispatch to secretary of state, October 9, 1947, all in *FRUS, 1947* (Washington, DC: Government Printing Office, 1972), 8:392–94. In addition, see Pawley, dispatch to Spruille Braden, August 16, 1946, DS 832.00/8-1646, RG 59, NA; "Policy Statement for Brazil," July 19, 1948, DS 711.321/7-248, RG 59, NA; and Flynn, *Brazil: A Political Analysis*, p. 140.
16. Daugherty, "Brazilian Policy towards the Soviet Union," p. 211; Pawley, dispatch to Department of State, 732.64/10-649, RG 59, NA.
17. Daugherty, "Brazilian Policy towards the Soviet Union," p. 205; Fernando de Carvalho, *O Communismo no Brasil* (Communism in Brazil) (Rio de Janeiro: Biblioteca do Exército, 1966–67).
18. Between 1947 and 1952 five Latin American countries severed relations with the Soviet Union. See Cole Blasier, *The Giant's Rival: The USSR and Latin America* (Pittsburgh: University of Pittsburgh Press, 1983).
19. Daugherty, "Brazilian Policy towards the Soviet Union," p. 97. See also Dutra, *O govêrno Dutra*; and Milciades Mourão, *Dutra, História de um Govêrno*

(Dutra, a history of his government) (Rio de Janeiro: Editôra Civilizacão Brasileira, 1955).

20. See Daugherty, "Brazilian Policy towards the Soviet Union," pp. 99–101. Oswaldo Aranha was the Brazilian representative to the United Nations in 1947. Eugênio Gudin was a leading Brazilian economist and at one time Dutra's finance minister. General Couto e Silva was a veteran of the Forca Expedicionaria Brasileira (FEB) and one of the founders of the Escola Superior de Guerra (ESG).

21. See Silva and Ribass Carneiro, *Dutra*, pp. 139–41; Frank D. McCann, "Brazilian Foreign Relations in the Twentieth Century," in Selcher, ed., *Brazil in the International System*, p. 12; and Baily, *Development of South America*, p. 134. In May 1949, Dutra visited the United States. He was the first Brazilian president to address the U.S. Congress. See Silva and Ribass Carneiro, *Dutra*, pp. 137–38. Dutra remained influential in Brazilian politics long after he left the presidency in 1950. He was frequently consulted after the coup of 1964 and remained a strong anti-Communist ally of the United States. He died in June 1974 at the age of ninety-two. See Flynn, *Brazil: A Political Analysis*, p. 125.

22. See Estes Kefauver to Dean Acheson, April 5, 1950, DS 732.11/4-550, RG 59, NA; and Hélio Silva, *O Ciclo de Vargas* (The Vargas cycle) (Rio de Janeiro: Editôra Civilizacão Brasileira, 1964), p. 470.

23. The records of key U.S. intelligence agencies, such as the CIA, NSA, and FBI, remain closed for this period.

24. See Skidmore, *Politics in Brazil*, p. 4; and Carvalho, *O Communismo no Brasil*, pp. 10–30. See also NSC 16, "U.S. Policy Regarding Anti-Communist Measures Which Could Be Planned and Carried Out within the Inter-American System," June 28, 1948, which concluded that communism was a potential danger in Latin America, but that, with a few exceptions, "it was not seriously dangerous at the present time," Records of the National Security Council (NSC), Record Group 273, National Archives, Washington, DC (hereafter cited as RG 273, NA).

25. See Pawley, dispatch to Braden, August 16, 1946, DS 832.00/8-1646, RG 59, NA; and Flynn, *Brazil: A Political Analysis*, p. 140. On the Emergency Advisory Committee for Political Defense see *FRUS, 1942* (Washington, DC: Government Printing Office, 1964), 5:74–107; *FRUS, 1943* (Washington, DC: Government Printing Office, 1966), 5:2–39; and *FRUS, 1944* (Washington, DC: Government Printing Office, 1967), 7:1–26. See also NSC 16, "Anti-Communist Measures," RG 273, NA.

26. "Policy Statement for Brazil," July 19, 1948, DS 711.321/7-248, RG 59, NA.

27. Memorandum by George F. Kennan, March 29, 1950, *FRUS, 1950* 2:598.

28. Ibid.

29. Fourth meeting of the foreign ministers, *FRUS, 1951* (Washington, DC: Government Printing Office, 1979), 2:932–33. For the text of the Alien Registration Act (PL 690) (Smith Act), approved June 28, 1940 see 54 *Statutes at Large* 670. For the text of the Internal Security Act of 1950 (PL 831) approved September 23, 1950 see 64 *Statutes at Large* 987.

30. See Paulo Brandi, *Vargas, da vida para a história* (Vargas, his life in history) (Rio de Janeiro: Zahar Editôres, 1985), pp. 233–85.

31. See Dulles, "The Contribution of Getúlio Vargas," p. 55.

32. W. T. Bennett, Jr. (Office of South American Affairs) to Cottrell, Thomas C. Mann, John Cabot, "Communism in Brazil," February 26, 1953, DS 732.001/2-2653, RG 59, NA.

33. Walter N. Walmsley, Jr., to Department of State, "Gradual Reorganization and Consequent Weakening of Anti-Communist Division of Federal Policy," October 29, 1953, DS 832.501/10-2953, RG 59, NA.

34. Walmsley, dispatch to Department of State, "Minister of Labor João Belcher Marques Goulart and His Importance in the Present Brazilian Political Scene," July 8, 1953, DS 732.521/7-853, RG 59, NA. See also Caspar D. Green (first secretary of embassy), dispatch to Department of State, "Strategy of the Brazilian Communist Party," October 2, 1953, DS 732.001/10-253, RG 59, NA; and Henry S. Hammond (labor attaché), dispatch, "Communist Activities in Brazilian Labor Groups," September 20, 1950, DS 832.062/7-853, RG 59, NA.

35. See Baily, *Development of South America*, pp. 70–72; and United States Department of State, *Report of the U.S. Delegation to the Tenth Inter-American Conference, Caracas, Venezuela, March 26 thru March 30, 1954* (Washington, DC: Government Printing Office, 1954).

36. R & A Report 8002, "Nationalism in Brazil," July 24, 1959, RG 59, NA.

37. Cottrell to Bennett, "Communism in Brazil," April 15, 1954, DS 732.001/4-154, RG 59, NA.

38. Memorandum from Secretary of Defense to Joint Chiefs of Staff, March 11, 1953, CCS 381 Western Hemisphere, Records of the Office of the Secretary of Defense, Record Group 330, Modern Military Branch, National Archives, Washington, DC (hereafter cited as RG 330, NA). On the phenomenon of revolutionary nationalism in Latin America and other areas of the underdeveloped world see Arthur Whitaker, *Nationalism in Latin America, Past and Present* (Gainesville: University of Florida Press, 1962); Silvert, ed., *Expectant Peoples: Nationalism and Development*; Silvert, *The Conflict Society: Reaction and Revolution in Latin America* (New York: American Universities Field Staff, 1966); and John D. Martz, ed., *The Dynamics of Change in Latin America* (Englewood Cliffs: Prentice Hall, NJ, 1965).

39. See Rabe, *Eisenhower and Latin America*, p. 30; and Robert H. Ferrell, ed., *The Eisenhower Diaries* (New York: W. W. Norton, 1981), diary entry, July 2, 1953.

40. Vargas Document—Request for Aid, Rio telegram, January 15, 1951, attached to memorandum from Edward G. Miller, Jr. (assistant secretary of state) to W. Averell Harriman (special assistant to the president for foreign affairs), February 6, 1951, Miller Files, Lot File 53D-26, RG 59, NA. See also McCann, "Brazilian Foreign Relations," pp. 22–23.

41. Memorandum of conversation among Brazilian Ambassador Carlos Martins and Braden, James H. Wright, Briggs, and Daniel Braddock, March 6, 1946, *FRUS, 1946* (Washington, DC: Government Printing Office, 1969), 11:709–10. See also R & A Report 7923, "Latin American Attitudes toward the U.S.," January 19, 1959, RG 59, NA; and Hilton, "The United States, Brazil, and the Cold War," pp. 599–624.

42. Randolph A. Kidder to Johnson (U.S. ambassador in Brazil), October 20, 1950, DS 611.32/10-2050, RG 59, NA.

43. See Henriques, *Ascensão e Queda de Getúlio Vargas* (The rise and fall of Getúlio Vargas), vol. 3, *Declíneo e Morte* (Decline and death), pp. 119–51, for a

discussion of the relationship between Perón and Vargas and the influence of Peronismo in Brazil. See also Flynn, *Brazil: A Political Analysis*, p. 130.

44. See memorandum by Edward G. Miller, August 19, 1949, Miller Files, RG 59, NA.

45. There was even concern among the Brazilian experts that the reorganization of the department, which consolidated the Office of Inter-American Regional Political Affairs (RPA) and the Office of Brazilian Affairs (BA) and placed Howard H. Tewksbury, chief of the Division of River Plate Affairs, in charge of the new Office of East Coast Affairs, would greatly upset the sensitivities of the Brazilian government. See memorandum by Miller, August 19, 1949, Miller Files, Lot File 53D-26, RG 59, NA.

46. Miller to Johnson, April 15, 1950, Miller Files, Lot File 53D-26, RG 59, NA. See also Miller to secretary of state, "Brazilian Reaction to Argentine Developments and Significance to Brazilian-American Relations of Possible Election of Vargas to Presidency," April 26, 1950, DS 732.00/4-2650, RG 59, NA.

47. See John A. Houston, *Latin America in the United Nations* (New York: Carnegie Endowment for International Peace, 1956), p. 36; Edward T. Rowe, "The United States, the United Nations, and the Cold War," *International Organization* 25:1 (1971): 59–78; McCann, "Brazilian Foreign Relations," p.11; and Baily, *Development of South America*, p. 156. On the China issue see Sheldon Appleton, *Eternal Triangle? Communist China, the United States and the United Nations* (East Lansing: Michigan State University Press, 1961); and Lincoln P. Bloomfield, "China, the United States, and the United Nations," *International Organization* 20:4 (1966): 653–76. See also USC 14 4/1, "U.S. Objectives and Courses of Action with Respect to Latin America," March 18, 1953, *FRUS, 1952–1954* (Washington, DC: Government Printing Office, 1983), 4:1–10.

48. R & A Report 4314, "Analysis of Policies Followed by the Other American Republics in the General Assembly of the United Nations," September 15, 1947, RG 59, NA; R & A Report 7433, "Brazil—Recent Developments and Probable Trends," February 20, 1957, RG 59, NA.

49. Pedro Leão Veloso was the first Brazilian member of the Security Council. See McCann, "Brazilian Foreign Relations," p. 11; and E. Bradford Burns, *A History of Brazil* (New York: Columbia University Press, 1980), p. 93.

Chapter Four

Cultivating the Military

One of the most consistent and important features of U.S. policy toward Latin America in general, and Brazil in particular, during the early Cold War years was Washington's cultivation of the Latin American military as a valuable ally in the anti-Communist struggle. Both the Truman and Eisenhower administrations sought to build up Latin American military establishments, to increase their ties to the United States, to guarantee U.S. predominance in supplying equipment and training, and to make the military an increasingly influential factor in the political life of the region. The Brazilian military was the chief focus of this effort.[1]

The Brazilian military was, and is, the most important force in Brazil. Although Getúlio Vargas dominated the 1930s, the 1940s, and the early 1950s, he nevertheless shared center stage with the military. A military junta installed Vargas in the presidency in November 1930, and the military elevated him to a dictatorship in 1937, summarily deposed him in 1945, and forced him to resign in 1954.[2] The military also engineered the countercoup of 1955 that allowed Juscelino Kubitschek to assume office. Seen in this light the intervention of the Brazilian military in 1964, which overthrew João Goulart and brought to an end the era of democratic politics begun ostensibly in 1945, was consistent with previous actions. The Brazilian military has been in the modern era the final arbiter in domestic politics. It is military men and not the politicians who are the ultimate custodians of power.[3] Brazilian Foreign Minister Oswaldo Aranha put it succinctly in an interview in 1939 when he said: "My dear fellow, you simply don't begin to know how much everything has to do with the army."[4]

It would be a dangerous oversimplification to view the Brazilian military as an encapsulated, unified professional body, monolithic in its thinking.[5] Certain rational and bureaucratic norms do stand out, however. Europeans, chiefly French and German, guided the pre-World War II professionalization of the Brazilian military. Brazil styled its military educational and training programs after those of Germany and France and used their manuals, instructors, and equipment. This European tutelage stimulated rather than lessened Brazilian military interest in politics and motivated the elite professional military officers to assume responsibility for the conduct of national affairs. The professional militarism instilled by the Europeans fostered a set of attitudes that pictured the armed forces as advanced and solid, a bulwark of modernity, and morally superior to civilian interest groups. The Brazilian military viewed itself as the technocratic nation builder in a backward and divided land where domestic order and internal security were prerequisites to progress and stability.

Although the army officer corps came overwhelmingly from the middle classes, unlike many Spanish American countries where members of the rural landowning class dominated the military, the Brazilian military looked upon itself as a classless group with no special interests to uphold. It was loyal to the state and the nation more than to a specific government or administration. These officers saw themselves as *o povo ferdado* (the people in uniform). They identified with all national problems and objectives and were an indispensable stimulator of development. And, with the 1930 revolution, the Brazilian armed forces were catapulted into the very center of national political life.[6]

Despite frequent conflicts within the officer corps over such issues as nationalism, development, communism, and the Korean War, the majority of the military was committed to national development, the necessity of industrialization and modernization, the absolute need for unity among the officer corps, the preservation of the military as a bastion of official anti-Communist ideology, and the prevention of any proletarian agitation.[7] The military believed it had a civilizing mission. It also desired to procure modern weapons to bolster its forces because of internal security concerns, fear of Perón's mass movement, and the knowledge that Brazilian industry did not have the capacity to manufacture modern implements of war. It looked to the United States for aid and support.[8]

The attitudes of the Brazilian military fit well with most American objectives for Latin America. What American policy planners wanted was a stable, prodemocratic Brazil capable of participating not only in the inter-American defense system but also in a worldwide anti-Communist security system. They sought to make over the Brazilian military in the American image and to use it as a strong component of the postwar world order envisioned by Washington.

Unlike other military groups in Latin America, the Brazilian armed forces maintained close contacts and relations with the United States military establishment. Cut off from German and French influences by the war, the Brazilian military relied more and more on U.S. training, techniques, and equipment. During World War II, Brazil was the only Latin American nation to send troops abroad to aid the Allies. A Joint Brazilian-U.S. Defense Commission (JBUSDC) coordinated defense policy in Washington and in Rio de Janeiro, and a variety of U.S. training missions exposed the Brazilians to American military doctrines. By the end of the war the United States had acquired a near-monopoly over the training and equipping of the Brazilian armed forces.[9]

World War II not only raised the professionalism of the Brazilian officer corps but also intensified its ongoing politicization.[10] The irony of a dictatorship sending an army across the seas to liberate oppressed people was not lost on the Forca Expedicionária Brasileira (FEB). But the favorable impression received by FEB members of the American economic system's conduciveness to both military and national development had more important consequences for future Brazilian policies. FEB officers were not only impressed with the organizational ability of the United States but also with the efficiency and productivity of the American system—capitalism could create a physically powerful and democratic nation. They developed an admiration for the United States and its technology and a strong belief that Brazil could profit from a close relationship with the United States.[11]

For their part, American policymakers believed that the Brazilian military stood aloof from politics and supported the democratic process. Ambassador Adolf Berle, for example, reported in 1945 that the army, because of its contacts with American military forces and its experience in Europe, had developed a "far wider point of view." It was, he said, extremely impressed with democratic institutions of which it previously had known nothing. Berle even interpreted the army's intervention in 1945 as "saving the democratic elections."[12]

To strengthen the U.S.-Brazilian military ties and generate goodwill General Mark W. Clark, who had directed Brazilian troops in Italy, visited Brazil in July 1945. He conferred medals on the FEB's top officers. In August, General of the Army Dwight D. Eisenhower paid a visit to Brazil and reviewed the Brazilian armed forces.[13] But despite such attention, the Brazilians felt somewhat neglected. Colonel Bina Machado expressed this attitude when he called on Ambassador Berle as President-elect Dutra's representative. Berle reported to Washington as a result of this conversation that there was a growing feeling in the Brazilian military that the United States was inclined to treat Brazil as a small brother rather than as an important nation pledged to full military cooperation.[14]

Despite such protests by the Brazilian officer corps, the Truman administration took few concrete actions to bolster the military's position in Brazil during the early postwar period. It was not so much lack of interest on the part of American planners as it was the radically changing world situation and bureaucratic in-fighting between the Department of State and military officials that prevented a more active U.S. role.

The end of the war in Europe and Asia brought a steady push from Washington for the continuation of the "American Way" in hemispheric defense. U.S. planners wanted to exclude all non-American military from the Western Hemisphere. They also wanted a supply monopoly on all military goods and equipment but achieved only limited results.

The Joint Chiefs of Staff first described postwar U.S. objectives in Latin America on February 6, 1945, in response to a request from the secretary of state for views on the subject for use at the Inter-American Conference in Mexico City. The Joint Chiefs pointed out the importance of arrangements for the common defense of the Western Hemisphere as part of a worldwide security system. They supported such a system, but nonetheless wanted "the Inter-American defensive structure . . . preserved within it." In the event the world security system proved ineffective, the security of the hemisphere would still be protected. They suggested that the U.S. delegation push for a program of standardization in organization, equipment, and training and for the maintenance and improvement of air and naval bases essential for hemispheric security.[15]

Following the conference, the Joint Chiefs took up the issue of postwar military aid to Latin America. Although they realized that military supplies and training for Latin America had been a relatively low priority during the war, they now called for a stepped-up program of aid, because the United States "was clearly the leader in the Western Hemisphere and should act to persuade the other nations involved to agree to adopt U.S. military doctrine, tactics, techniques, practices, equipment, and weapons."[16] President Truman gave his approval to this approach in August 1945.[17]

U.S.-Brazilian military cooperation was already close. In 1942, Brazil had signed a secret agreement with the United States for the operation and protection of bases in Brazil. This agreement had also called for the establishment of the JBUSDC and charged it with the implementation of the agreement and with advising and assisting the Brazilian armed forces in adopting American methods, doctrines, organization, and equipment.[18]

Proceeding on the assumption that "it was the desire of the United States that Brazil be able to play a strong and cooperative role in the maintenance of hemispheric defense as a component of the postwar world order," U.S. Army, Navy, and Air Force officials initiated staff conversations with the Brazilians. They envisioned a vast program of aid that would make the Brazilian military the strongest force in Latin America and give it great international prestige. If adopted, the program would foster hemispheric defenses, provide an outlet for excess U.S. equipment, and give Brazil unquestioned supremacy so that no nation or group of nations in Latin America could oppose it. For example, the navy proposed making available to Brazil two battleships of the *Nevada* class, two light aircraft carriers of the *Independence* class, four cruisers of the *Cleveland* class, fifteen destroyers, nine submarines, and a variety of auxiliary craft.[19]

When Ambassador Berle discovered these proposals he found them "unrealistic and overly ambitious." Moreover, the U.S. military missions had already overextended their authority and scope of operations, according to Berle, by not reporting to the embassy. Berle's protest was symptomatic of the problems and divisions between the Department of State on the one hand and the War Department (later the Department of Defense) on the other. This dispute over military aid to Brazil continued for the next ten years.[20]

Despite the lofty goals of the U.S. military in 1945, the Truman administration provided little aid to Brazil. The staff conversations failed to result in any agreement for military equipment, and Truman abruptly terminated Lend-Lease, except for "pipeline" orders, in July 1945. Those in favor of providing military aid to Brazil fell back on an interim program offering limited amounts of surplus equipment for sale under the Surplus Property Act.[21]

In 1946 the Joint Chiefs, concerned about the growing Soviet military threat and the lack of progress in the defense of the hemisphere, called for more positive action to ensure military capability in Latin America. They warned that "the ultimate security of the United

States has become far more dependent than heretofore upon the maintenance of the strategic unity of the Western Hemisphere" because of Soviet domination of the Eurasian continent and the development of long-range aircraft and the atomic bomb. Building an adequate hemispheric defense system was of "cardinal importance to the security of the United States."[22] Accordingly, the Joint Chiefs recommended a systematic program of military aid to the American republics. Although the Department of State concurred reluctantly, and even Admiral Ernest J. King expressed some doubts about being pushed into sponsoring "unsound military expansion," the State-War-Navy Coordinating Committee (SWNCC) approved draft legislation for Inter-American Military Cooperation, and President Truman submitted the bill to Congress in May. It authorized measures to support the training, organizing, and equipping of the armed forces of Latin America. Congress, however, adjourned without taking action on the bill.[23] The Republican party controlled the first postwar Congress (1946–1948), and it was determined to cut government spending. The Republicans refused to pass any legislation to build up the inter-American defense system.[24]

Despite such opposition, Truman reintroduced the bill in 1947. The War and Navy departments believed that a strong, coordinated inter-American defense under the leadership of the United States was essential to national security. The War Department fought hard to complete standardization of equipment, organization, and training projects and to become the sole supplier of South American military hardware. Secretary of War Robert P. Patterson, for example, in congressional hearings, stressed the importance of excluding all non-American military participation from the Western Hemisphere:

> We learned from World War II that the introduction of foreign equipment, foreign training methods, are a hazard, a definite hazard to the security of the United States, a definite hazard to the security of the Panama Canal. If we do not furnish them, someone else will, and I think that it is wise policy to remove the existing impediments.[25]

It was not only the Republicans who initially objected to any attempts to build up the Latin American military establishments but also the Department of State, which believed such a buildup would undermine democratic government in South America and impose economic hardships on the American republics. The War Department countered, however, that the Latin American governments would build up their military establishments regardless of what the United States did. Furthermore, according to the War Department, U.S. support for the military was one of the best ways of fighting communism. Patterson reasoned that "it would seem that we are playing into the hands of the Communists if by our own decisions we disable ourselves from the tender of military assistance."[26] He then proposed an entire program of assistance including the sale of arms, the standardization of equipment, military missions and training, and visits to the United States by top-ranking Latin American military officers. Such a program, according to the secretary, would ensure U.S. influence in the hemisphere and prevent Communist infiltration.[27]

Despite such arguments, however, events in Greece, Turkey, and the rest of Europe relegated arms programs for Brazil and Latin America to the background of U.S. policy considerations. In the early months of 1947 the War Department still had large stocks of surplus equipment that it desired to ship to Latin America. But by late 1948, because of demands for arms elsewhere, budgetary limitations dictated by the overshadowing requirements of the North Atlantic Alliance, and the buildup of American forces, the military found itself short of equipment and recommended that all programs for aid to the American republics be postponed. Even the Surplus Property Act program was terminated in 1948.[28]

Concerned that they could not make even token shipments of arms to Brazil, American officials increased their efforts to court the Brazilian military. At the invitation of the Truman administration, General Salvador César Obino, the chief of the Joint Staff of Brazil, visited various U.S. military installations. Although American officials avoided making any commitments to Brazil because of urgent strategic interests elsewhere, they nevertheless stressed to Obino the "special relationship" between the United States and Brazil and affirmed that Brazil would receive special considerations at a later time.[29] Despite such attempts to pacify Brazilian officials, the status of Brazil as well as the rest of Latin America was clearly outlined in a State-Army-Navy-Air Force Coordinating Committee (SANACC) paper of 1949. This report ranked priorities into three categories. The Western Hemisphere was in the third category for long-term military considerations, in the second category for long-term political considerations, and in the third category for combined considerations. In a separate ranking, of the seven categories into which countries were grouped, Brazil was relegated to category six, which meant that it should receive only a limited degree of assistance in the future.[30]

By 1949 the only American source of military assistance open to Brazil was the Mutual Defense Assistance Act. Congress designed the act to promote U.S. foreign policy and to provide for the defense and general welfare of the United States by furnishing military assistance to foreign nations.[31] But here, again, American policymakers warned that the greater share of limited resources available for foreign military assistance would be made to those countries outside the hemisphere that were immediately exposed to the threat of aggression. By virtue of its geographical and political situation Brazil did not qualify. It faced no threat of aggression comparable to that experienced by many other countries. Dean Acheson put it succinctly when he instructed U.S. Ambassador to Brazil Herschel V. Johnson to "soft pedal any request for military assistance at this time."[32]

Unable to supply Brazil with large amounts of equipment, American planners searched for other ways to maintain and strengthen Brazilian military support and cooperation. When General Obino proposed to General Dwight D. Eisenhower in December 1946 that the United States help establish a Brazilian war college, Eisenhower was delighted to offer assistance. After all, Brazil was the best and strongest friend the United States had in South America, Eisenhower reasoned, and the two countries had much in common.[33]

Modeled on the National War College in the United States, the Brazilian war college (Escola Superior de Guerra) was officially founded in 1949 with an American advisory mission.[34] American officials thought it was a great step forward for the Brazilian services. The intellectual focus of the ESG was the interrelationship of national security and national development. Drawing on American source materials and instructional techniques, the college stressed modern war strategy and economic theories, the impact of science and technology upon the art of war, and high-level political and strategic problems. The curriculum sought to integrate, using Cold War theories, all aspects of internal and external security—military policy, economic development, education, politics, agriculture, and industry. Known as the Sorbonne, the school was led by former officers of the FEB. Its first commanders, Generals Oswaldo Cordeiro de Farías and Juarez Távora, promoted the idea of interdependence with the United States, saw Brazil firmly aligned with the West, accepted the concept of Communist worldwide subversion, and projected a firm anti-Communist policy with strong support for the leadership of the United States in the Cold War. The enemy for these officers was not a nation or a group of nations but rather an ideology. This Cold War view of the world, encouraged by the United States, prompted these officers to view their own role as encompassing the control and direction of all aspects of national life.[35] Each graduating class toured the United States as guests of the government.[36]

In counseling the Brazilian military to become increasingly involved in all stages of society, American advisers implicitly encouraged, much like their earlier European counterparts, deeper involvement of the Brazilian military in domestic politics, and thus promoted military "managerial activism." Although the influence of ESG doctrine was not pervasive within the military in the early 1950s, it had a profound effect on later military governments as it became increasingly anti-Communist and committed to rapid economic development. In Castello Branco's government in the 1960s, for example, 80 percent of the core group of policymakers had attended either the college or United States military schools. The belief, shared by most American officials, that the U.S. military training of Brazilian officers inculcated apolitical professional values among the officer corps seems insupportable.[37] Such training, Washington insisted, exposed Brazilian officers to "democracy at work" and the "bureaucratic ethos." More often, it exposed them to the power and opulence of the United States military without stressing its submission to civilian authority.[38]

Yet, the myth persisted. According to most American officials the Brazilian military formed the core of stability in that country. It was the upholder of the democratic order and, although somewhat overly nationalistic, the promoter of free enterprise. While recognizing that the Brazilian army had taken the decisive action against the Vargas regime in 1954, a 1956 State Department Research and Analysis Report saw the Brazilian military as performing a new and moderating role in its nation's life. The report maintained that the army threw its weight against a revival of extremist elements in national politics and against a bankrupt Vargas regime. It took such action with restraint and with some reluctance, because it was the protector of the constitutional and democratic process. According to this report, the military shared the concerns of the middle class about the increasing radical movement, tended to eschew force, and played a "moderating role in the national life."[39]

The outbreak of the Korean War further limited the ability of the United States to provide military equipment and aid to Brazil and the rest of Latin America. It also brought a reassessment of U.S.-Brazilian relations and American security objectives.[40] Believing that a global war was a distinct possibility, American planners began to stress the need for access to the resources of Latin America as essential to any transoceanic projection of U.S. offensive power. Washington needed to ensure the uninterrupted availability of raw materials upon which any major U.S. war effort would depend and to minimize U.S. military manpower requirements in Latin America under emergency conditions. During the Second World War the United States had diverted considerable manpower and materiel to the defense of Western Hemisphere areas. American planners did not want a repeat performance.[41]

Although all of the Latin American republics supported the UN action in Korea, officials in the Truman administration were disappointed with their level of active military cooperation. The United States desired to tap the manpower resources of Latin America in order to avoid too great a commitment of U.S. troops.[42] Moreover, the effective development of Latin American forces, went this line of thinking, would be valuable for countering future Communist aggression in other areas as well as in their home area.[43] Edward Miller, the assistant secretary of state for Inter-American Affairs, was particularly disappointed with Brazil, supposedly the United States' leading ally in Latin America. Miller contrasted Brazil's apathetic position in the Korean crisis with its enthusiastic support for the Allied cause in 1942.[44]

Something had to be done. Although severely limited by the demand for military equipment elsewhere, U.S. planners wanted to make some gesture to Latin Americans and especially to the Brazilian military. They encouraged the Brazilians to build six destroyers in Rio under the guidance and supervision of U.S. naval authorities and initiated discussions about the sale of two cruisers to Brazil. Even the State Department favored such action, reasoning that the navy was one of the most pro-U.S. institutions in Brazil. It cautioned, however, that it was "almost criminal for Brazil to spend money on armaments when it needed other things so badly" and that under present legislation it was almost impossible to transfer military equipment to Latin American countries except on the basis of 100 percent cash reimbursement.[45]

When American officials learned, however, of British sales of jet aircraft to Argentina, despite reservations they considered the possibility of providing the Brazilian air force with jet planes. To Ambassador Johnson, the "worst possible thing from the local point of view would be for the Argentines to get more than Brazil or to get all she wanted while Brazil got nothing or only part of what she wants."[46] While sympathetic to Johnson's argument, department officials were wary of providing military equipment of an offensive character. Moreover, since the Brazilians had not officially requested jet aircraft it was best not to broach the subject with them.[47]

The Korean crisis continued to cause problems for American planners concerned with U.S.-Brazilian relations. When the National Security Council approved an army recommendation asking for Latin American ground forces to participate in the Korean action, Miller responded: "In my opinion, the key to the question in South America is Brazil. If Brazil contributes troops, the chances are that one or more of the other countries will follow suit." Accordingly, the State Department considered negotiations with Brazil on this matter to be vitally important.[48] To State, active Brazilian participation would make it difficult for other reluctant states like Mexico to postpone making similar contributions.[49]

During the fourth meeting of American foreign ministers held in Washington in March and April of 1951, Secretary of State Dean Acheson and General Charles L. Bolté, deputy chief of staff for planning in the Department of the Army and Chairman of the Inter-American Defense Board, held frank and apparently successful discussions with the Brazilian foreign minister, João Neves da Fontoura, and his principal military advisers about the pressing need for ground troops in Korea. They stressed the common responsibility of all UN nations to repel aggression and the importance of a Brazilian contribution.[50] President Truman also broached the subject in a letter to President Vargas in which he stressed the need for close military cooperation. The U.S. Army invited Brazilian Minister of War Major General Estillac Leal to tour U.S. installations, in part at least to promote Brazilian participation in the war.[51] America's hopes were high as the Brazilians returned home.

Subsequently, however, the Brazilian foreign minister, in a discussion with Assistant Secretary of State for Inter-American Affairs Miller, advanced the idea of sending a Brazilian commission to Korea to study the ways in which Brazil could fulfill its international commitments. According to Fontoura, Brazilian public opinion was not prepared to support the shipping of a substantial contingent of Brazilian ground forces to Korea. The commission would have the announced purpose of studying the various ways Brazil could contribute to the UN effort. But the real purpose behind the formulation of the commission, Fontoura confided, would be to place its members in position, upon their return to Brazil, to come out strongly in favor of sending troops to Korea. The trip envisioned by Fontoura would be brief, the commission would proceed first to UN headquarters in New York, and it would then go to Tokyo and Korea, returning to Brazil by way of Washington for conferences with the Unified Command.[52]

While Fontoura's proposal was considerably less than what the Truman administration wanted from Brazil, Miller's initial reaction was favorable. Such a commission "would materially enhance the possibility of Brazil's contribution of ground forces to Korea."[53] Preliminary informal discussions with the Pentagon revealed extreme coolness to the suggestion, however. The Joint Chiefs of Staff argued that there were great administrative difficulties in the theater with regard to the handling of VIPs and extreme shortages of transportation between Tokyo and Korea and adequate housing in Korea. They were also extremely reluctant to establish a precedent that other nations might wish to follow of sending exploratory or inquisitory missions to Korea without having made any commitment to fight. The Joint Chiefs pointed out that none of the nations that had committed troops to Korea had previously sent exploratory missions.[54] Miller thus wired Johnson to tell the Brazilians in no uncertain terms that they should not send the mission to Korea unless there was a bona fide intention to send troops. At some point thereafter, the Brazilians stopped mentioning their proposed mission to Korea.[55]

Instead, President Vargas presented the United States a fait accompli by announcing publicly that he was sending General Pedro A. Góes Monteiro, chief of the Brazilian joint general staff, to the United States to discuss military cooperation in the present crisis.[56] Vargas's announcement caught U.S. officials by surprise and set off a minor flap between the State Department and the army about who would organize General Góes Monteiro's visit and who would pay for the social obligations associated with the visit. The army objected to acting as host on the grounds that there had recently been too many visits of military officials of other countries and that the social obligations were too burdensome. Moreover, the expense of entertaining visiting military officials fell too heavily on the army, which believed that the navy, air force, and State Department were not paying their share. State responded that if the army did not show Góes Monteiro proper consideration not only the general but also President Vargas would be deeply resentful, and this would jeopardize chances of getting Brazilian troops. State added that it was legally impossible for itself to finance parties at military facilities such as Fort Meade. General Omar N. Bradley finally settled this bureaucratic skirmish by agreeing that the army would do all- in its power to make Góes Monteiro welcome.[57]

Arriving in the United States in late July, Góes Monteiro held extensive discussions regarding Brazil's military cooperation. Time and again U.S. planners pressed on the Brazilian military leader the concept that Brazil now had a great opportunity to project its leadership in Latin America by contributing to the end of Communist aggression in Korea. According to Assistant Secretary of State Miller, Brazil was in a position to achieve several advantages by acting promptly: "She could increase her prestige, obtain special and very valuable training for some of her troops, and improve her opportunity to obtain military equipment." Miller closed his argument by stating that "the United States would consider it a privilege to be able to cooperate with Brazil in achieving these ends."[58] Góes Monteiro, although he spoke in terms of a firm Brazilian policy of cooperation, was wary of any direct commitment. Speaking in great detail, the general described the difficulties Brazil faced in the areas of transport and communication facilities, problems with inflation and basic economic development, and the troubles Brazil had with its own Communists. Góes Monteiro made it clear that Brazil's first priority was its own internal stability and its second priority was economic development.[59]

As the talks with Góes Monteiro continued, Miller became increasingly convinced that the Brazilian government was not going to take action. The Americans, nevertheless, continued to press for a commitment. Brigadier General Edwin L. Sibert, director of the staff of the Inter-American Defense Board, outlined to Góes Monteiro the military priorities assigned by the Department of Defense to the principal geographical areas of the world: 1) Korea, 2) Europe, 3) Far East and Southeast Asia, 4) Middle East, 5) Northern part of the Western Hemisphere, and 6) the rest of Latin America. Sibert emphasized that Brazilian participation in Korea would lift Brazil from category six to category one. He went on to add that the United States would supply such a force with everything it needed except replacement personnel, including technical assistance, training, and transportation.[60] Sibert even offered jet pilot training for up to twenty-five Brazilian volunteers who would serve in American units in Korea and hinted about the favorable results for Brazil of such collaboration in connection with its balance of military power vis-à-vis Argentina.[61] Góes Monteiro responded that Brazilian assistance in Korea in the defense of the free world, if a third world war should break out, would depend upon the amount and speed of the economic and military assistance received from the United States. The greater the help received from the United States, the sooner Brazil could act.[62]

Although the U.S. offer seemed generous, the talks dragged on into September with little progress. The Americans even produced two secret draft military assistance agreements. The first, "Military Assistance to the United Nations," called for Brazil to offer to the

Unified Command an infantry division for deployment as part of the UN force serving in Korea. It also stipulated that the United States would train, equip, and furnish logistic support to this division.[63] The second, "Brazil-U.S. Military Cooperation," was made contingent on the passing of the Mutual Security Act of 1951. It proposed U.S. assistance to Brazil in developing a rearmament program consistent with Brazil's hemispheric defense responsibilities and U.S. defense needs.[64]

After being entertained in New York by Nelson A. Rockefeller, General Góes Monteiro flew to Brazil with the draft agreement, but nothing ever came of the proposals. Brazil sent no troops to the Korean theater.[65] Washington's lack of success was due primarily to differing priorities. For U.S. planners the global situation and preventing the spread of international communism predominated. The Brazilians' primary objectives were internal stability and economic development. A war in the Far East held little attraction for a regime attempting to consolidate its power internally and to industrialize.[66] Moreover, the rallying cry of the Brazilian Communists had become "Not one soldier for Korea."[67]

The Brazilian military was also sharply divided on the issue of economic development and militant nationalism as politics in the Clube Militar (the military club of Brazilian army officers) clearly illustrated. One faction, led by Generals Estillac Leal and Luis Hildebrando Horta Barbosa, advocated moving away from a close relationship with the United States and promoted economic nationalism. These officers dominated the Clube's directorate in the early 1950s. In what American officials considered a major setback for Vargas and the "nationalistic forces" these officers were defeated in Clube elections in 1952, and "moderates" backing a more liberal economic development policy and favoring close ties with the United States gained dominance. These "moderates" were primarily from the Brazilian Expeditionary Force and the ESG. When Vargas appointed Leal his war minister, this further alienated most members of the officer class, and they forced Leal to resign.[68]

While military ties with the United States tightened and military officers favorable to American concepts of development increased their influence and power, the Brazilian military nevertheless preferred, where possible, to acquire locally produced weapons and equipment. It wanted to "liberate itself from foreign dependency." Although often divided on the issues of nationalism and foreign policy, the Brazilian armed forces consistently were united in advocating heavy industry as a base for autonomous armaments production.[69]

Despite this attitude and the setback on the Korean proposal, American policy planners continued to focus on Brazil as the key to their Latin American policy. When Congress approved the Mutual Security Act of 1951 authorizing $40 million for military aid to the other American republics, Brazil received over one third of the total amount available.[70] American policymakers considered Brazil to be the cornerstone of any U.S. collective military plans for Latin America and the Brazilian military to be pro-U.S. In addition, the U.S. military wanted to increase its base rights and expand its facilities in Brazil. The army and navy sought to set up and operate worldwide communications stations in Brazil. And the air force wanted surveillance stations for missile flights.[71]

At a meeting held in Rio de Janeiro during September 1952, representatives of Brazil and the United States worked out a draft agreement on closer military cooperation. In addition to reviving the almost dormant Joint Military Commission in Rio de Janeiro and the JBUSDC, the draft agreement notes provided for the creation of a Permanent Joint Board on Defense, Brazil-United States, composed of high-level defense officials of the two governments who would meet annually, alternating between Washington and Rio. The purpose of the board was to give guidance to and coordinate the work of the two existing commissions.[72] The United States also signed agreements with Brazil for army and naval missions to be dispatched to Brazil for training purposes and for a bilateral military assistance program.[73]

The Eisenhower administration accepted the general assumptions of the military aid program developed by Truman, and U.S. military policy with regard to Brazil did not change. Officials viewed the small investment in equipment and training of Brazilian forces as extremely successful. Aside from the obvious advantages of training future leaders and their personnel in the doctrines of the United States military, Washington anticipated nonmilitary benefits from the effort as well. Such aid, it was believed, not only helped in the development of technically trained specialists, health and sanitation procedures, and organizational skills—all of which could be of value in improving the country, but it also would pay benefits in a crisis by having the Brazilians familiar with U.S. techniques and methods of operation. And it would provide "useful friends in the military."[74]

Relations seemed to be improving. Grants and credits to Brazil mounted under the revised military assistance program in the first Eisenhower administration. Between 1952 and 1955 the United States provided $93.3 million worth of assistance,[75] but problems again surfaced. On the American side, first the Office of European Affairs of the

Department of State and then the Canadian government objected to the name of the new organization because it so closely approximated the Permanent Joint Board on Defense, Canada-United States. A joint meeting of the Department of State and the Joint Chiefs of Staff resolved this issue quickly by agreeing to a name change, the Combined Board on Defense, Brazil-United States.

A much more difficult issue flared up, however, and prevented establishment of the board. After reviewing the draft agreement notes, the State Department recommended that it and the Ministry of Foreign Relations of Brazil should have full membership on the board. The draft provided only that they should be present as advisers "when deemed necessary." The Joint Chiefs rejected State Department membership on the grounds that "it would alter the concept of the Board to that of a Government-to-Government body, thus opening the way to include political and economic matters as well as setting an unwanted precedent and paving the way for other Latin American nations to follow." Formal State Department representation, according to the Joint Chiefs, was not only unnecessary but also undesirable.[76] The issue was never resolved. In 1955 the United States and Brazil exchanged notes perpetuating the joint military and defense commissions without the Board.[77]

Bureaucratic infighting between the Department of State and the U.S. military continued over proposals for supplying the Brazilians with increased quantities of war materials. State constantly complained that the Pentagon never kept it informed of its plans, recommendations, or negotiations. State officials found out about the transfer of ships and the sale of airplanes to Brazil only through informal channels. Moreover the U.S. military, according to State Department authorities, rarely took into account the consequences of such actions on U.S. relations with Brazil or with other Latin American states.[78]

For its part, the Joint Chiefs thought that the political arguments advanced by State regarding Brazilian unhappiness were unconvincing in the absence of an accompanying rationale involving military necessity. Even the Joint Chiefs, however, eventually rejected Brazilian requests for aircraft carriers, submarines, and aircraft. With its other commitments around the world, U.S. military resources were already stretched too thin.[79]

Despite such bureaucratic bickering and some unhappiness on the part of the Brazilian military about its share of U.S. military aid, relations between the armed forces of the two countries continued to improve during the Eisenhower administration as American military missions provided U.S. techniques, organization, and equipment to their Brazilian counterparts. Under U.S. supervision the Brazilian military became the most modern and developed sector of Brazilian society and a major component of the overall modernization process. Washington held up the Brazilian military as exemplary not only in its training and organization but also in its civil-military relations. According to officials in both the Truman and the Eisenhower administrations, Brazil was stable, conservative, pro-American, anti-Communist, and proprivate enterprise. Not until 1964 did the Brazilian military cast doubts on its image in the minds of U.S. officials by overthrowing the civilian government.

Notes

1. See Baily, *Development of South America*, pp. 67, 73; and Rabe, *Eisenhower and Latin America*, p. 34.
2. See Carvalho, "Armed Forces and Politics in Brazil."
3. Skidmore, *Politics in Brazil*, pp. 53, 76, 325. See also Alfred Stephan, *The Military in Politics: Changing Patterns in Brazil* (Princeton: Princeton University Press, 1971), p. 10.
4. As quoted in McCann, *Brazilian-American Alliance*, p. 131.
5. See Peter S. Smith, *Oil and Politics in Modern Brazil* (Toronto: Macmillan of Canada, 1976), p. 55.
6. Stephan, *Military in Politics*, pp. 34–42; Frederick M. Nunn, "Effects of European Military Training in Latin America: The Origins and Nature of Professional Militarism in Argentina, Brazil, Chile, and Peru, 1870–1940," *Military Affairs* 39:1 (February 1975): 1–7. See also Nunn, "Military Professionalism and Professional Militarism in Brazil, 1870–1940: Historical Perspectives and Political Implications," *Journal of Latin American Studies* 4:1 (May 1972): 29–54; and Carvalho, "Armed Forces and Politics in Brazil," p. 20.
7. Skidmore, *Politics in Brazil*, p. 321; Stephan, *Military in Politics*, p. 131; Cláudio Moreira Bento, "Getúlio Vargas e a Evolucão Da Doutrina Do Exercito" (Getúlio Vargas and the evolution of army doctrine), *Revista do Instituto Histórico e Geografico Brasileiro* (The Brazilian institute of history and geography review), 339 (1983): 63–71.
8. See John D. Wirth, *The Politics of Brazilian Development, 1930–1954* (Stanford: Stanford University Press, 1970), pp. 128–30.
9. Jan Knippers Black, *United States Penetration of Brazil* (Pennsylvania: University of Pennsylvania Press, 1977), p. 191.
10. See Samuel P. Huntington's criteria of professional corporateness, expertise based on specialized education and training, and a sense of responsibility, plus career orientation in Huntington, *The Soldier and the State: The Theory and Politics of Civil-Military Relations* (Cambridge: Harvard University Press, 1957), pp. 8–18.
11. Wirth, *The Politics of Brazilian Development*, p. 221; Stephan, *Military in Politics*, pp. 240–46; Burns, *Brazil*, p. 411.

12. Telegram from Adolf Berle to secretary of state, October 30, 1945, DS 832.00/10–3045, RG 59, NA. See also Berle and Jacobs, eds., *Navigating the Rapids*, p. 67.

13. In August 1950, President Dutra made Clark a general in the Brazilian army. See Baily, *Development of South America*, pp. 134, 146.

14. See Berle, dispatch, October 7, 1945, *FRUS, 1945* (Washington, DC: Government Printing Office, 1952) 9:603–5.

15. James F. Schnabel, *The History of the Joint Chiefs of Staff: The Joint Chiefs of Staff and National Policy* (Washington, DC: Government Printing Office, 1982). The delegates in Mexico City reached an agreement in principle only. See JCS to secretary of war, February 6, 1945, and the enclosure to the JCS 1233/2, January 31, 1945, CCS 092 (1-18-45), Records of the United States Joint Chiefs of Staff, Record Group 218, National Archives, Washington, DC (hereafter cited as RG 218, NA); and U.S. Department of State, *Inter-American Conference on Problems of War and Peace February 23–March 8, 1945 Final Act of Chapultepec* (Washington, DC: Government Printing Office, 1945).

16. Schnabel, *History of JCS*, pp. 364–66.

17. See SWNCC 4/10, Records of the State-War-Navy Coordinating Committee, July 7, 1945, Records of the Interdepartmental and Intradepartmental Committees (State Department), Record Group 353, Diplomatic Branch, National Archives, Washington, DC (hereafter cited as RG 353, NA).

18. For the text of the secret agreement see *FRUS, 1942* 5:662. See also memorandum to the Chiefs of Staff, March 13, 1946, PO 091 Brazil, Records of the War Department General and Special Staffs, Record Group 165, National Archives, Washington, DC (hereafter cited as RG 165, NA).

19. Berle, dispatch to secretary of state, July 26, 1945, *FRUS, 1945* 9:600–21.

20. Ibid. See also memorandum from Philip O. Chalmers to Fletcher Warren, "Coordination of Military and Naval Missions with the Embassy," August 11, 1945, Records of the American Republic Affairs Division, RG 59, NA.

21. For the text of the act see 58 *Statutes at Large* 765. See also National Security Council report to the president, "U.S. Policy toward Inter-American Collaboration," May 18, 1950, *FRUS, 1950* 1:628–29.

22. Memorandum from JCS to SWNCC, April 3, 1946, CCS 092 Sec. 2, RG 218, NA; Schnabel, *History of JCS*, 1:375.

23. Memorandum from Admiral William Leahy to JCS, March 20, 1946, CCS 092 Sec. 2, RG 218, NA.

24. Baily, *Development of South America*, p. 65.

25. See U.S. Congress, House Foreign Affairs Committee, *Hearings on Inter-American Military Cooperation Act, 1947*, 80th Cong., 1st sess. (Washington, DC: Government Printing Office, 1947), pp. 26–44. See also the remarks of Fleet Admiral Chester Nimitz and General of the Army Dwight D. Eisenhower at the same hearings; and Baily, *Development of South America*, p. 65.

26. *FRUS, 1946* 1:86–110; *FRUS, 1947* 1:101–36. See also David Green, *Containment*, p. 163. For a general discussion of U.S. military aid policies toward Latin America see Harold Hovey, *United States Military Assistance: A Study of Policies and Practices* (New York: Praeger, 1965); and Edwin Lieuwen, *Arms and Politics in Latin America*, 2d ed. (New York: Praeger, 1963).

27. Green, *Containment*, p. 169. See also Rabe, *Eisenhower and Latin America*, p. 2.

28. Secretary of state to diplomatic representatives in the American republics, July 30, 1948, *FRUS, 1948* (Washington, DC: Government Printing Office, 1972), 9:218–19; memorandum from Carl M. Marcy (assistant legislative counsel) to acting secretary of state, October 19, 1948, *FRUS, 1948* 9:224–25.

29. Memorandum from Gordon Grey (secretary of the army) to secretary of defense, July 26, 1948, DDS 092 (15-1-29), RG 330, NA.

30. For the text of SANACC 360/11, March 16, 1949, see *FRUS, 1949* 1:257. Only one other Latin American country, Mexico, was listed, and it also was placed in category 6. See memorandum from Lt. Col. J. F. Franklin to the chief of staff, May 21, 1948, PO 1948, PO 091 Latin America, Records of the Army Staff, Record Group 319, National Archives, Washington, DC (hereafter cited as RG 319, NA).

31. For the text of the act see 63 *Statutes at Large* 714.

32. General Omar Bradley to General William H. H. Morris, Jr., July 14, 1948, JBUSMC, PO 091 Brazil, RG 319, NA; secretary of state to diplomatic offices in the American republics, January 16, 1950, *FRUS, 1950* 1:620–22. The Department of State even opposed this minimal assistance as diverting U.S. aid from the main effort. See army memorandum, April 4, 1949, PO 319.1TS, RG 319 NA; and Schnabel, *History of JCS*, p. 353.

33. Conference between Eisenhower and General Salvador César Obino, December 4, 1946, PO 337, RG 319, NA.

34. See memorandum from Allen Dawson to Spruille Braden, May 15, 1947, DS 711.32/5-1547, RG 59, NA, for the State Department's view on the issue. State was not consulted until the negotiations had reached an advanced stage.

35. See Black, *United States Penetration of Brazil*, pp. 188–227; Bourne, *Getúlio Vargas of Brazil*, pp. 175–77; Flynn, *Brazil: A Political Analysis*, p. 152; Alves, *Military Brazil*, p. 7; and Baily, *Development of South America*, pp. 146–47. Stephan points out in *Military in Politics* that the ESG differed from its American counterpart in two major ways: 1) it focused on the danger of subversive warfare and Soviet indirect attacks and 2) it included not only military but also upper-class civilians among its regular staff, visiting scholars, and students. See also Alexandre de Barros, "The Brazilian Military: Professional Socialization, Political Performance, and State Building" (Ph.D. diss., University of Chicago, 1978).

36. Mission of U.S. Army officers to Brazil for the foundation of high command school, February 12, 1947, P.O. 350.1 Case 20, RG 319, NA. The new Brazilian war college, unlike its American counterpart, combined the functions of the U.S. Industrial College of the Armed Forces and the National War College and increasingly emphasized the internal aspects of development and security to a far greater degree than the U.S. war college. The Brazilians also encouraged civilian participation, a key aspect not found in the U.S. example. See Stephan, *Military in Politics*, pp. 175–78.

37. The U.S. advisory mission remained until 1960, and in 1970 the United States was still the only country with a liaison officer with faculty status at the war college. See Stephan, *Military in Politics*, p. 129.

38. See Stephan S. Kaplan, *U.S. Military Aid to Brazil and the Dominican Republic: Its Nature, Objectives, and Impact*, Department of the State Foreign

Affairs Research Series, no. 16217 (Washington, DC: Government Printing Office, 1972), pp. 179–87.

39. R & A Report 7116, "Latin American Recent Developments and Future Prospects," RG 59, NA.

40. See NSC 56/2 "U.S. Policy toward Inter-American Military Collaboration," May 18, 1950, RG 273, NA. U.S. defense planners assumed that the United States was locked in a momentous global struggle with the Soviet Union, and with this policy paper they outlined a design for hemisphere defense.

41. Draft report by the National Security Council of the position of the U.S. with respect to the military aspects of the implementation of the inter-American treaty of reciprocal assistance, FRUS, 1950 1:643.

42. Draft memorandum by John C. Dreier for NSC, "Military Assistance for Korea from Latin America," August 3, 1950, ibid. 1:643.

43. Memorandum from Bradley to secretary of defense, January 2, 1951, CCS 381 Western Hemisphere, RG 330, NA.

44. Memorandum from Edward G. Miller to Paul Nitze, September 26, 1950, FRUS, 1950 1:654–56.

45. See memorandum of conversation by Sheldon T. Mills, minister counselor of U.S. embassy, October 19, 1950, DS 732.5621/10-2750, RG 59, NA; DuWayne G. Clark to Herschel Johnson, August 7, 1950, DS 732.5-MAP/8-150, RG 59, NA; and memorandum by U.S. naval attaché, September 22, 1950, attached. Two light cruisers, the Philadelphia and the St. Louis, were eventually transferred to Brazil. See Department of State memorandum, January 30, 1951, DS 732.5621/1-3051, RG 59, NA. See also memorandum by John Elliott and F. T. Murphy, "Report of Sale of Naval Vessels to Brazil," May 5, 1950, DS 732.562/5-550, RG 59, NA; memorandum from Dreier to Clark, July 18, 1950, DS 732.5-MAP/8-152, RG 59, NA; Clark to Johnson, August 7, 1950, DS 732.5-MAP/8-152, RG 59, NA; and memorandum of conversation among Clark, Juan Trippe, Pan Am Airways, July 19, 1950, DS 732.5-MAP/7-1450, RG 59, NA.

46. Johnson to Fletcher Warren, director, Office of South American Affairs, September 26, 1950, DS 732.5621/4-2650, RG 59, NA.

47. Department of State memorandum, "Military Assistance for Korea," March 16, 1951, FRUS, 1951 2:1008–9.

48. Ibid.

49. Memorandum by Miller, "Special Mission to Brazil," May 31, 1951, Miller Files, Lot File 53D-26, RG 59, NA.

50. Memorandum of conversation with João Neves da Fontoura, Dean Acheson, Edward Miller, General Charles L. Bolté, Maurício Nabuco (Brazilian ambassador to the United States), General Paulo de Figueredo (Brazilian army), April 1, 1951, DS 732.13/4-551, RG 59, NA.

51. Memorandum by Philip E. Barringer (Office of Foreign Military Affairs) [n.d.], Miller File, Lot File 53D-26, RG 59, NA.

52. See Brandi, Vargas, pp. 248–53.

53. Miller to General Bolté, May 4, 1951, Miller Files, Lot File 53D-26, RG 59, NA.

54. Miller to Johnson, May 3, 1951, Miller Files, Lot File 53D-26, RG 59, NA; Miller to General Matthew B. Ridgway (Supreme Commander of UN Forces in Korea), August 10, 1951, Miller Files, Lot File 53D-26, RG 59, NA.

55. Miller to Johnson, May 3, 1951, Miller Files, Lot File 53D-26, RG 59, NA; Miller to Ridgway, August 10, 1951, Miller Files, Lot File 53D-26, RG 59, NA.

56. Brandi, *Vargas*, pp. 253–58.

57. Memorandum by Thomas C. Mann, July 13, 1951, DS 732.5811/7-1351, RG 59, NA; memorandum from Miller to secretary, "Background Information for Call of General Góes Monteiro," July 31, 1951, DS 732.5811/7-3151, RG 59, NA. General Góes Monteiro was Chief of Staff of the rebel forces that brought Vargas to power in 1930. He served as minister of war from 1934 to 1945 and was in 1951 chief of the Brazilian joint general staff. Prior to Brazil's entry into World War II, Washington regarded Góes Monteiro as pro-Nazi and as an admirer of the German military machine. However, according to U.S. officials, upon Brazil's entry into World War II on the side of the Allies, the general completely changed his viewpoint and had since been a wholehearted supporter of the United States and bitterly anti-Communist. See biography statement on Góes Monteiro attached to memorandum from Miller to secretary of state, July 31, 1951, DS 732.5811/7-3151, RG 59, NA.

58. Memorandum by Miller of conversation with Góes Monteiro, August 2, 1951, *FRUS, 1951* 2:1206.

59. Discussion with General Góes Monteiro, August 17, 1951, DS 732.5811/8-1751, RG 59, NA; memorandum of conversation, "Korean War and the Need for Peace Aid from Brazil," August 2, 1951, DS 732.5811/8-251, RG 59, NA. See also Lourival Coutinho, *O General Góes depõe* (General Góes speaks), 2d ed. (Rio de Janeiro: Livraria Editôra Coelho Branco, 1956).

60. Memorandum by Edward L. Sibert of conversation with Góes Monteiro, August 3, 1951, Miller Files, Lot File 53D-26, RG 59, NA. See also Miller to Ridgway, August 10, 1951, *FRUS, 1951* 2:1211; and Department of State, memorandum of conversation, "Discussions with General Góes Monteiro on his Mission to U.S.," August 17, 1951, *FRUS, 1951* 2:1213–16.

61. Memorandum from Johnson to Miller, August 17, 1951, DS 732.5/8-1751, RG 59, NA; memorandum by Miller of conversation with Góes Monteiro, August 14, 1951, Miller Files, Lot File 53D-26, RG 59, NA.

62. Memorandum of discussions with Góes Monteiro, August 17, 1951, DS 732.5811/8-1751, RG 59, NA; memorandum, "Discussions with Monteiro," August 22, 1951, DS 732.5811/8-2251, RG 59, NA; Coutinho, *Góes*, p. 206.

63. See DS 732.551/9-2651, RG 59, NA. For a draft of this agreement, see also "Brazil-U.S. Military Talks," September 29, 1951, Miller Files, Lot File 53D-26, RG 59, NA.

64. Miller to secretary of state, "Background for Your Meeting with General Monteiro," October 12, 1951, DS 732.551/10-1251, RG 59, NA.

65. For the draft "Military Assistance to the U.N.," see Bolté (deputy chief of staff for plans, Department of the Army) to Góes Monteiro, September 27, 1951, *FRUS, 1951* 2:1224–28. See also Coutinho, *Góes*, p. 206.

66. For U.S.-Brazilian negotiations see DS 732.5, 732.5 MSP, 732.5811, and 795B.5, RG 59, NA.

67. Dulles, "Post-Dictatorship Brazil," p. 23.

68. See Flynn, *Brazil: A Political Analysis*, p. 166; Peter S. Smith, *Oil and Politics*, p. 86; and Nelson Werneck Sodré, *História Militar de Brasil* (Military history of Brazil), p. 239.

69. See Wirth, *The Politics of Brazilian Development*, pp. 128–29; and Jose Teixeira Oliveira, *O govêrno Dutra* (Rio de Janeiro: Editôra Civilizacão Brasileira, 1956), p. 28.

70. For the text of the Mutual Security Act of 1951 see 65 *Statutes at Large* 373. See also memorandum by Miller, August 12, 1951, *FRUS, 1951* 2:1026–27; R & A Report 5830, "Factors Affecting the Negotiations of Bilateral Military Assistance Agreements with Selected Latin American Countries," July 25, 1952, RG 59, NA; and Michael J. Francis, "Military Aid to Latin America in the U.S. Congress," *Journal of Inter-American Studies* 6 (July 1964): 389–404.

71. Henry F. Holland to Deputy Undersecretary Francis T. Murphy, "U.S. Military Relations with Brazil," July 12, 1954, DS 733.5 MSP/7-1254, RG 59, NA.

72. Holland to Robert D. Murphy, "Proposed Defense Organization with Brazil," April 7, 1954, attached notes, DS 732.5/4-754, RG 59, NA.

73. For the text of these agreements see *U.S. Treaties and Other International Agreements, 1955* (Washington, DC: Government Printing Office, 1956), 6:pt.3:3506–7.

74. Military attaché report, October 4, 1952, PO 091 Brazil, RG 319, NA. See also Rabe, *Eisenhower and Latin America*, p. 36.

75. See Kaplan, *U.S. Military Aid to Brazil and the Dominican Republic*, p. 169. On general U.S. military aid to Latin America see Lieuwen, *Arms and Politics*; Hovey, *United States Military Assistance*; and Frank Pancake, "Military Assistance as an Element of U.S. Foreign Policy in Latin America, 1950–1968" (Ph.D. diss., University of Virginia, 1969).

76. Holland to secretary of state, "Proposed Combined Board on Defense, Brazil-U.S.," July 6, 1954, Miller Files, Lot File 53D-26, RG 59, NA.

77. For the text of these notes see *U.S. Treaties and Other International Agreements, 1955*, 6:pt.3:4103–5.

78. George Spencer to Sterling Cottrell, May 11, 1954, DS 732.5621/5-1154, RG 59, NA; Robert F. Woodward to Holland, June 10, 1954, DS 732.5622/6-1054, RG 59, NA.

79. Holland to Murphy, "U.S. Military Relations with Brazil," July 12, 1954, DS 733.5 MSP/7-1254, RG 59, NA; memorandum by Cottrell, "Brazilian Navy Request for Vessels," August 9, 1954, Cottrell Files, Lot File 58D-42, RG 59, NA.

Chapter Five

Financing Brazilian Development

Firmly committed to the Wilsonian liberal concept that expanding foreign trade was necessary for full domestic employment and prosperity, the Truman and Eisenhower administrations promoted an "open world," expansion of American private enterprise, and the use of American private capital at home and abroad.[1] Most American policymakers had an unqualified belief that private entrepreneurs, unrestrained and encouraged by government, could duplicate the American success story in other areas of the world. For these officials, the gains of unregulated private business were synonymous with the advancement of society as a whole. Most American policymakers looked on the U.S. economic order as a universal model for successful development. All an underdeveloped nation needed was to follow the American model as a "blueprint for success."

The formula put forward by American leaders was somewhat simplistic and a distortion of the historic role the federal government played in the development of the United States. American policymakers knew perfectly well that the New Deal was an experiment in state intervention. Yet, both the Truman and Eisenhower administrations ignored this aspect of American development and focused instead on the primary role of private enterprise and private capital.[2] This is readily apparent in their dealings with Brazil.

Both administrations defined Brazilian development in traditional liberal economic terms—that is, it should come about through the use of private capital free of government restrictions, the creation of a good investment climate, and the maintenance of monetary and political stability. In general, they opposed economic nationalism, statism, and "excessive" industrial development, and they condemned government intervention and interference in the economy. According to these officials economic nationalism weakened respect for private property and individual initiative. It injured U.S. business and smacked of communism. Moreover, state enterprises had the potential to become bloated with bureaucracy and responsive to political whims rather than to sound economic analyses.[3]

Intertwined and often inseparable from the American promotion of private capital as the way to achieve a prosperous, expanding economy in Brazil was the attempt by U.S. policymakers to avoid government-to-government loans to help finance development. The issue provoked long and bitter debates not only between the two nations' officials but also within the U.S. government itself. The Department of State found itself constantly at odds with the International Bank for Reconstruction and Development (IBRD), the Treasury Department, and the Department of Commerce over the role of government funds for development projects. Only as a last resort did the Truman and Eisenhower administrations consider the use of public loans for Brazilian development. When officials did consider such aid they demanded that Brazil follow a strict financial course designed to benefit U.S. corporations and private investors.[4]

These views collided with Brazil's determination to use nationalist and statist techniques in promoting growth and to seek U.S. government loans for its development plans. Seeing the United States as the richest and most powerful nation in the world, Brazil constantly pushed, prodded, and pleaded for financial aid and assistance in promoting its economic development and modernization.[5] Brazilian policymakers fluctuated, however, between acceptance of the American advice and commitment to a strong nationalistic approach to development. Determined to catch up with the more advanced nations, the governments from Getúlio Vargas to João Café Filho saw rapid industrialization and economic growth as the solution to their problems. Although committed to a capitalist mode of development, these governments came to see the promotion of national development as a major role for the central government. All relied on a mixed strategy of promoting private and public investment of foreign and domestic capital to develop the industrial base deemed necessary for a modern economy. For example, Vargas's Estado Novo faithfully adhered to a general course of economic liberalism, but nevertheless increased the power of the central government and its participation in the economy.[6]

In contrast, the Dutra government, strongly encouraged by the Truman administration, pursued, during its first two years in office, policies based on economic liberalism and free trade. Determined to avoid even the limited state intervention and state controls of the Estado Novo, it reversed Vargas's nationalist restrictions on foreign participation in the economy and attempted to attract private foreign investment. It generally followed the neoliberal, noninterventionist policies of the conservative economist Eugênio Gudin, who basically accepted the American arguments. He believed that the optimum use of resources would result from private initiative operating in a free market economy.[7]

Following these guidelines, the Dutra government allowed the free entry of consumer goods into Brazil in 1946. The result was that the large foreign reserves built up during the war were soon drained. Rethinking its development strategy, the Dutra government in 1947 adopted a strong nationalist approach to development. It imposed a rigid system of import controls including both a priority system and a fixed exchange rate. The priority system was designed to favor the importation of machinery and to discourage the importation of consumer goods. This system reserved for national producers the domestic market for consumer goods and permitted the expansion of basic industries. By maintaining an exchange barrier to the importation of manufactured consumer goods, it also guaranteed a relatively low exchange rate for imports necessary to Brazilian industry. Although officials in both the Truman and Eisenhower administrations were unhappy with many of its regulations and restrictions, the system prevailed until the end of the decade and was regarded as being highly successful in encouraging Brazilian development.[8]

Despite U.S. prodding, few Brazilian leaders accepted laissez faire economics or liberal capitalism outright. Most believed in an integrated approach to development by means of a tripartite alliance between the state, multinational corporations, and foreign and domestic capital. The state was the coordinator of the effort and became the driving force behind industrialization. Unlike their American counterparts, the Brazilians came to view statism and economic nationalism as effective tools in their quest for rapid modernization. State ownership or control of the nation's major economic resources was often a common denominator in the thinking of various Brazilian political factions, including the military. The Brazilian efforts seemed to work. Total industrial output grew 122 percent between 1947 and 1955 and the public sector grew from 17.1 percent in 1947 to 23.9 percent in 1956. Brazil's policies also produced real problems. While the growth rate steadily increased, real minimum wages steadily declined from a base of 100 in 1944, to 58 in 1948, to 50.9 in 1950. Brazil also incurred rapid inflation and huge foreign debts.[9]

The Brazilians walked a tightrope. Not wanting to offend the United States, the only nation with sufficient funds to aid their country's development, and desiring large U.S. government loans, they often paid lip service to American advice while continuing to expand the role of the state in the economy. The result was that Brazilian plans and concepts often mixed with American proposals and ideas to produce a kaleidoscopic picture of economic development and industrialization in Brazil.

Only after the Second World War did Brazil embark on a deliberate, all-embracing and sustained industrialization drive that markedly altered the structure of its economy. Outlining a comprehensive program of economic development in 1946, the SALTE plan, the Dutra government requested U.S. financial and technical assistance to put the program into effect. The Dutra government, however, desired large amounts of U.S. capital at a time when American and European postwar demands preempted most of what was available.[10]

In presenting the request to U.S. officials, Brazilian Ambassador Celso Raul Garcia took the offensive, stating that Brazil had been led to believe by the U.S. government and leading American industrialists that the immediate postwar period would be the most favorable time to undertake its development program. He hoped, the ambassador added, to be able to carry out the development program with American capital and the purchase of American equipment.[11]

The official Department of State response reflected an attitude and tone that would dominate American thinking toward Brazilian proposals for the next ten years. "While the United States government is alive to the efforts of the Brazilian government to strengthen the economic structure of Brazil and will be glad to give careful and sympathetic study to the plans for the realization of the Brazilian development program," it began, "Brazil should seek out private financing as the best way to initiate the program."[12]

When President Dutra visited the United States in May 1949, President Truman reaffirmed his interest in Brazil but stressed the use of private capital for development purposes. In his message to Congress in June 1949, Truman devoted considerable attention to the encouragement of private American capital investment abroad. He emphasized that development aid had to come from the private sector. Unfortunately, in the late 1940s, American private capital tended to bypass less developed regions such as Brazil in favor of Western Europe, Canada, or quick profit areas such as oil.[13]

Privately, although some in the Truman administration believed that Brazil's development program was desirable and deserving of assistance both for political and economic reasons, they thought it did not have the same claim of urgency that the war-devastated countries of Europe had.[14] The Truman administration was determined to avoid committing large-scale economic aid outside Western Europe. In a response to the Brazilian request, Daniel Braddock of the Brazilian Affairs Division sought to clarify the position of the United States by stating that the lack of enthusiasm on the part of the United States was not due at all to "any lack of willingness on our part or wish to help, but rather because of the multitude of demands with which this Government was confronted."[15] Spruille Braden put it more bluntly: the time had come for countries like Brazil to realize that the U.S. Treasury was not an inexhaustible reservoir of funds.[16] The Federal Reserve, the Treasury Department, and the Export-Import Bank also opposed the Brazilian request on the grounds that the United States had to reserve its funds for more urgent reconstruction loans, and because Brazil's needs were not urgent and could wait for International Bank funds, or Brazil could draw on its large gold and dollar reserves.[17] This attitude of "rehabilitation of Europe and Asia first" and a disinclination to commit public funds for Brazilian development remained constant throughout the 1940s despite the concern among some officials that the United States should do something more for "its best Latin American friend."[18] Writing in the Department of State *Bulletin,* Dean Acheson put the Truman administration position succinctly: "The U.S. has been built by private initiative, and it remains a land of private initiative. The United States would not approve loans for development projects when private capital was available."[19]

As postwar economic problems in Brazil became increasingly critical in the late 1940s because of the exhaustion of wartime accumulated international reserves, difficulties in production and marketing, and increasingly widespread popular demands, Brazilian pressure upon the United States for more economic support mounted. Prior to the opening of the Bogotá Conference in 1948, for example, Brazilian officials expressed the hope that the United States would initiate a Latin American Marshall Plan.[20] Secretary of State George C. Marshall's announcement at Bogotá that Latin American economic problems had to take second place to European recovery was a harsh blow to the Brazilians. They believed that, as one of the active allies of the United States in both world wars, Brazil should have been a beneficiary of Marshall Plan funds equally with U.S. European allies and certainly before former enemies received help. They reasoned that their economy, too, had suffered a setback during the war. Brazil, they said, had postponed major development plans during the war to provide the United States with a stable source of raw materials. U.S. officials were unsympathetic. "Unlike Europe, Latin America did not seem threatened by the Soviet Union," Ambassador Herschel Johnson explained to the Brazilian press, "the situation might be graphically represented as a case of smallpox in Europe competing with a common cold in Latin America."[21]

The Department of State's Office of American Republic Affairs was more supportive of the Brazilian loan request. It argued forcefully for a change in policy, stating that Brazil "had gotten a very small amount of the total pie." Yet, little changed.[22] American officials, in general, believed that the Brazilians were inclined "to place too much emphasis upon outside assistance whereas many of Brazil's problems were subject to solution by the Brazilians themselves."[23] Moreover, according to the official American position, the aid the United States provided the European Cooperation Agency (ECA) for European reconstruction was of a temporary character and in no way prejudiced U.S. interest in Brazilian development. ECA aid was an emergency gesture, not a long-term policy.[24]

Despite such reassurances, Brazilian officials continued to view with growing concern the extension of U.S. aid to other parts of the world. They were not convinced by the Department of State argument that the reconstruction of Europe would benefit all.[25] They feared that U.S. aid, especially to Africa and Asia, would stimulate commercial economic activities in such commodities as coffee, cotton, and cocoa, directly competing with Brazilian production and jeopardizing Brazil's trading position. The Truman administration tried to reassure the Brazilians that their fears were unfounded. According to the Department of State, any development in these areas was designed to improve the standard of living of the areas' inhabitants and was not directly related to the exploitation of resources that could be immediately translated into exportable surpluses. "Practically all of these expansion programs are intended to increase supplies which will be used to meet the requirements of the local population," the department explained.[26] Despite the rhetoric, Brazilian fears were well-founded. Great Britain, France, Belgium, and the Netherlands all diverted a portion of ECA financing to development projects in Africa and Asia in hopes of stimulating a commercial market that they could control. This was potentially damaging to the Brazilian export market.[27] In addition, whereas Europe received over $25 billion in economic and military aid during the Truman administration, Brazil and the rest of Latin America received less than $1 billion.[28]

The question of providing loans to Brazil also provoked major differences in the inner circles of the U.S. government. The announcement of major Export-Import Bank loans of $150 million to Mexico and $125 million to Argentina in 1950 for general development purposes prompted the Brazilian minister counselor in Washington, Afrânio de Melo Franco, to protest the shabby treatment of Brazil by the United States. Melo Franco pointed out that during the entire Dutra administration no new Export-Import Bank loans had been made to Brazil. "It was a rather sorry record," he complained.[29] Meeting later with State Department planners to review economic aid to Brazil in the light of the Brazilian reaction, Assistant Secretary of State for Inter-American Affairs Edward Miller stressed Brazil's importance as a Western Hemisphere nation traditionally and reliably friendly to the United States. He indicated that it would be desirable to "spectacularize" U.S. economic aid to that country in a manner that would make the Brazilians feel better.[30]

Following a review of Brazilian loan applications for economic development projects pending at the Export-Import Bank and the IBRD, the group agreed that the total amounts involved would be substantial enough to compare favorably with the other loans and would allay Brazilian fears of being neglected.[31] The group then discussed the merits of packaging together as many of these credits as possible and announcing the total in one large and impressive amount. Willard Thorp, the assistant secretary for economic affairs, pointed out that there was not much more publicity value in a $50-million loan than in a $10-million loan. To help alleviate Brazilian unhappiness, he argued, it would be more effective to announce the loans individually as they came up.[32]

In a confidential letter to Ambassador Herschel Johnson, Miller later admitted that the $150-million loan to Mexico, which included aid for the development of the Mexican petroleum industry, put the United States in an embarrassing position vis-à-vis Brazil since the United States constantly denied such loans to the Brazilian petroleum industry.[33] But Miller again set forth the argument that the Brazilians had little concept of the magnitude of the U.S. effort to help them largely because aid had been "dribbled out in relatively small quantities." Even more would have been done for Brazil, Miller lamented, were it not for the jurisdictional dispute between the IBRD and the Export-Import Bank. This dispute regarding the exact spheres of operation of the two banks along with differences between the Departments of State and Treasury plagued both the Truman and the Eisenhower administration's efforts to develop a specific loan policy for Brazil.[34]

When Brazilian Ambassador Mauricio Nabuco met with Secretary of State Dean Acheson and President Truman in October 1950, he again brought up his country's difficulties in obtaining financial assistance from the United States. Truman expressed to Nabuco his personal interest in Brazil's problems and requested the Department of State to provide new guidance on the issue of loans. Miller, outlining the department's position for Secretary Acheson, highlighted Brazil's importance as a potential supplier of key strategic materials, and stressed that the jurisdictional conflict between the Export-Import Bank and the IBRD hindered financial assistance to Brazil. Miller recommended that immediate discussions with the banks and the Treasury Department be initiated to resolve the issue and that Eugene Black, president of the IBRD, announce publicly his bank's desire to proceed with a $250-million program in Brazil.[35]

Meeting with Department of State representatives, Black claimed that his institution was the chosen instrument for long-term development lending programs and that the Export-Import Bank should, in the case of Brazil, confine itself to short-term financing directly related to U.S. trade promotion. Proclaiming himself "bullish about Brazil's future," Black stated that the bank was prepared to announce publicly that it would commit over $250 million in loans over the next five years if Brazil accepted the bank as its investment banker. Black added, however, that the $250-million figure was not a firm commitment but a working figure for planning purposes.[36]

Black submitted his ideas in a draft agreement of understanding to the Department of State.[37] Although encouraged by Black's response, State officials believed it to be unduly restrictive of the Export-Import Bank. Ivan White of the Economic Section thought that Black's concept of Brazil's financial requirements was on the low side. Brazil, he argued, was "going ahead by leaps and bounds and with the right kind of financial support could become the southern counterpart of Canada as a source of hemisphere economic strength." There was so much to be done in Brazil that there was plenty of room for both banks to operate. Leroy Stinebower of the department observed that if the IBRD obtained a monopolistic position in Brazil "it would be very slow in getting on with the job."[38] Miller wanted any agreement with the IBRD to be broadened to include emergency loans by the Export-

Import Bank for projects deemed essential to U.S. foreign policy goals. In brief, he argued that the Export-Import Bank was an agent of U.S. foreign policy and should be used in pursuance of the national interest, especially with such essential projects as strategic materials development and loans for which the Export-Import Bank already had established creditor-client relationships.[39]

Despite continued discussions between State, IBRD, and Treasury nothing came of Black's proposal for the duration of 1950. Only with the inauguration of Vargas in January 1951 and a renewed push on the part of the Brazilians for long-term development support did the talks bring results. Urged by President Truman to resolve the territorial dispute between the two lending institutions, the National Advisory Council (NAC) made the decision in February to recognize the IBRD as the institution of first recourse for Brazilian development loans.[40]

Like his predecessor, President Dwight Eisenhower accented the concept that the keys to world peace and prosperity were free trade, private investment, and private enterprise. These concepts, if adopted throughout the world, Eisenhower believed, would "allow backward people to make a decent living and help secure America's freedom." The NSC document "U.S. Objectives and Courses of Action with Respect to Latin America" reflected Eisenhower's line of thinking. According to this study, the primary economic objective of the United States was to encourage Latin American governments to recognize that the bulk of the capital required for their economic development can best be supplied by private enterprise and that their own self-interest required the creation of a climate that would attract private investment.[41]

The general agreement on policy, however, did not prevent continued infighting and bitter disagreements between State, the IBRD, and Treasury over development aid to Brazil. The debate continued within the Eisenhower administration. The State Department, although opposed to outright grant aid, viewed an adequate flow of government funds into economic development projects as the biggest problem the United States faced in its relations with Brazil. Assistant Secretary of State for Inter-American Affairs John Cabot (Cabot replaced Edward Miller in this position in February 1953) laid out the department's position in a briefing memorandum prepared for Undersecretary of State Walter Bedell Smith for a meeting at the White House. For Cabot, private investment, while it could greatly stimulate development, could not carry the entire burden. It was essential to make public financing at reasonable interest rates available for such basic infrastructure development as roads, airports, harbors, railways, and utilities. Cabot argued that such development was in the national interest of the United States because it would facilitate the development of strategic resources and would actually help rather than harm private investment by providing the infrastructure needed for expansion. Such a policy, Cabot concluded, would convince the Brazilians that we were concerned with their well-being and that "our democratic capitalism is far better for them than Communism with its rosy promises."[42]

Secretary of the Treasury George Humphrey took a much more narrow approach. He insisted that if Brazil and the rest of Latin America "behaved properly they could obtain adequate amounts of capital from private sources for their development." The United States was not in the business of subsidizing potentially competitive development, Humphrey argued.[43] He was sure that if the United States could find a few first-rate businessmen and send them as ambassadors to the key Latin American nations, it would "do far more good than any amount of money we could dole out." Commerce Secretary Sinclair Weeks agreed that what was needed was technical assistance and U.S. business expertise, not money from the Treasury. From his own experience as a private businessman in Latin America, Weeks added, "the efforts of private enterprise needed to be backed up more strongly than in the past by the Department of State."

Humphrey also took a narrow view of the role of the Export-Import Bank. According to the secretary, loans by the Export-Import Bank should have a direct relation to U.S. exports. The IBRD was the lender to governments, and the role of the Export-Import Bank was to facilitate U.S. exports and imports. It was to supplement and encourage but not compete with private capital.[44] President Eisenhower expressed general sympathy and agreement with his Secretaries Weeks and Humphrey, but reminded the latter that "the United States was not merely doing business in Latin America, but was fighting a war there against communism."[45]

The issue remained unsettled. State Department officials continued to advocate a more vigorous Export-Import Bank role. They argued that the bank's lending policies should be far more than the simple promotion of U.S. exports and should "look towards participating in a healthy development of the economics of friendly countries" such as Brazil. Reasoning that there were cases where "the IBRD will not or cannot make development loans which we wish to see made in our national interest," State pushed the idea that the Export-Import Bank was an instrument of national policy and should be allowed to operate on a much wider scope.[46] State Department officials saw the IBRD as infringing on their authority to set foreign policy guidelines. As an international organization the IBRD did not, theoretically, have to follow U.S. policies. State had far more influence on the Export-Import Bank, where the secretary of state played a major role in policymaking decisions.

After Milton Eisenhower returned from his fact-finding mission to the countries of South America during the summer of 1953 (he visited Brazil from July 22 to July 27) and reported to the president that the "Brazilians were furious and made no effort to hide their anger," it appeared that the internal dispute would be settled.[47] Although he recommended that Brazil and the rest of Latin America follow a policy of "fiscal responsibility, balanced budgets, and hard money" and that they refrain from economic nationalism, he also advocated an expansion of all types of U.S. assistance programs. President Eisenhower added his endorsement to his brother's proposal and the president's Commission on Foreign Economic Policy, commonly referred to as the Randall Commission, issued a report that encouraged private investment but also called for the expansion of United States contributions to development. Even Secretary Humphrey seemed prepared to permit the Export-Import Bank to operate on a somewhat wider scale. Yet, the disagreements persisted.[48]

U.S. bureaucratic infighting was not confined to the role of the Export-Import Bank. As Brazil pressed its development programs sharp differences of opinion occurred not only between American and Brazilian officials but also between various U.S. agencies and the IBRD over the types of loans to be made available, the amounts, and the political repercussions of such loans. The Department of State saw U.S. loan policy as part of its overall foreign policy domain and wanted to incorporate all loans and negotiations into a long-range policy of maintaining close relations with "the major nation of Latin America." Treasury and the IBRD, which were more business oriented, wanted to use loan funds to push the Brazilians toward reforms that would create a climate attractive to private U.S. investment. According to them, this was the best way of obtaining the capital needed for economic development. Brazil was to be kept on a short leash, and aid was to be given out with an eye dropper.[49]

Despite some State Department protests, the Eisenhower administration differed little from the Truman administration with regard to financing development in Brazil, especially during its first term.[50] U.S. officials continued to stress investment guarantees, a healthy investment climate, profit maximization, and monetary stability rather than government-to-government loans for general social and economic improvement. Brazil would do best by expanding private investment opportunities and encouraging private enterprise.[51]

Although Vargas campaigned openly during the 1950 election against the domination of Brazilian resources by foreign monopolies, he basically believed that private foreign capital had its place as long as it behaved responsibly. In October 1950, Vargas declared that he had always favored the flow of foreign capital into Brazil and added that such investments were indispensable to Brazil's progress.[52] In his message to the Brazilian congress in 1951 he specified that his government would "facilitate the investment of foreign private capital, especially in association with domestic capital, as long as it does not damage the fundamental political interests of our country."[53]

After reviewing statistics that showed the inflow of venture capital into Brazil averaging 15 million per year from 1947 to 1952 while profit remittances averaged 47 million per year, however, Vargas attempted to curb excessive profit remittances. On January 3, 1952, Vargas issued a decree establishing much stricter regulations to remedy the problem.[54] He told the nation that foreign investors had been bleeding Brazil by excessive, illegal, and scandalous remittances. Vargas, under growing domestic pressure from nationalists who railed against "parasitical foreign capital," tried to appease his own political base, which was becoming increasingly restless for signs of economic improvement. Vargas was attempting a delicate balancing act. He hoped to placate the Americans and their demands for reform and his own internal supporters as well as his domestic opposition.[55] The United States, however, held the trump cards—the economic and technological resources Brazil needed. Desiring large amounts of economic aid, Vargas was forced to adopt an anti-inflation economic program and to back away from his profit remittance reforms. Still pursuing financial aid from the United States, Vargas attempted to placate further U.S. banks, investors, and the Eisenhower administration by appointing a fiscal conservative, Horácio Lafer, as his finance minister. Lafer attempted a number of belt-tightening measures designed to control prices and credit emissions, but inflation remained out of control. The cost of living index in Rio de Janeiro, for example, taking 1940 as 100, was 179 in 1945, 289 in 1950, and 550 in July 1954.[56]

Despite Vargas's appointment of Lafer, U.S. companies doing business in Brazil bombarded the Eisenhower administration with protests about the new profit remittance decree. Although worried that the decree would discourage the entry of private capital into Brazil, State Department officials preferred not to rock the boat. They wanted to give the Brazilians a chance to change their position. Too much pressure on the proponents of Brazil-U.S. collaboration, State officials argued, would give fuel to the Communists. They reasoned it was better to let Lafer, a strong supporter of the United States, work the matter out. "If we are patient," Ambassador Johnson wrote Secretary Acheson, "and can convince Vargas of our sincere intent to assist the economic development of Brazil, I am certain we shall work out a solution of the remittance decree problem which we can accept."[57]

Under the direction of Eugene Black, the IBRD also put pressure on Vargas and the Brazilians by threatening to withhold approval of development loans already negotiated unless Vargas's remittance decree was changed. To show the Brazilians he meant business, Black directed that all work be stopped on processing Brazilian loan requests. In discussions with Black, Brazilian Finance Minister Lafer assured the IBRD president that a free market bill would soon be introduced into the Brazilian legislature to allow foreign capital to come and go without restriction. Black stuck religiously to his position, however, that no further loans would be made until a free market bill passed. He also pointed out to Lafer that Brazil's increasingly poor credit position further complicated the picture and that the restrictions prevented new venture capital from entering Brazil.[58]

Black's position touched off a storm in the Department of State. According to Merwin L. Bohan, interim U.S. commissioner of the Joint Brazil-U.S. Development Commission, Black and the IBRD were dictating U.S. policy. Because of Black's coercive position the United States and Brazil were "going hat in hand to bid for favors." A program undertaken by the strongest country in the world and the strongest country in Latin America, Bohan wrote, depended for its implementation on the whims of officials of an international organization that prided itself on being uninfluenced by national interests.[59]

Bohan was not the only one upset. Ambassador Johnson, a businessman himself, believed that the bank's position was logical but that it greatly oversimplified the Brazilian situation and was based on "extremely conservative purely banking principles."[60] Cabot characterized Black's tactics as "outrageous." It was not only prejudicial to Brazil, he suggested, but to U.S. national interests as well.[61] Most State Department officials believed that the "loan package" required to restore some measure of confidence in U.S.-Brazilian economic collaboration was "tragically short." If the United States could give some assurances to Lafer on firm loan commitments, they argued, Lafer could obtain the backing of President Vargas on the free market bill.[62]

The Brazilians considered Black's position as an attack on the Vargas government's financial and economic policies. According to Brazilian members of the Joint Commission, Ari F. Torres and Valentim Boucas, it reawakened all of Vargas's suspicions and undid much of the good work of the Joint Commission. They concluded that the bank's representatives were invariably well-meaning, competent, and sincere but unsuited to dealing with Brazilians. Characterizing the IBRD's dealings as "moralizing in tone, with a note of pedantry" with a "disposition to move the bait forward just as the taker expects to taste it," the Brazilians stressed that the bank had to realize it was not dealing with a private client but with a sovereign nation that was passing through a difficult political, economic, and social crisis. It was not easy either to obtain legislation to carry out worthy objectives or to solve problems immediately.[63]

Under U.S. pressure for economic reforms and domestic pressure for signs of growth and development, the Vargas regime, with no realistic alternative to U.S. financial assistance, passed a free exchange market bill in February 1953 permitting remittances of foreign investments. Black and the bank seemed to have won their point, but the issue left a bitter feeling with members of the State Department and with many Brazilians.[64]

At the same time that Washington and Brazil squabbled over remittance legislation, Brazil's financial situation continued to worsen. Reacting to the crisis the Vargas government applied to the Export-Import Bank for a three-year $350-million loan to enable it to liquidate the commercial backlog it owed to U.S. exporters. Although Treasury and Commerce were skeptical about such a large loan, Department of State officials again considered the request "in the national interest of the U.S." State Department official Thomas C. Mann believed that if the Brazilian request went unheeded, "the risk that Brazil would become extremely nationalistic in its dealings with us and would adopt a policy of neutralism in the free world's struggle with Soviet imperialism would be greatly increased." According to Mann, denial also would have serious consequences for the whole inter-American system and would make it extremely difficult for the United States to achieve its objectives not only in Brazil but also with other Latin American countries.[65]

Although Mann and other State Department officials agreed with the Treasury Department's arguments that Brazil needed to institute many fiscal and economic reforms to improve its credit worthiness and general economic health, they did not believe that these reforms could be brought about by an ultimatum or by economic coercion. Reacting to a Treasury Department suggestion that perhaps Brazil could be made to make a deal to permit foreign participation in its petroleum development in return for a backlog loan, Mann thought the idea politically impossible. He responded: "Brazil is a horse we can lead to water, but we can't force her to drink. We can persuade her in time. We should not abandon her. We need her in reasonably good temper to work with us." The United States could not by limiting its cooperation force Brazil to do things it was not prepared to do.[66]

At first, State Department officials attempted to limit the loan to $100 to $150 million in an effort to gain Treasury support. Such a loan, they reasoned, would provide an adequate psychological boost to the opening of the free market and would make it clear to U.S. exporters that Washington was not prepared to bail them out completely when they had taken the risk of overexporting to a country that was managing its affairs inefficiently.[67]

After discussions at the White House in which Treasury Department officials claimed that granting the full $300 million would establish a precedent for a series of such requests from the other less-developed nations, the Eisenhower administration nevertheless decided to go ahead with the entire amount. Eisenhower did not want his administration open to possible charges from the Latin Americans of bad faith with regard to commitments made by the prior administration. Accordingly, on February 21, 1953, the Export-Import Bank announced a line of credit to the Banco do Brasil, S.A., of $300 million to assist Brazil in liquidating its past due U.S. dollar accounts.[68]

Treasury and State Department fears about the Brazilian economy were not unfounded. With imports continuing to multiply and the export sector stagnating, Brazilian commercial payments quickly ran into enormous arrears despite the $300-million bailout. Brazil faced a payment backlog of over a billion dollars to all countries and projected a dollar deficit of $197 million for 1954 and $380 million in 1955.[69]

In an attempt to reassure U.S. investors and the Eisenhower administration that Brazil was making a sincere effort to bring inflation under control and to avert the growing crisis of balance of payments, Vargas appointed Oswaldo Aranha to the Ministry of Finance in mid-1953. Aranha was an old friend of the United States and knew many U.S. businessmen. Aranha's moderate and distinctly orthodox strategy to stabilize the economy recommended itself to foreign bankers and officials in the Eisenhower administration. Aranha proposed to cut public spending, limit credit, provide stringent exchange controls to help Brazilian exports, and limit nonessential imports. Yet Aranha, like most Brazilian leaders, was determined to continue with rapid industrialization. He placed a higher value on development, for example, than on attempts to control inflation, despite the fact that the control of inflation was a major U.S. policy goal for Brazil.[70]

Despite Aranha's efforts, the Eisenhower administration remained skeptical of Brazil's commitment to private investment and development by the private sector.[71] By 1954 the Brazilians were back asking for an extension of the terms of the previous year's loan. Marcos de Sousa Dantas, president of the Bank of Brazil, and João Carlos Muniz, the Brazilian ambassador to the United States, meeting with Department of State officials, emphasized that Brazil was prepared to meet its payments on the $300-million loan on schedule but added that it would mean curtailing dollars for imports from the United States.[72]

Brazilian officials were not above playing off the United States against other industrialized nations if they could. Sousa Dantas pointed out that U.S. exports to Brazil were decreasing and that in 1953 only about 23 percent of his country's imports came from the United States, while 72 percent were from Europe. In 1952, 50 percent of its imports had come from the United States. Brazil, Sousa Dantas emphasized, preferred U.S. goods, but much of its supply of dollars would have to be used to meet the terms of the $300-million loan, and consequently Brazil would have to turn to Europe for an increasing quantity of imports.[73] "The choice was really up to the United States," Sousa Dantas argued, "if the United States wanted Brazil to make more dollars available to its exporters it could extend the loan payments over a longer period of time."[74]

Washington was not impressed. Even with Vargas's death and the distinctly right-wing focus of the Café Filho regime (Café Filho appointed a noted conservative, Eugênio Gudin, his minister of finance) little changed. Both countries remained frustrated. When Gudin traveled to Washington in late 1954 to discuss Brazil's serious balance of payments problem, he requested U.S. cooperation in meeting estimated dollar deficits of $160 million in 1954 and $380 million in 1955.[75] He was soon disgruntled. According to Gudin, the only thing Secretary of the Treasury Humphrey would discuss was the usefulness of foreign private investment for Brazilian development.[76]

The Treasury Department, for its part, was unmoved by Gudin's request. According to Humphrey, Brazilian figures were notoriously inaccurate. His own estimates indicated that Brazil could get through calendar year 1955 without aid. Humphrey further believed that a stabilization credit was uncalled for at this time. Even the Department of State was unimpressed with the new Brazilian request. When Brazilian Ambassador Muniz asked for a public statement from State in support of Gudin, indicating that U.S. financial aid was necessary, the department refused.[77]

In internal discussions, department officials expressed their discouragement with Brazil's lack of progress in adopting a sound, comprehensive financial program. According to these officials, Brazil was simply attempting to shift the burden of responsibility to the United States for once again bailing Brazil out of its financial problems. Gudin's argument was the same old story—the United States must support his position with statements and loans to counteract internal Brazilian opposition and permit him to put his program into effect,"otherwise the roof falls in and the Commies take over." The United States had heard this story before and each time Brazil returned in worse shape. According to Sterling J. Cottrell, "It was becoming increasingly difficult to justify to the American people pouring more money into that country if Brazilians were not willing to do what they and we know is necessary to straighten out their affairs."[78]

In a later meeting with Export-Import Bank officials and representatives from the Treasury Department, Assistant Secretary of State Henry Holland suggested that in return for a new loan the United States extract a quid pro quo from Brazil. Holland believed that the time had come for the United States to assume a "certain responsibility" and to maintain a close scrutiny over any credit extended to the Brazilians. Although this approach might open the United States to charges of meddling in Brazilian internal affairs, it would also provide a lever to bring them back to a course of "righteousness and sobriety."[79] Cottrell, Holland's assistant, went even further. Frustrated that the Brazilians "demand respect even though they don't earn it and make assurances that were next to worthless," Cottrell believed that only by "sweating" Brazil on loans and hammering at the idea that "all Brazil's economic ills would be solved" by foreign private investment would the United States get any results. One could not "force them into doing anything"; the only effective technique in moving them, according to Cottrell, was the "carrot" approach: "This is all we can spare now, but whenever you change your petroleum policy, for example, there's lots more where this came from: private, public, and IBRD."[80] Cottrell believed that the two nations' relations would never be on a sound basis until Brazil "put its house in order." As long as they postponed reforms, they would be broke and crying for help.[81]

General Glen E. Edgerton of the Export-Import Bank agreed. Although the bank was "in pretty deep," the United States was in effect financing past Brazilian errors, which set a dangerous precedent for other Third World clients. It gave them the impression that if they got into balance of payment difficulties they could look to the United States to pull them out.[82]

Despite these arguments and a growing disillusionment about the Brazilians ever producing the "necessary reforms," the NAC recommended that the Federal Reserve Board consider a loan of $160 million against Brazil's gold collateral on deposit with the Federal Reserve Bank of New York. The Eisenhower administration extended the term of the $300-million Export-Import Bank loan from two to six years, and the IBRD approved an additional $89-million development loan.[83]

Eisenhower was not about to allow Brazil to sink into default even if this required a fundamental change in thinking. Faced with an increasing world crisis and a rising tide of Third World nationalism, American policymakers increasingly turned to major government-to-government loan programs for Brazil and other Third World countries to help solve pressing economic problems of development.[84]

Despite this change in thinking the Eisenhower administration continued its rhetoric of liberalized world trade and reliance on private capital and private foreign investment to ensure world economic growth and prosperity. At the Rio Economic Conference held in September 1954, for example, the U.S. delegation reiterated its goals of fostering private enterprise, expanding U.S. trade, and encouraging Latin America "to create a political and economic climate conducive to private investment."[85]

The rhetoric of the Rio Conference notwithstanding, 1954 witnessed a major change in policy as the Eisenhower administration came to support increased government loans and public financing to promote economic growth abroad. Justifying the entire program of economic assistance as serving national security interests, officials in the Eisenhower administration came to see foreign aid as leading to economic development and prosperity. This in turn would prevent the spread of communism by promoting economic growth along capitalist lines—along American lines.[86]

Although the Brazilians saw the beginning of this shift in 1954, Washington remained pessimistic about the situation. Even with

American loans Brazil appeared unwilling to institute the major reforms U.S. policymakers deemed essential in order to set Brazil on the right course and to attract private investment.

In spite of Washington's skepticism, private investment in Brazil increased dramatically. Major U.S. corporations such as Du Pont, ITT, Borden, Monsanto, Squibb, Firestone, Goodyear, Bendix, IBM, Ford, Chrysler, General Motors, Westinghouse, and Sears Roebuck poured investment money into the "new Brazil." Measured in constant dollars, U.S. direct private investment in Brazil for the 1946–1954 period was almost twice as much as in 1919–1929. For American business, Brazil in the early 1950s was now the land of opportunity. Brazilian law, due in large part to pressure from Washington, allowed the transfer of income by U.S. branches and subsidiaries to their American parent companies, and there seemed to be an ever-increasing demand in Brazil for American products.[87] There was an economic boom in Brazil, and U.S. corporations and private investment helped fuel it.

In summary, during the late 1940s and early 1950s both the Truman and Eisenhower administrations advocated a classic liberal approach to development. They promoted private capital and private initiative, not government loans, as the best way to economic development. Brazil had only to remove the barriers that hindered the flow of this capital. However, as its economic situation continually worsened, officials in both the Truman and Eisenhower administrations reluctantly accepted a more direct involvement in financing Brazil's development. Perceiving them as financially incompetent or unwilling to deal with harsh economic realities, U.S. officials became more and more disillusioned with the Brazilians. Even the Department of State, which had strongly supported most of their requests for loans, came to the conclusion that they were simply out of control.

Both the Truman and Eisenhower administrations believed that Brazil would have to put its own house in order to achieve economic prosperity. This meant adhering to American advice regarding sound financial policies, promotion of the private sector and private investment, not pursuing a monopolistic, statist approach to economic development, and not relying on massive U.S. loans. Despite the rhetoric, both Truman and Eisenhower committed increasing amounts of government loans to Brazil's development. In addition, despite Brazil's reluctance to introduce reforms advocated by the United States and despite the many nationalistic initiatives of the Brazilian government in its rush to achieve a modern, industrialized status, U.S.

private capital did flow into Brazil. The nation leaped ahead with a mixed economy.

Notes

1. Green, *Containment*, pp. 38–39. See also William A. Williams, *The Tragedy of American Diplomacy*, rev. 2d ed. (New York: Dell, 1972).
2. Green, "The Cold War Comes to Latin America," p. 155; Rabe, *Eisenhower and Latin America*, p. 68.
3. Emily Rosenberg, *Spreading the American Dream: American Economic and Cultural Expansion 1890–1945* (New York: Hill and Wang, 1982), pp. 9–11, 233. See also Rabe, *Eisenhower and Latin America*, pp. 76, 177.
4. Baily, *Development of South America*, pp. 54–55; Green, "The Cold War Comes to Latin America," pp. 176–78; Bresser Pereira, *Development and Crisis in Brazil*, p. 35; McCann, "Brazilian Foreign Relations," p. 15; Wirth, *The Politics of Brazilian Development*, p. 167; Green, *Containment*, p. 421.
5. Skidmore, *Politics in Brazil*, p. 360; Werner Baer, *Industrialization and Economic Development in Brazil* (Homewood, IL: Richard D. Irwin, 1965), p. 61; Joint Brazil-U.S. Economic Development Commission, *The Development of Brazil* (Washington, DC: Government Printing Office, 1954); U.S. Senate, Committee on Foreign Relations, U.S.-Latin American Study, no. 4, "U.S. Business and Labor in Latin America," January 22, 1960, Senate Document 1656, 86th Cong., 2d sess. (Washington, DC: Government Printing Office, 1960), p. ix. See also Maria Celina Soares D'Araujo, *O Segundo Govêrno Vargas, 1951–1954, Democracia, Partidos e Crise Politica* (The second Vargas government, 1951–1954, democracy, parties, and political crises) (Rio de Janeiro: Zahar Editôres, 1982), p. 26; Henriques, *Ascensão e Queda de Getúlio Vargas* (The rise and fall of Getúlio Vargas), 3:285; and Vera Alice Cardoso-Silva, "Foreign Policy and National Development: The Brazilian Experiment under Vargas, 1951–1954" (Ph.D. diss., University of Illinois, 1984).
6. Jaguaribe, *Economic and Political Development*, p. 144.
7. Flynn, *Brazil: A Political Analysis*, p. 141; Werner Baer, *The Brazilian Economy: Growth and Development*, 2d ed. (New York: Praeger, 1983), p. 33.
8. Bresser Pereira, *Development and Crisis in Brazil*, p. 23; Flynn, *Brazil: A Political Analysis*, p. 141. Import substitution policies are described in detail by Celso Furtado in "Political Obstacles to Economic Growth in Brazil," *International Affairs* 41 (April 1965): 253–55.
9. See Bresser Pereira, *Development and Crisis in Brazil*, pp. 24, 53; and Flynn, *Brazil: A Political Analysis*, p. 141.
10. Daugherty, "Brazilian Policy towards the Soviet Union," p. 108. On the SALTE plan, which was a wide-ranging economic development plan developed by the Dutra administration, see Charles W. Adair, Jr. (first secretary of embassy) to Department of State, "The SALTE Plan Becomes Law," May 24, 1950, DS 832.00 Five Year/5-2450, RG 59, NA; Albert Port (finance officer), "Continuation of SALTE Plan Vetoed by President," May 21, 1954, DS 832.00 Five Year/11-1754, RG 59, NA; Heitor Ferreira Lima, *História político-econômica e industrial do Brasil*, 2d ed. (A political-economic and industrial history of Brazil) (São Paulo: Companhia Editôra Nacional, 1976), pp. 367–74; and Manuel Correia de Oliveira Andrade, *História econômica e administrativa do*

Brasil (Economic and administrative history of Brazil) (São Paulo: Editôra Atlas, 1976), p. 163. Because of inadequate financing the program was virtually abandoned by 1951.

11. Memorandum by Daniel Braddock of conversation with Celso Raul Garcia, April 22, 1946, *FRUS, 1946* 11:489, 494.

12. Department of State memorandum to the Brazilian embassy, March 27, 1946, ibid., p. 487.

13. See Paterson, "Foreign Aid under Wraps," 124; and McCann, "Brazilian Foreign Relations," p. 15. For Truman's remarks see Harry S. Truman, *Public Papers of President Harry S. Truman* (Washington, DC: Government Printing Office, 1963), pp. 329–33. See also Jeanette P. Nichols, "Hazards of American Private Investment in Underdeveloped Countries," *Orbis* 4 (Summer 1960): 174–91.

14. Memorandum from Braddock to Spruille Braden, June 5, 1946, *FRUS, 1946* 11:496.

15. Memorandum by Braddock of conversation, May 1, 1946, ibid., p. 473; memorandum from Braddock to Braden, April 8, 1946, DS 832.51/4-846, RG 59, NA.

16. Green, "The Cold War Comes to Latin America," pp. 173–76.

17. Memorandum from Norman Nes (director of the Office of Financial and Development Policy) to Assistant Secretary of State for Economic Affairs Henry Clayton, August 12, 1946, *FRUS, 1946* 11:498.

18. Green, *Containment*, p. 271.

19. Dean Acheson, "Waging Peace in the Americas," Department of State *Bulletin* 21 (September 26, 1949): 462–66.

20. Lieuwen and Jarrin, *Political Development in Latin America*, p. 45; R & A Report 4747, "Reaction in Certain Latin American Countries to the Economic Aspects of the Bogota Conference," August 16, 1948, RG 59, NA.

21. Johnson is quoted in Hilton, "The United States, Brazil, and the Cold War," 559–624.

22. Memorandum from Edward Miller (assistant secretary of state for inter-American affairs) to acting secretary of state, October 5, 1950, *FRUS, 1950* 2:672–73; memorandum from Miller to Paul Nitze, September 27, 1950, ibid., pp. 680–81.

23. See memorandum by DuWayne G. Clark, April 11, 1950, DS 832.00TA/1-2050, RG 59, NA.

24. Department of State, memorandum of conversation, November 28, 1949, *FRUS, 1949* (Washington, DC: Government Printing Office, 1975), 2:583.

25. Paterson, "Foreign Aid under Wraps," p. 119.

26. Memorandum by Clark, April 11, 1950, DS 832.00TA/1-2050, RG 59, NA.

27. Department of State, memorandum of conversation, November 28, 1949, *FRUS, 1949* 2:583; Lieuwen and Jarrin, *Political Development in Latin America*, p. 52; memorandum by Harold Midriff, May 26, 1949, *FRUS, 1949* 2:575.

28. Baily, *Development of South America*, p. 55.

29. Memorandum by Clark of conversation among Assistant Secretary Miller, Afrânio de Melo Franco, Joâo Baptista Pinheiro (second secretary of the Brazilian embassy), and Clark, May 19, 1950, 832.11/5-1950, RG 59, NA.

30. Memorandum by Miller, "U.S. Economic Aid to Brazil," May 19, 1950, DS 832.11/5-1950, RG 59, NA.

31. For a listing of the individual projects and credit amounts see ibid.

32. Ibid.

33. For a discussion of U.S. policy with regard to the development of the Brazilian petroleum industry see Chapter 6.

34. See Miller to Herschel Johnson, August 23, 1950, DS 832.10/8-2350, RG 59, NA.

35. Miller to Dean Acheson, October 26, 1950, DS 832.10/10-2650, RG 59, NA. For a review of the origins and purposes of the IBRD see Robert W. Oliver, *International Economic Cooperation and the World Bank* (London: Holmes and Meier, 1975).

36. Miller to secretary of state, October 30, 1950, Miller Files, Lot File 53D-26, RG 59, NA.

37. See Miller to secretary of state, October 30, 1950, draft copy attached, Miller Files, Lot File 53D-26, RG 59, NA.

38. Memorandum from Ivan White to Miller, November 8, 1950, Miller Files, Lot File 53D-26, RG 59, NA.

39. See memorandum by Miller, October 26, 1950, DS 832.11/10-2650, RG 59, NA.

40. The NAC, established in 1945, had responsibility for coordinating the policies and operations of all federal agencies involved in making foreign loans or engaged in foreign financial exchange or monetary transactions. The NAC consisted of the secretary of the Treasury as chairman, the secretaries of State and Commerce, the chairman of the Board of Governors of the Federal Reserve System, the chairman of the board of directors of the Export-Import Bank, and, originally, the administrator of the Economic Cooperation Administration (followed by the successive administrators of U.S. agencies for foreign aid). For a review of the discussions leading up to his decision see Miller to Acheson, January 25, 1951, Miller Files, Lot File 53D-26, RG 59, NA. See also Sterling Cottrell to Robert P. Terrill, counselor of embassy, June 4, 1953, Cottrell Files, Lot File 58D-42, RG 59, NA.

41. See Ferrell, ed., *The Eisenhower Diaries*, diary entry, July 2, 1953; and NSC 144/1 "U.S. Objectives and Courses of Action with Respect to Latin America," March 18, 1953, RG 273, NA.

42. Memorandum from John Cabot to Walter Bedell Smith, January 20, 1954, DS 820.00/1-2054, *FRUS, 1952–1954* 4:203–5. For a discussion of U.S. policy regarding improving the Brazilian infrastructure see Chapter 7.

43. See memorandum of conversation by Edward G. Cole (director of the Office of Regional American Affairs), "Foreign Aid for Latin America for Fiscal Year 1955," October 2, 1953, DS 720.5MSP/10-253, *FRUS, 1952–1954* 4:197–201.

44. Minutes of the 214th meeting of NAC, Washington, September 22, 1954, ibid., pp. 250–51.

45. Quoted in Rabe, *Eisenhower and Latin America*, p. 71. See also memorandum of discussion at 13th meeting of NSC, March 18, 1953, NSC Records, Whitman File, Dwight D. Eisenhower Library, Abilene, Kansas.

46. Memorandum from Cabot to Smith, January 20, 1954, *FRUS, 1952–1954* 4:203–5; memorandum by Cabot, "Summary of Meeting at White House," January 21, 1954, 103XMB/1-2145, ibid., pp. 206–7; memorandum by Samuel C. Waugh (assistant secretary of state for economic affairs) to secretary,

"Policies with Respect to Export-Import Bank," October 28, 1954, ibid., pp. 255–57.

47. Milton Eisenhower, *The Wine Is Bitter: The United States and Latin America* (New York: Doubleday, 1963), p. 152.

48. For documentation on Milton Eisenhower's mission see DS 120.220, RG 59, NA; DS 611.20, RG 59, NA; and Eisenhower, *The Wine Is Bitter*. His report on the mission was published as Milton Eisenhower, *U.S.-Latin American Relations, Report to the President* (Department of State Publication 5290, Washington, DC: Government Printing Office, 1953). A supplement to his report, which contains an analysis of certain specific economic problems of the respective countries he visited, is found in DS 120.220/1-1354, RG 59, NA. President Eisenhower requested Secretary of State John W. F. Dulles to take the lead in studying the report by the Defense and Treasury departments, the Export-Import Bank, IBRD, and the Office of Defense Mobilization. See memorandum from Eisenhower to Dulles, June 12, 1954, DS 120.220/1-1254, RG 59, NA.

The recommendations of the Randall Commission are contained in Randall Commission, *Report to the President and Congress* (Washington, DC: Government Printing Office, 1954). For President Eisenhower's endorsement see memorandum from Robert F. Woodward (deputy assistant secretary of state for inter-American affairs) to acting secretary of state, "Presidential and Cabinet Support of Eisenhower Report Recommendations for Strengthening Latin American Relations," March 2, 1954, DS 611.20/3-1054, *FRUS, 1952–1954* 4:217. See also memorandum of conversation with President Eisenhower, Milton Eisenhower, General Smith, Andrew N. Overby, General Glen E. Edgerton (Export-Import Bank), Waugh, Cabot, George Humphrey, Sinclair Weeks, and Robert Anderson, "Summary of Meeting at White House," January 21, 1954, 103XMB/1-2154, ibid., pp. 206–7; and Clarence R. Randall, *A Foreign Economic Policy for the United States* (Chicago: University of Chicago Press, 1954).

49. See Ronald M. Schneider, foreword to Selcher, ed., *Brazil in the International System*, p. xvi; and memorandum by Waugh, "Policies with Respect to Export-Import Bank," October 28, 1954, *FRUS, 1952–1954* 4:255–57.

50. See Rabe, *Eisenhower and Latin America*, p. 84.

51. Baily, *Development of South America*, p. 69. See also Eisenhower, *The Wine Is Bitter*, pp. 128–29.

52. See Adair (first secretary of the embassy), dispatch 572, October 19, 1950, DS 732.00/10-1950, RG 59, NA.

53. Richard Bourne, *Getúlio Vargas of Brazil*, p. 166; Flynn, *Brazil: A Political Analysis*, p. 153; Smith, *Oil and Politics*, p. 74; Getúlio Vargas, *A política nacionalista do petróleo no Brasil* (The nationalistic oil policy of Brazil) (Rio de Janeiro: Tempo Brasileiro, 1964), pp. 61–65.

54. A translation of the decree can be found in Department of State, dispatch 1098, January 5, 1952, DS 800.05132/1-552, RG 59, NA. Under the provisions of the decree, a firm's profit remittance was limited to 8 percent annually on capital actually brought into Brazil. Anything in excess of 8 percent was regarded as repatriation of capital and the remittance limited to 20 percent of the registered amount annually. It was an attempt to establish the principle that reinvested profits were not foreign capital but "national Brazilian capital" owned by foreigners. See U.S. embassy dispatch, Annual Economic Report, 1951, DS 832.00/2-652, RG 59, NA.

55. Bourne, *Getúlio Vargas of Brazil*, p. 166.

56. Ibid.

57. See memorandum from Stanley Metzger (deputy assistant legal adviser for economic affairs) to Assistant Chief for Exchange Restrictions and Payment Agreements Mortimer D. Goldstein, January 8, 1952, DS 832.131/1-852, RG 59, NA; Johnson, dispatch to State Department, January 5, 1952, DS 832.131/1-552, RG 59, NA; Miller to Johnson, March 4, 1952, Miller Files, Lot File 53D-26, RG 59, NA; telegram from Johnson to Department, March 11, 1952, DS 832.00TA/3-1152, *FRUS, 1952–1954* 4:573; and Johnson, dispatch to department, May 8, 1952, DS 800.05132/5-852, ibid., p. 575.

58. See Miller to Mervin Bohan (president, U.S. Section, Brazil-U.S. Economic Development Commission), "Brazil," October 11, 1952, Miller Files, Lot File 53D-26, RG 59, NA.

59. Bohan to Miller, October 1, 1952, Miller Files, Lot File 53D-26, RG 59, NA. For a discussion of the Joint Brazil-United States Development Commission see Chapter 7.

60. Telegram from Johnson to secretary of state, January 26, 1953, DS 932.512/1-2653, RG 59, NA.

61. Memorandum by Cabot, "IBRD Loans," June 6, 1953, Miller Files, Lot File 53D-26, RG 59, NA.

62. Telegram from Johnson to department, May 22, 1952, DS 832.00TA/5-2252, RG 59, NA.

63. Memorandum from Harold F. Linder to Thomas Mann, "Causes for Present Deadlock between Brazil and IBRD," January 29, 1953, Miller Files, Lot File 53D-26, RG 59, NA.

64. See Edward N. McCully (second secretary of embassy), dispatch 969, "Analysis of the Free Exchange Market Legislation Promulgated on January 7, 1953," January 9, 1953, DS 832.131/1-953, RG 59, NA. The Portuguese text of the bill can be found in dispatch 1784, May 2, 1952, DS 832.131/5-252, RG 59, NA.

65. Memorandum by Mann, February 19, 1953, DS 832.10/2-1953, RG 59, NA. See also John W. Dulles, *Vargas of Brazil, A Political Biography* (Austin: University of Texas Press, 1967), p. 311.

66. Ibid. See also memorandum by Mann, February 20, 1953, *FRUS, 1952–1954* 4:608.

67. See Linder to Mann, February 19, 1953, DS 832.10/2-1953, RG 59, NA; and Mann to secretary of state, February 20, 1953, DS 832.10/2-2053, *FRUS, 1952–1954* 4:607–8.

68. See minutes of secretary's staff meeting, February 24, 1953, ibid., pp. 608–9; and Export-Import Bank of Washington, *Sixteenth Semiannual Report to Congress for the Period January-June 1953* (Washington, DC: Government Printing Office, 1953), pp. 7–8.

69. See Cottrell, "Brazil—Basic Economic Problems," October 12, 1954, Cottrell Files, Lot File 58D-42, RG 59, NA.

70. Daland, *Brazilian Planning*, p. 174; Flynn, *Brazil: A Political Analysis*, p. 164; Raouf Kahil, *Inflation and Economic Development in Brazil, 1946–1963* (Oxford: Clarendon Press, 1973), pp. 330–34.

71. See Flynn, *Brazil: A Political Analysis*, p. 164.

72. Memorandum by Miller of conversation with Marcos de Sousa Dantas, João Carlos Muniz, and Miller, "$300 Million Loan to Brazil," May 10, 1954, DS 832.10/5-1054, RG 59, NA.

73. Memorandum of conversation, "U.S.-Brazil Financial Relations," May 10, 1954, DS 832.10/5-1054, RG 59, NA.

74. Memorandum of conversation, "$300 Million Loan to Brazil," May 10, 1954, DS 832.10/5-1054, RG 59, NA.

75. See memorandum from Woodward to secretary of state, October 8, 1954, Miller Files, Lot File 53D-26, RG 59, NA. See also Cottrell memorandum, "Progress Report on Latin American Policy," November 30, 1954, DS 832.10/11-2054, RG 59, NA.

76. See Flynn, *Brazil: A Political Analysis*, p. 165; and Daugherty, "Brazilian Policy towards the Soviet Union," p. 106.

77. See Cottrell to Henry Holland, "Brazil's Balance of Payments Crisis," October 27, 1954, Cottrell Files, Lot File 58D-42, RG 59, NA.

78. Ibid.

79. Memorandum by Holland, "Brazil's Financial Situation," January 26, 1955, Records of the assistant secretary of state for inter-American affairs (Henry F. Holland) 1953–1956, Lot File 57D-295, RG 59, NA.

80. Memorandum by Cottrell, "Political and Economic Situation in Brazil," May 24, 1955, *FRUS, 1955–1957* 7:668–69.

81. Ibid.

82. See memorandum of conversation, "Brazil's Financial Situation," January 26, 1955, Holland Files, Lot File 57D-295, RG 59, NA; memorandum by Rudolph E. Cohen to Holland, "Brazil: Program of Economic Reform," October 14, 1955, *FRUS, 1955–1957* 7:670–71; and Jack C. Corbett (Office of Financial and Development Policy, Bureau of Economic Affairs), "Brazil's Request for Financial Assistance," November 17, 1954, DS 832.10/11-1754, RG 59, NA.

83. Memorandum by Cottrell for press conference, May 7, 1955, Cottrell Files, Lot File 58D-42, RG 59, NA; Smith to U.S. embassy in Rio, September 30, 1954, DS 832.10/9-3054, RG 59, NA.

84. For the development of this concept during the Eisenhower years see Burton I. Kaufman, *Trade and Aid: Eisenhower's Foreign Economic Policy, 1953–1961* (Baltimore: Johns Hopkins University Press, 1982). See also Hilton, "The U.S., Brazil, and the Cold War," pp. 599–624. Hilton argues that the Eisenhower administration's neglect of Brazil brought about an eclipse in the "special relationship." See also Rabe, *Eisenhower and Latin America*, pp. 177–78. Rabe argues that the Eisenhower administration adopted this approach after 1958.

85. On the Rio Conference see NSC 5432/1, "U.S. Policy toward Latin America," September 3, 1954, *FRUS, 1952–1954* 4:313; and Stephen G. Rabe, "The Elusive Conference: United States Economic Relations with Latin America, 1945–1952," *Diplomatic History* 2:3 (Summer 1978): 279–94.

86. See Kahil, *Inflation and Economic Development in Brazil*, pp. 333–34; and Daland, *Brazilian Planning*, p. 171.

87. See U.S. Senate, Committee on Foreign Relations, U.S.-Latin American Study, no. 4, "U.S. Business and Labor in Latin America," p. 296; and U.S. Department of Commerce, *U.S. Investment in the Latin American Economy* (Washington, DC: Government Printing Office, 1957). See also E. T. Kelsey (American consul, São Paulo), dispatch, "International Business Machines Company Moving Plant to São Paulo," June 1, 1953, DS 832.343/6-153, RG 59, NA; George T. Coleman, Alfonso V. Hidalgo (American consuls, Belem, Para), dispatch, "Tire Manufacturers Starting Experimental Rubber Plantations in

the Brazilian Amazon Valley," October 20, 1954, DS 832.2395/10-2054, RG 59, NA; and Alexander L. Peaslee (American vice consul, Pôrto Alegre), "American-owned Telephone Company Situation," May 25, 1951, DS 932.30/5-2551, RG 59, NA. By 1959 U.S. private investment in Brazil was exceeded only by U.S. capital in Venezuelan oil, Cuban sugar, and Chilean coffee. See *U.S. Investments in the Latin American Economy*, p. 121.

Chapter Six

Developing Brazil's Natural Resources

Wedded to the concepts of private enterprise and private invest-ment for Brazilian development, U.S. policymakers consistently argued that Brazil's vast natural resources could best be exploited by allowing private capital, especially that of American corporations, to develop them. Both the Truman and Eisenhower administrations held to this position and constantly pressured the Brazilians to adopt it. Despite the increasing concerns of U.S. military officials over securing adequate supplies of vital raw materials in Brazil during times of crisis, both the Truman and Eisenhower administrations, in general, simply urged American private enterprise to take the lead in the development of these strategic resources in Brazil.[1] Unlike during World War II, when the United States signed many commodity and procurement agreements to ensure the availability, production, delivery, and stockpiling of strategic materials, neither Truman nor Eisenhower aggressively pursued agreements that might be commercially unprofitable. Both of their administrations merely pressed the Brazilians for legislation to promote foreign private capital participation in Brazilian mining and drilling efforts and encouraged American companies to become more involved in the development of these resources.[2] Advocating a neocolonial, neomercantilist policy, U.S. officials desired to create and maintain a flow of unprocessed, unfinished raw materials from Brazil. They did not wish to see Brazil develop a competitive industrial capacity, especially with regard to the processing of strategic materials.

The Brazilians had a somewhat different outlook and attitude regarding the development of their nation's strategic resources. Most Brazilians, including the military, viewed national development rather than private development as the way to exploit their country's wealth of resources and to protect the nation from foreign exploitation. Moreover, Brazilian officials wished to develop an industrial base and create a domestic processing and manufacturing capability. They did not want Brazil to be simply an exporter of raw materials with little or no control of the market. Sensitive to their World War II experience, in which the Brazilian economy often suffered shortages of imported heavy manufactured goods, Brazilian leaders pressed Washington for guarantees regarding finished heavy industrial items. With the onset of the Korean War, Brazilian officials feared their development plans would be curtailed as the United States reduced its exports.

The Brazilian leaders also wished to protect and expand the local industries that had been started up during the Second World War. They believed that they had sacrificed a great deal during the war for the common cause by supplying raw materials to the United States. They had accepted shortages and postponed major economic development; now they wanted financial aid to establish their own industries.[3]

The differences in the overall objectives and plans for the development of Brazil's resources held by U.S. and Brazilian officials became increasingly clear during the 1940s and early 1950s as negotiations dragged on over the development of such strategic materials as manganese, monazite, quartz crystal, industrial diamonds, iron ore, and petroleum. However, for a variety of reasons, these differences never led to any major break in relations.

The postwar period saw U.S. policymakers increasingly concerned over the production and safeguarding of vital raw materials in Brazil. American defense planners believed that the continental United States was rapidly emerging as a "have not" nation regarding mineral resources and energy sources. World War II had put a tremendous drain on its resources, and domestic demand and consumption exploded after the war. According to a U.S. Bureau of Mines report, the United States was self-sufficient in only eleven of the fifty most critical industrial minerals and had serious deficiencies in zinc, tin, mercury, manganese, lead, cobalt, vanadium, tungsten, chromite, industrial diamonds, nickel, asbestos fiber, bauxite, petroleum, and copper.[4]

Moreover, the continuing confrontation with the Soviet Union, the growing instability of the world, and the outbreak of the Korean conflict brought a crisis atmosphere to Washington. American planners envisioned Soviet communism dominating the Eurasian land mass and preventing U.S. access to strategic raw materials vital to America's war-making potential. From the point of view of the Department of Defense, the uninterrupted delivery of strategic raw materials from Western Hemisphere nations to the United States was therefore essential to any future major war effort.[5]

The perceived threat of the Soviet Union in the eastern Mediterranean and in the Persian Gulf also pushed U.S. officials to reexamine their overall oil policy. They feared that petroleum supplies in the Middle East could be cut off by the Soviets. Under such circumstances the principal supply of oil for the Western world would have to come from the Western Hemisphere. It thus became U.S. policy, in so far as possible, to make the Western Hemisphere independent of the rest of the world in the matter of petroleum supply.[6] Even the new U.S. atomic capabilities were threatened, according to this line of thinking. The United States required easy and secure access to fissionable materials in the Western Hemisphere.[7] Nevertheless, at the various inter-American conferences from Chapultepec in 1945 to Caracas in 1954, U.S. delegates advocated relatively traditional economic development policies that stressed private capital, not government monopoly, as the best way to develop resources.[8]

Officials in both the Truman and Eisenhower administrations considered Brazil to be the key to a successful U.S. drive for access to Latin American strategic materials. Viewing Brazil as rich in many critical and highly strategic materials, these officials pressed Brazil to allow U.S. companies to develop these resources. With regard to the development of Brazil's petroleum resources, for example, time and again the United States and private American petroleum industry officials stressed the need for private American enterprise to participate in all phases of the Brazilian oil industry. Washington argued that only U.S. companies had the technical knowledge, expertise, and capital to develop Brazil's oil resources. They also believed that if Brazil accepted the American program for development, especially development of its oil resources, the rest of Latin America would follow.

The first step for planners in the Truman administration was the general identification of Brazil's resources. Although everyone believed that Brazil was rich in mineral resources, little information existed on specific minerals and their availability. In addition, little actual exploration or exploitation had taken place. To correct this problem, U.S. officials used President Truman's Point Four proposal, which was designed to provide technical assistance and expertise to friendly countries around the globe, to foster a collaborative program of aeronautic charting and topographic mapping in Brazil.[9] This program was designed to identify potential new sources of such strategic materials as manganese, iron ore, lead, phosphate, tin, tantalite, tungsten, uranium, and oil. Careful to avoid charges of spying on Brazil's resources, Washington played down the value of these studies to the United States and private American corporations and emphasized the benefits that up-to-date geological mapping programs held for Brazilian development proposals. U.S. policymakers reasoned that such studies provided important information on the location of minerals essential to Brazilian industry and on the availability of these commodities for export. The development of these resources for export, U.S. experts proclaimed, would improve Brazil's economy by strengthening its purchasing power abroad. Left unheralded was the potential benefit to the United States in the event of a worldwide crisis.[10]

As a part of this overall effort, the Truman administration also agreed to bring Brazilians to the United States for specialized training in geology, mining, mineral chemistry, and metallurgy.[11] Again, Washington stressed the benefits for Brazil, not the possible advantages to U.S. war planning.

A close examination of U.S. efforts to influence and direct the development of Brazil's natural resources strikingly illustrates the differences between the two nations' positions and the consistency of U.S. policy. During the 1940s and early 1950s, Washington worked tirelessly to provide a more favorable climate in Brazil for private exploitation of its resources. For a century prior to 1932 there were no restrictions against the participation of foreign capital in Brazilian mining or the extraction of Brazil's mineral resources. However, because other parts of the world were far more attractive for development, foreign companies showed little interest in Brazilian mining or oil exploration. The Brazilians themselves exhibited little desire to exploit their own mineral resources. Only when Getúlio Vargas, during his first administration (1932–1945), excluded foreigners from direct ownership of Brazilian mines did the United States express any official concern.[12]

With regard to petroleum, during the 1930s Brazil had two options for establishing a national oil industry. Lacking enough private internal capital to undertake the enterprise, Brazilian leaders could either encourage private foreign capital (primarily from the international oil companies) or use state funds and create a state oil monopoly. Although private foreign capital had shown an interest in the development of Brazilian oil resources in the early 1930s and had actually constructed a number of small refineries in Brazil, Vargas used the constitution of 1937 and the Decree laws of 1938 and 1939 to exclude non-Brazilians from petroleum exploration and development operations. He confined foreign capital in the petroleum industry to marketing activities. The early Vargas regime held firmly to this policy of de facto state monopoly of the Brazilian petroleum industry. Despite pressure from the U.S. government to change, Vargas resisted throughout the war years.[13] On various occasions between 1938 and 1945 private U.S. oil companies such as Jersey Standard also strongly urged the Vargas government to permit foreign capital to participate in expanded petroleum activities and emphasized their readiness to enter Brazil if a "proper climate" were established.[14] Despite such prodding, Vargas held fast.

The Brazilian military played a crucial role in Vargas's decision. There had long been a connection in their thinking between security concerns and the control of Brazilian oil resources. The security aspects of Brazil's heavy dependence on foreign oil sources did not go unnoticed by the Brazilian armed forces. This concern for national security and the protection of energy supplies led Vargas, with most of the military's support, to establish a controlling agency for oil policy in the 1930s, the Conselho Nacional de Petróleo (CNP). Headed by General Luis Hildebrando Horta Barbosa, the CNP sought greater state intervention and control of Brazil's oil industry. Horta Barbosa looked favorably upon the corporatist state monopoly policies developed in Argentina and Mexico. He saw them as a model for Brazil. For him it was essential that Brazil control its own resources.[15]

Despite Vargas's position, after the war American policymakers renewed pressure on Brazil to change its oil policies. For example, Secretary of State James F. Byrnes urged Ambassador Adolf Berle "to find a way to open Brazil to petroleum production on a commercial scale." Byrnes outlined the department's position with respect to Brazil. In his view, the Brazilians had been too willing to subordinate the real economic interest of Brazil in securing adequate supplies of petroleum from foreign sources to misdirected nationalist feelings. Byrnes did not believe that exclusive reliance on Brazilian capital could produce the desired results in the petroleum field. What was needed was American capital, technology, and organization. He pointed to the contract between the Venezuelan government and private U.S. firms as an excellent example of petroleum development.[16] Byrnes asked

Berle to intensify his efforts to persuade the Vargas government to "modernize its petroleum legislation in such a manner as to guarantee to the oil companies, within proper limits, security in their concessions, freedom in their operations and the enjoyment of the fruits of their enterprise."[17] The official attitude of the department held that the Brazilian government should enter into arrangements with private concerns for the development of its petroleum industry. Following this policy, the department further instructed Berle to hint in his discussions that U.S. loans for Brazilian development might be examined more closely in the future if Brazilian petroleum laws did not change.[18]

While Berle favored the development of Brazilian oil resources by private capital he also believed that such American companies as Standard Oil of New Jersey and Atlantic Refining were not without faults in their exploration for oil in Brazil. In his diary he wrote: "If Brazilians wanted oil fast they could simply open the country to exploitation by the private companies. But that does something else besides get oil—and the something else is not too nice."[19] Despite Berle's reservations, the Truman administration continued to press Brazil hard for the adoption of legislation designed to permit foreign companies to enter the country on "a reasonable basis." U.S. officials urged that, "properly controlled," the investment of foreign capital would be an asset to Brazil's economy and would facilitate its self-sufficiency. The Department of State reminded Brazil that Export-Import Bank credits for development would be curtailed unless it modified its laws antagonistic to the entry and activity of American corporations. Policymakers in the Truman administration implied that Brazil's "progressive nationalization" programs had rendered foreign capital investment in this type of enterprise unattractive and speculative.[20]

A new study by the Army-Navy Petroleum Board in 1946 for the Joint Chiefs of Staff found that, in the event of a future national emergency, petroleum sources available to the United States from the Western Hemisphere would not be sufficient to meet military requirements. World War II had drained U.S. petroleum reserves, and the United States was still consuming its petroleum at a rate vastly greater than that of any other country or any other oil-producing area in the world. The report found that the United States was becoming increasingly dependent on foreign sources of supply. Because of the vulnerability of the Middle East under emergency conditions, the U.S. military recommended acceleration and expansion of the exploration and development of the petroleum resources of Latin America.[21] The time seemed opportune for a change in Brazilian policy.

Brazilians in 1945 were tired of rationing, the black market, and shortages brought on by the war. Owners of automobiles and trucks wanted gasoline, industrialists wanted more fuel oil for development, and commuters wanted cheaper means of transportation. Brazilian fuel requirements climbed at a rate of 16 percent a year. In 1943 national production reached 300 barrels per day (BPD), which was 1 percent of consumption. By the end of 1945 production averaged only 217 BPD or 0.7 percent of Brazilian consumption.[22]

As Brazil's dependence on foreign oil sources increased, debate among its military leaders also intensified over the best approach to developing their country's oil resources. Led by General Juarez Távora, a minority of the military now advocated a more liberal petroleum law that would open up the country to private foreign oil companies for exploration and development. Távora saw the vital role oil played in World War II and strongly believed Brazil needed foreign capital, equipment, and technicians to develop a modern oil industry. Even Vargas seemed to favor some form of mixed corporation with both private and government funds for the development of petroleum resources.[23]

The election of 1946 signaled a relaxation of the strict controls of the Estado Novo. The government of Eurico Gaspar Dutra looked more favorably on foreign participation and seemed more willing than the Vargas administration had been to create a receptive environment for American petroleum interests. The Department of State quickly renewed its attack on Brazilian restrictions.

Truman's new ambassador to Brazil, William Pawley, immediately took up the issue with President Dutra. Pawley impressed on Dutra that developing an oil industry required large amounts of venture capital and a willingness to take present risks for a relatively remote return, and that the supply of capital and technical competence in Brazil was not sufficient for this task. For Pawley, there was no way that the desired development of a Brazilian oil industry could take place unless Brazil was willing to open its doors to foreign oil companies. Pawley then related his own experience in Peru, stating how the American firm of Herbert Hoover, Jr., and John Curtis had assisted in writing Peru's new petroleum laws to the advantage of all parties. "While the job of devising a proper law for Brazil is one that the Brazilians themselves must undertake," Pawley advised, "in doing so they would be wise to hire the advisory services of private people who have had extensive experience with foreign oil operations."[24]

Pawley also attempted to show Dutra the "great and logical development of the petroleum industry in the United States because of the liberal laws which provided equal opportunity for all." He pointed to the immense investment of Shell Oil in U.S. refineries, roads, and filling stations, and the development of the automotive industry because of the farsighted planning of legislation. Dutra responded that the Communists and Vargas were responsible for retarding Brazil's progress in this area. Pawley heartily agreed, as did the Department of State, which contended that "dog-in-the-manger" nationalism kept Brazilian petroleum resources locked uselessly under the ground. Such nationalism, Pawley believed, was contrary to both Brazilian and American interests.[25]

The new Brazilian constitution of 1946 encouraged Washington. It seemed to open the way for broader foreign participation in the Brazilian oil industry. Its only restriction on petroleum development was that such activity be carried out by Brazilians or "companies organized in the country." There was no stipulation about the nationality of the shareholders of the companies.[26]

The new constitution of 1946 also allowed non-Brazilians to acquire mineral rights and to engage in any phase of mineral production in Brazil by establishing a company under the laws of the country. With this change the Dutra administration hoped to placate U.S. officials. Citing this provision of the new constitution, the Department of State promoted private participation in developing Brazil's extractive resources. According to an internal department memorandum, such involvement would aid overall Brazilian modernization and help ensure that the United States had an adequate supply of strategic materials in times of crisis.[27]

Despite the new constitution, there was no rush by major U.S. companies to invest in Brazil's natural resources. The CNP continued to impose harsh terms for profit remittance, and the oil companies were not particularly interested in Brazil, which had a relatively unattractive geology and a relatively small market.[28]

Ambassador Pawley, nevertheless, after full consultation with the oil industry and the Department of State, personally presented to President Dutra a draft for a new petroleum law that encouraged private development with such provisions as the granting of areas of sufficient size as to justify the investment required for an efficient exploratory effort, security of concession rights (including the right to develop any discoveries made), managerial control of operations, and allowances for a fair profit if the exploratory effort were successful.[29] In 1947, President Dutra appointed a committee, under the chairmanship of Odilon Braga, a noted Brazilian jurist and former cabinet member, to draft suitable petroleum legislation. Taking Pawley's suggestion, Dutra also engaged Hoover and Curtis to report on the committee's work.

The committee, adopting a somewhat liberal approach to development, proposed to allow foreign participation in oil refining but restricted foreign ownership to 40 percent. The Dutra government believed that this mixed ownership would stimulate the Brazilian economy, satisfy national defense requirements, and help save valuable foreign exchange.[30]

The Americans, however, were highly critical of the work of the committee. It did not go far enough. Hoover and Curtis objected that the Brazilian report "openly discriminated against foreign capital through limiting its possible ownership in refining and transportation enterprises to forty percent of voting stock; lacked a guaranteed right to develop a discovery; lacked security for concession rights; produced restrictions on the size of exploratory areas; and placed in the hands of the Brazilian Petroleum Council instead of the independent operator the ultimate detailed control of operations."[31]

Standard Oil of New Jersey officials also found the report objectionable and "most unworkable." They made their point of view clear: "The venture must offer us a reasonable chance to make a profit. The management of a business in which we risk our money must be left in our hands." To the company's way of thinking it would be foolish to commit vast sums of money to operations in Brazil without a better legal basis than presently existed. What the company wanted was an agreement comparable to that instituted in Venezuela.[32]

Dutra and his advisers were more sympathetic to the arguments of the Truman administration than the Vargas regime had been. Under the guidance of the Hoover-Curtis mission, the Brazilian government redrafted the petroleum laws to meet most of the American objections. However, because of strong political pressures and Brazilian military opposition, the Dutra government took no action to push the laws through congress.

Most of the Brazilian military officers strongly backed a state monopoly. Generals Júlio Caetano and Horta Barbosa represented this line of thinking. Quoting President Woodrow Wilson, Horta Barbosa claimed that "the value of a nation depends on the quantity of petroleum it possesses," and "national resources should be at the service of the state." Horta Barbosa rejected the American argument that Brazil should follow the Venezuelan example. According to Horta Barbosa, under the policy developed in Venezuela only the exploiting companies, not the people, enriched themselves. By the end of Dutra's term, the petroleum statute and the liberal, American-supported approach to development of Brazil's oil resources were pretty much dead issues in Brazilian politics.[33]

Nevertheless, Washington continued to push the idea that past experience showed that the best way to develop an oil industry was by private enterprise free of undue restrictions. They proclaimed that this was how the U.S. oil industry, the most successful and largest in the world, had been developed. Its creation had included participation by companies controlled abroad. To their way of thinking, the oil industry was so complex that only experienced companies with appropriate technical skills, personnel, and resources could engage in major oil development with maximum efficiency. U.S. officials further argued that government intervention in such operations had generally proved unsuccessful. They pointed to Mexico and Argentina, where production under government control and administration had made no progress toward meeting those countries' oil and foreign exchange needs. On the other hand, they pictured Venezuelan development as a resounding success story. Private foreign capital had been given a relatively free hand that benefited not only the oil companies but also the government and the country as a whole, they argued. Through royalties and taxation Venezuela was thriving.[34] Such development in Brazil, according to the Americans, would bring self-sufficiency in petroleum, allow lower prices for local consumers, reduce or eliminate the drain on foreign exchange, and create a possible petroleum export trade. It also would expand Brazilian industry, increase employment, aid in the development of a transportation network, help expand health and sanitation measures, and provide greater military security.[35]

Not all American officials saw the private development of oil resources as a perfect solution to all of Brazil's problems. DuWayne G. Clark of the Brazilian Division of the Department of State believed that the issue was given more prominence than it deserved, particularly in view of the fact that, with the exception of a small field in Bahia, no exploration had taken place. The whole subject, according to Clark, was based on hopes, dreams, and expectations.[36] Robert Eakens of the Petroleum Division of the Department of State agreed with Clark. With regard to the oil potential of Brazil, he indicated that Brazil had only 6 percent of the sedimentary formations of the world compared with 12 percent in the United States. In his opinion, the potential of Brazil was much less promising than that of areas such as the Texas-Louisiana Gulf Coast, Venezuela, and the Middle East. He suggested that Brazil might be considered comparable in oil resources to such areas as Kansas, Illinois, and Michigan.[37] Harold Midriff of the Brazilian Division also questioned the appropriateness of U.S. government representation before the Brazilian government on behalf of private companies. For Midriff it was a dangerous policy that would lead to Washington's entanglement in any future controversies between Brazilian and American private interests.[38]

Despite such reservations, the Truman and Eisenhower administrations both continued to press for the liberalization of Brazilian petroleum laws and the opening up of the country to private petroleum firms. According to U.S. officials, private money was ready to go into Brazil if the Brazilian government created more favorable conditions. Without a petroleum law along the lines outlined by the U.S. experts, however, private capital would not be attracted to Brazil, and the oil industry would languish. This would be disastrous for the country's economy and development prospects.[39]

Such arguments did not stop Brazil from pressing the Americans for Export-Import Bank loans for the development of petroleum resources.[40] U.S. planners were adamant in their opposition to such loans, however. Department of State officials reasoned that it would be counterproductive to provide loans to strengthen monopolistic practices in Brazil at the same time as it was lobbying for changes in Brazilian oil legislation.[41]

Officials from both the Truman and Eisenhower administrations also pointed out that Brazil had a growing dependence on the import of finished petroleum products. Petroleum, U.S. officials stressed, was such an important dollar exchange consuming item that failure to develop vigorously domestic sources of crude and refined oil would be cataclysmic. Demand was increasing at a rate of 22 percent per year, and by 1952 approximately 25 percent of all dollar imports would be consumed in paying for imported petroleum products.[42]

Such pressure from the United States seemed to be succeeding when the Vargas administration in 1951 proposed moderate petroleum legislation providing for the participation of both public and private capital in the development of Brazil's oil reserves. On December 6, 1951, Vargas sent a new proposal for a comprehensive oil law to the chamber of deputies. It called for the creation of a mixed company, Petróleo Brasileiro Sociedade Anônima (Petrobrás), and permitted foreign participation in the oil industry. Vargas was determined to modernize the Brazilian economy, and a reliable national source of energy was vital to his plan. Moreover, Vargas was set on reducing dependence on oil imports, which were a crippling burden on Brazil's foreign exchange reserves. Brazilian officials predicted that oil consumption would more than double from 1950 to 1955.[43]

Nevertheless, Vargas's proposal came under immediate attack by nationalists from all sides, and the slogan "The petroleum is ours" ("o petroleo é nosso") became a national shibboleth. A national oil industry, to most of the military as well as to the general population, represented sovereignty, independence, power, and well-being.[44] According to Michael W. Johnson, president of the Standard Oil Company of Brazil, "many Brazilians had reached a stage similar to Pavlov's dog. The moment you mention the word 'oil' they practically foam at the mouth."[45]

Washington, however, continued to press Vargas for favorable action. During his visit to Brazil, Assistant Secretary of State Edward Miller, for example, pictured its petroleum policy as totally inadequate and stressed that unless Brazil changed it would never realize its economic potential. Standard Oil agreed with Miller's assessment. According to Eugene Holman, president of Standard, only by the rapid development of its oil resources could Brazil achieve any substantial relief from its growing balance of payments problems. The very development projects advocated by the Brazilian government exacerbated the petroleum problem. Holman emphasized that American private capital, management, and know-how could provide the most efficient development of Brazil's petroleum industry. In the long run, following the American way would be the least costly and would eventually provide the greatest benefit to Brazil.[46]

In a letter to Miller, Holman also recommended that Washington withhold Export-Import Bank and IBRD loans for development until Brazil worked out a different petroleum policy.[47] Although Miller disagreed with such a drastic action as "extremely unwise and playing into the hands of nationalist elements," he nevertheless pushed Vargas for a favorable response consistent with past American suggestions.[48]

Reacting to the domestic pressure, which accused him of being an *entreguista*,[49] rather than to Miller's arguments, Vargas in 1953 made the exploration, exploitation, transport, and refining of petroleum (all activities connected with the oil industry except distribution and marketing) a monopoly of the federal government. Petrobrás, the government agency that operated this monopoly, became a touchstone for Brazilian nationalism, and few politicians dared to attack it.[50] Although Vargas entered the presidency in 1951 with no firm idea about oil policy beyond his commitment to solving the energy crisis and to assuring government control of any new oil industry, after his suicide in 1954 he became known as the champion of a state oil monopoly.[51]

Many U.S. businessmen and bankers, however, regarded the creation of the state-owned oil-producing monopoly as a triumph of irresponsible radicalism. *Fortune*, for example, editorialized that Petrobrás was "only dancing a samba with the basic petroleum problem." What was needed was American expertise. The editorial claimed that Vargas and the Communists were mortgaging Brazil's future by responding to demoniac nationalist sentiments. From the standpoint of enlightened self-interest, *Fortune* concluded, it would seem to Brazil's advantage to support private development of the indigenous "vast oil reserves."[52]

Department of State officials had a more balanced reaction, evaluating the creation of Petrobrás in terms of growing Brazilian enthusiasm for statism, and as having the solid support of the military and professional classes. Nonetheless, basic U.S. policy did not change. Officials in the Eisenhower administration continued to hammer at Brazilian petroleum policy as mistaken and even suicidal. According to these officials only the participation of private foreign (read American) capital could turn the situation around.[53]

These efforts to modify Brazilian petroleum legislation were uniformly unsuccessful, however, just as the Truman administration's attempts had been. Even after Vargas's suicide the new president, João Café Filho, could not gather much support for his position that foreign capital, with proper safeguards for the nation's interest, would benefit the development of Brazil's petroleum resources. He introduced a bill to amend the existing petroleum law to permit the participation of private firms, but it failed. The bill had little chance of success even with Café Filho's support. The military stood firmly behind the state petroleum monopoly. General Henrique Teixeira Lott, the war minister, announced that "Brazil will simply not turn over its petroleum resources for development by foreign companies which will in their operations be guided by their international interests and not those of Brazil." Lott believed strongly, as did most of the military, that the only way Brazil would "emancipate" itself was through the nationalization of its mineral resources, especially oil.[54] Even General Távora changed his position as the military closed ranks in support of Petrobrás. General Canrobert Pereira da Costa spoke for this unified front when he declared that it would be "inopportune" to alter the state monopoly on petroleum without a trial period for Petrobrás.[55]

Undeterred, American policymakers continued to seek a change in Brazil's petroleum policy. For many in the Eisenhower administration the petroleum issue was the most important link in any solution to Brazil's financial and economic development problems. It was not until 1959, when outgoing President Juscelino Kubitschek stated, "No Brazilian government can alter Petrobrás' statutes, which constitute an emotional state of the Brazilian people. Its success was a question of national honor,"[56] that American policymakers gave up. They finally admitted to themselves that the view that constant U.S. pressure and economic necessity would lead to a revision of Brazil's petroleum policy was "largely wishful thinking."[57]

Despite the U.S. military's concern about securing adequate oil supplies in the Western Hemisphere for national security reasons, officials in both Truman and Eisenhower administrations refused to institute a centralized, government-initiated plan for the development of the hemisphere's oil resources. Instead they relied upon private industry to exploit the needed resources and rejected Brazil's nationalistic, state-controlled plans for petroleum development. They reasoned that acceptance of such policies would set a dangerous precedent for other emerging areas. The creation of Petrobrás was a major setback for American policymakers, and they continually attempted to overturn the Brazilian decision. However, large petroleum deposits were never discovered in Brazil despite concentrated efforts on the part of its government, and petroleum policies seldom became a major bone of contention between the United States and Brazil. Petroleum development, however, remained a major problem for Brazil throughout the next three decades. Even today, a large portion of that nation's budget goes toward the importation of petroleum.

The overall attitude of U.S. officials regarding the development of Brazil's petroleum resources is consistent with all strategic materials negotiations between Washington and the Brazilians. For example, during the late 1940s planners in the Truman administration expressed both to the Dutra administration and to private U.S. corporations their keen interest in the rapid development of Brazilian manganese deposits.[58] Concerned over the loss of its Russian source and the rather questionable status of its supply from India, the Truman administration wanted to safeguard a supply of this critical resource in the Western Hemisphere.[59]

Interested in the development of the Brazilian deposits for their own use, American corporations such as United States Steel and Bethlehem Steel Corporation began negotiations with Brazilian firms for expanding manganese operations. United States Steel formed a joint company with the Chamma brothers of Brazil, the Sociedade Brasiliera de Mineracao Ltds (Sobrami), to finance the acquisition and installation of the equipment and facilities required to mine and deliver to an ocean port three million tons annually of manganese ore. The Export-Import Bank provided a $30-million credit to the new company to help initiate the project.[60]

The fact that the plan to form the new Brazilian corporation gave the Chamma interests 51 percent control in the venture did not bother either United States Steel officials or the Truman administration because, as a State Department memorandum explained, the agreement covered both manganese and iron ore deposits. The iron ore deposits were located in Brazil's national security zone, which was theoretically off-limits for foreign development. (The area in question held the Urucum deposits, located near the Bolivian border.) Moreover, that United States Steel would not have majority control of the stock would be offset by the fact that technical direction was wholly in the hands of the U.S. company. A further advantage of the plan, at least to steel company executives, was that they would no longer have to pay the annual $200,000 royalty to the Chamma brothers for reserving to United States Steel the right to buy manganese ore from Chamma mines.[61] Bethlehem Steel concluded a similar agreement with the Brazilian ICOMI Company for the development of the Amapá deposits. Bethlehem received loans from both the Export-Import Bank and the IBRD for their project.[62] This pleased Washington.

With the onset of the Korean War the principal objective of the United States in Brazil became the production and delivery of essential strategic materials. As late as 1951, however, no real program for the expansion of strategic materials production existed, and, as the State Department Bureau of American Republics reported, production goals had not been established to meet the requirements of both current consumption and stockpiling. To officials in the bureau, the United States was simply pursuing a day-by-day policy of dealing with the problems as crises arose.[63]

For its part, the Vargas government showed reluctance to go along with the defense production programs of the Truman administration unless they were to be integrated into an economic development program that would take into account Brazil's essential wartime requirements and the adverse effect on its economy of the eventual termination of these programs. The chief concern of the Brazilians was their own national economic development rather than the political and economic security of the United States. When Assistant Secretary of State for Inter-American Affairs Edward Miller visited Rio de Janeiro as part of a five-country tour of South America in 1951, Brazilian officials pressed him for a "supply agreement." They wanted to ensure an adequate flow of scarce U.S.-manufactured products such as turbines and earth-moving equipment in exchange for producing the strategic materials required by the United States. Although the discussions were inconclusive, both parties agreed to establish at Rio a Joint Group on Emergency Supply Problems to determine Brazilian needs for scarce equipment and material from the United States and to consult on measures for facilitating the export of raw materials from Brazil to the United States.[64]

Finally, in 1952, the two nations signed a military assistance agreement that, in part, provided for technical and financial cooperation between the two countries in order to increase the production of strategic materials and to provide one another with materials, products, and services required for their common defense.[65] This agreement, however, failed to remedy many of the major problems that had surfaced in the negotiations over strategic materials. Increasing nationalist sentiments for the protection and exploitation of Brazil's resources by Brazilians, differing views on development, and changing market conditions plagued the discussions. For American planners, the fear of foreign competition and Soviet economic expansion compounded the problem.

The birth of the atomic age saw the United States scrambling to secure adequate sources of rare earths and thorium, which could be made into fissionable materials. As early as 1945 the Truman administration signed a secret agreement with Brazil for the exportation of monazite to ensure the production in the United States of rare earth elements necessary for military purposes.[66]

At the end of the war, American officials sought formal assurances from Brazil that the agreement would continue and that the United States would monopolize any Brazilian production. Washington not only wanted to deny the materials to the Soviet bloc but also to allies such as the French. According to a State Department memorandum a diversion of monazite or beryl to the French or French interests would "tend to increase the already important interest of the French in world sources of these materials."[67] The Truman administration thought France was attempting to dominate the world market for rare earth compounds. It kept a close eye on French activities in Brazil.[68]

Brazilian officials attempted to use Washington's desire for monazite as a bargaining point for increased financial aid. In 1951, Foreign Minister João Neves da Fontoura gave his categorical assurance to Ambassador Johnson that neither monazite nor any other substance that could be processed into fissionable material would be exported to any foreign destination other than the United States. In return Fontoura wanted U.S. aid in the construction and operation of a monazite processing plant in Brazil that would enable the Brazilians to sell the finished fissionable product.[69]

Fontoura's assurance delighted Johnson. However, U.S. officials were wary of Brazil's request for a processing plant. Department officials in Washington believed that such a plant would seriously compete with American products and would therefore not be desirable. Moreover, they doubted that Brazil could set up and run an effective industry in this area. Other government officials agreed.[70] The United States had to protect its own industry by first obtaining its minimum requirements of crude monazite. According to this line of reasoning, it would be "most unwise to jeopardize U.S. industry by relying on the ability of the Brazilians to provide skill, know-how, and performances equal to our own technologists and workmen in such a highly specialized industrial project."[71]

The Truman administration, making an exception to its general policy of simply advocating private exploitation of strategic materials, pushed for a supply agreement with Brazil. Its desire for such an agreement was heightened by the embargo placed on monazite by India and then by Brazil itself in 1950. (India was the principal supplier of monazite to the United States until 1945.) Under pressure to ensure monazite supplies, the Truman administration agreed to assist Brazil in expanding its monazite processing facilities if Brazil would sell the United States twenty-five hundred tons of monazite sand annually for three years. These complex negotiations ended on February 21, 1952, when the United States and the Vargas government signed a one-year commercial contract for the delivery of monazite and rare earth compounds derived from monazite and exchanged notes covering three years during which they agreed to carry out the sale and purchase of monazite and its derivatives.[72]

In spite of the agreement, monazite continued to be a problem in U.S.-Brazilian relations. With the discovery of large deposits of monazite sands in Idaho and California the United States was no longer dependent upon foreign sources. The Atomic Energy Commission (AEC) now refused to buy anything except thorium, and the General Services Administration eliminated monazite from its stockpile requirements. In short, the United States lost interest in additional purchases of rare earth compounds.

At the same time as U.S. interest in Brazilian monazite decreased, Brazil discovered large additional deposits of monazite in 1953 and desired to sell its expanded supply to the United States. Although the AEC was basically indifferent, the State Department argued that a refusal to renew the monazite contracts would seriously damage U.S.-Brazilian relations.[73] Under Department of State urging the two nations reached tentative agreements on the price for the monazite sand, but the negotiations failed when a U.S. producer of rare earth compounds, the Lindsey Chemical Company of Chicago, offered to sell Washington quantities of monazite at a lower price. Federal regulations prevented the government from purchasing from a foreign supplier if it could obtain the same material from a domestic source.[74]

The acquisition of monazite was not the only atomic energy matter that concerned U.S. planners, who also wanted a monopoly on all uranium exploration programs in Brazil and pushed for a contract between Brazil and Union Carbide for uranium exploration. The Brazilians wanted to exchange raw materials for technical information and assistance related not only to the exploration, mining, and treatment of ores used in atomic energy research, but also to reactor development and the training of Brazilian scientists in the field. Washington was reluctant at first to sanction such ventures, citing the relatively unimportant contributions to date of any South American country in this area and the fear of opening the atomic door too wide.[75]

With the United States dragging its feet, the Vargas administration turned to the French and signed a formal contract in November 1953 for atomic energy cooperation. When the U.S. embassy inquired about the agreement, the Brazilian foreign minister indicated that the French were in a better position to provide the necessary technology because of U.S. legal restrictions. Prodded into action the Eisenhower administration offered a cooperative program of its own in which the Atomic Energy Commission agreed to furnish technicians, equipment, and laboratory services, train Brazilian scientists and technicians, and provide to the National Research Council of Brazil technical information in the fields of reactor technology and atomic energy. Such assistance would help prepare Brazil "for the time that its peaceful economic atomic power may be developed," Washington reasoned. Technical military information was excluded from the agreement.[76] The Eisenhower administration was not about to let the French gain an advantage any more than it would tolerate Soviet penetration in such a strategic area or such an important technology.

Similar problems plagued efforts to procure quartz crystal from Brazil. During World War II the United States depended on Brazil for essential supplies of quartz crystal, a vital component in radio and radar equipment. It signed a commodity agreement in which Brazil sold its entire production to the United States for a fixed price. Despite decreased demand at the end of the war, the Dutra government pressed for a renewal of the purchasing program in order to maintain its country's extractive industry. Brazilian officials argued to their American counterparts that such a program was necessary in order to keep up the industry's potential capacity to be ready for possible emergency conditions. Talks began in 1949 to work out terms for new contracts.[77]

The Department of State was somewhat shocked to learn, however, that the Interdepartmental Stockpiling Committee was recommending to the Munitions Board, which had control over U.S. stockpiling requirements, that the quartz crystal stockpiling objectives of 4 million pounds be reduced to one and a quarter million pounds. Since the present stockpile was almost twice the recommended revised objective, the board no longer had any interest in further discussion with the Brazilians. State officials again argued that such a decision would have unfortunate political repercussions and would endanger or jeopardize the much more important monazite sand talks. Furthermore, the sudden termination of the purchasing program, according to State Department officials, would destroy an industry that the United States had been responsible for building up.[78]

Further complicating the problem was the Truman administration's general policy of not purchasing finished or semifinished products abroad. What the United States wanted from Brazil was unfinished raw quartz, but the Brazilians continued to push for aid in developing semiprocessing capabilities. Although negotiations dragged on, little progress was made until the U.S. embassy in Rio discovered that the Dutra government was on the verge of signing a contract to deliver quartz crystal to Czechoslovakia. Disturbed at the possibility that such a strategic material might be shipped to the Soviet bloc, the Truman administration issued a formal note to the Brazilian Ministry of Foreign Affairs citing "increasing concern over the movement of commodities of a strategic nature to Soviet bloc countries."[79]

Official U.S. policy was to prevent the export of quartz crystal to the Soviet Union and Soviet bloc countries. In fact, Truman administration officials had succeeded in including this strategic resource on the International List I, which embargoed certain commodities to the Soviet bloc area. The embassy also pointed out to the Brazilians that such a sale would be inconsistent with the General Agreement on Tariffs and Trade (GATT), to which Brazil became a party in 1948.[80] When the Truman administration agreed to the continued purchase of quartz crystals Brazilian authorities "readily and promptly" issued instructions that no further licenses be issued for the export of quartz crystal to Czechoslovakia or other Soviet bloc destinations.[81] The development of synthetic materials in this area, however, soon made the United States entirely independent of the supply of natural crystals.

U.S. officials had similar concerns about industrial diamonds. They feared that Soviet agents were acquiring diamonds from sources in Brazil. Comparing the situation to the Brazilian diamond market in 1941, when all first-quality merchandise went to German and Japanese agents at prices far above the norm, U.S. Economic Attaché Sterling Cottrell recommended a solution similar to the one introduced in 1941, when the United States instituted a purchasing program with the complete cooperation of the Brazilian government. This agreement had made it illegal to sell industrial diamonds except to the United States or to U.S.-approved purchasers. Cottrell granted, however, that even this did not entirely solve the problem of keeping diamonds from going to the Axis. It was only the offering of competitive prices that brought the situation under control.

Due to the methods of production and the inaccessibility of the mines, it was almost impossible to control diamond sales in Brazil. In addition, heavy taxes made it almost impossible for legitimate dealers to make a profit; therefore, smuggling was endemic to the trade. The detection of smugglers would, according to Cottrell, demand a police force "beyond the realm of reason." A system of informers also would not work, because "there is an odd kind of loyalty and mutual trust that makes diamond trading a unique business in Brazil." It was a fallacy, therefore, to hope to control smuggling by policing and informing. The only means of acquiring the diamonds was by offering prices that made it more profitable to deal with the United States. Despite Cottrell's recommendations, however, the Truman administration could find no direct proof that the Soviets were involved in the diamond market. Reluctant to undermine an apparently free market, the Truman administration refused to set up a monopolistic purchasing program.[82]

Brazilian iron ore presented U.S. officials with yet another problem. Unlike its treatment of the sale of diamonds, a strategic material that was difficult to trace, Brazil openly promoted expansion of its export of nonstrategic items, including iron ore, to Soviet bloc countries. This Brazilian policy greatly upset the Eisenhower administration, despite the fact that iron ore was not on the list of exports to the Soviet Union prohibited under the Battle Act.[83] The Soviet bloc countries were offering $18.50 per ton for Brazil's high-grade iron ore, while U.S. importers were paying $12.50 per ton or not seeking foreign supplies at all. When the Vargas government announced that the Vale de Rio Doce Company (CVRD) had signed contracts with Poland and Czechoslovakia for the export of 300,000 tons of iron ore, the U.S. embassy in Rio protested the decision as a serious breach of faith on the part of Brazil. The embassy pointed out that the Export-Import Bank had provided over $17.5 million in credits to CVRD on a priority basis, predicated on production for the free world. Policy planners in the Eisenhower administration suggested that Brazil, although it might be tempted to deal with the Soviet bloc countries since they offered $18.50 per ton, would fare far better economically through large long-term contracts with U.S. importers on a "run of the mine" basis at lower prices. The Brazilian government replied that it was under growing pressure to expand its trade, that it was disturbed at its inability to sell Rio Doce ore in the United States and that it had a perfect right to look for markets elsewhere, especially since Britain and other European countries were trading with the Soviet bloc, furnishing material much more strategically important than iron ore. Besides, Brazilian officials reminded the Eisenhower administration, they had scrupulously refrained from exporting truly strategic materials to the Soviet bloc.

Reasoning that, if private business expected the department to "make the world safe" for their operations abroad, the government should call on private business reciprocally to help with its problems, the Department of State approached United States Steel about making a firm offer, at any price, to take Brazilian ore. Such an offer, Sterling Cottrell related, would put the United States in a much better position to encourage Brazil to turn down the Poles and the Czechs. Despite government pressure, United States Steel refused to go along with the proposal. It was neither economical nor commercially profitable.[84]

The Department of State believed that increased Brazilian trade with the Communist bloc promoted more tolerance of Communist political inroads and provided arguments for diplomatic recognition of those Soviet bloc countries not already recognized by Brazil, including the USSR, Hungary, and Romania, and that such trade promoted closer economic ties and gave the Soviets added respectability in Brazil. Nonetheless, it reluctantly concluded there was little the United States could do. Iron ore was not a Battle Act item or even a "strategic material," and the Eisenhower administration could not force United States Steel to purchase the iron ore. Accepting this, a State Department memorandum rationalized that it was doubtful that the lack of Brazilian iron ore would much decrease the war-making potential of the Soviets in an atomic age.[85]

In summary, U.S. policymakers in the early postwar years increasingly considered the protection, development, and exploitation of strategic resources in Brazil to be a major U.S. defense concern. As the world situation worsened and the United States became involved in the Korean conflict, Washington tried to ensure that Brazilian resources were reserved for American use. Unwilling to institute monopolistic commodity or purchasing agreements, however, the Truman and Eisenhower administrations primarily relied on U.S. corporations to develop Brazil's resources. They continuously urged the Brazilian government to promote private exploitation rather than nationalist development and encouraged private U.S. firms to take a more active role in Brazilian development. Time and again the American government and private firms, especially in the petroleum industry, stressed the need for private American enterprise to participate in all phases of Brazilian extractive industries. When faced with Soviet bloc and French initiatives to exploit Brazilian resources, however, both the Truman and Eisenhower administrations acted quickly to prevent these nations from expanding their interests in Brazil.

What Washington desired was a neocolonial relationship, with Brazil providing the raw materials and the United States processing these raw materials for its industries and maintaining Brazil as a major market for its finished goods. The Brazilians, however, sought to protect and expand their processing and manufacturing capabilities.

Brazilian leaders were intent on industrializing and thus escaping from a neocolonial status. They looked to the United States more for developmental loans and aid in developing their industries than as a market for simple unprocessed raw materials. As for its petroleum reserves, as Brazil industrialized and used more energy resources, nationalism and oil became inextricably linked. Convinced that their country was rich in oil and that the American oil companies would stop at nothing to get it, the Brazilians supported state control of petroleum reserves. With the creation of Petrobrás in 1954 as a strictly national company that excluded all foreign capital, the debate in Brazil for all intents and purposes ended. The Brazilian oil industry would be uniquely Brazilian.[86] Despite this setback and the increasingly clear differences between the two countries' positions regarding the development of Brazil's natural resources, U.S.-Brazilian relations remained strong. In general, Brazilian officials needed the United States to help promote their country's industrialization, and the United States needed Brazil's strategic materials. Moreover, changing market situations, the development of new products and new technologies, and the fact that no major oil fields were discovered in Brazil served to push the differences between the two countries' goals to the background.

Notes

1. See Emerson Innis Brown (minerals attaché), "Possibilities for Mineral Development in Brazil by Private Enterprise," May 21, 1953, DS 832.25/5-2153, RG 59, NA. This dispatch also lists all embassy dispatches and reports on minerals in Brazil for the period 1944 to 1952.

2. Ibid.

3. Smith, *Oil and Politics*, p. 111; Baily, *Development of South America*, p. 108.

4. See Thomas G. Paterson, "The Quest for Peace and Prosperity: International Trade, Communism, and the Marshall Plan," in Bernstein, ed., *Politics and Policies of the Truman Administration*, p. 91.

5. NSC 56, "U.S. Policy Concerning Military Collaboration under the Inter-American Treaty of Reciprocal Assistance," August 30, 1949, RG 273, NA.

6. Report of Army-Navy Petroleum Board, "Petroleum Reserves in the Western Hemisphere," April 17, 1946, ABC 463.85A, RG 165, NA. See also JCS study, "Problems of Procurement of Oil for a Major War," February 1947, RG 218, NA.

7. NSC 56, "U.S. Policy Concerning Military Collaboration under the Inter-American Treaty of Reciprocal Assistance," August 30, 1949, RG 273, NA.

8. See Baily, *Development of South America*, p. 53.

9. Memorandum from Harold M. Midriff to Eldred D. Kuppinger (second secretary of embassy), "Proposed Agreement Regarding Charting and Mapping in Brazil," August 20, 1951, DS 732.002/8-205, RG 59, NA.

10. Robert H. Groves (acting director of technical cooperation), "Latin American Technical Assistance Programs FY 1954 Budget Narrative for Brazil," April 1, 1953, DS 832.00-TA/4-153, RG 59, NA; William A. Wieland (first secretary of embassy), dispatch to Department of State, September 2, 1952, DS 732.022/9-252, RG 59, NA. For a discussion of the Point Four program see Paterson, "Foreign Aid under Wraps," 119–26. See also the discussion in Chapter 7.

11. Ibid, all references in note 10.

12. Bresser Pereira, *Development and Crisis in Brazil*, p. 29; Jaguaribe, *Economic and Political Development*, p. 178; Bourne, *Getúlio Vargas of Brazil*, p. 166; Baily, *Development of South America*, p. 41.

13. Department of State memorandum, "Background Information for Discussion with Brazilian Officials," DS 832.001 Dutra, Gaspar/5-1749, RG 59, NA; Berle and Jacobs, eds., *Navigating the Rapids*, p. 559; Wirth, *The Politics of Brazilian Development*, p. 135. The Brazilian military played a leading role in the development of this policy, unlike its Latin American counterparts.

14. Charles E. Dickerson (counselor of embassy for economic affairs), "Recent Developments in the Interest of American Companies in the Brazilian Petroleum Industry," April 18, 1950, DS 832.2553/44850, RG 59, NA.

15. Smith, *Oil and Politics*, p. 55; Flynn, *Brazil: A Political Analysis*, pp. 156–57.

16. James F. Byrnes to Adolf Berle, August 10, 1945, DS 832.6363/8-1045, RG 59, NA. On the development of Venezuelan oil and United States relations with Venezuela see, Stephen G. Rabe, *The Road to OPEC: United States Relations with Venezuela, 1919–1976* (Austin: University of Texas Press, 1982); Franklin Tugwell, *The Politics of Oil in Venezuela* (Stanford: Stanford University Press, 1975); Juan Pablo Pérez Alfono, *Petroleo y dependencia* (Oil and dependency) (Caracas: Síntesis Dos Mil, 1971); and Betancourt, *Venezuela: Oil and Politics*.

17. Byrnes to Berle, August 10, 1945, DS 832.6363/8-1045, RG 59, NA. See also Berle, dispatch to Byrnes, July 12, 1945, DS 832.6363/7-1245, RG 59, NA.

18. See Philip O. Chalmers to Paul Daniels, June 16, 1945, *FRUS, 1946* 11:529–31; and Berle and Jacobs, eds., *Navigating the Rapids*, p. 531.

19. Berle to Chalmers, December 3, 1945, DS 832.6363/12-345, RG 59, NA; Berle to Chalmers, December 5, 1945, DS 832.6363/12-545, RG 59, NA.

20. Memorandum from Dean Acheson to Daniels, "Department Policy Concerning Brazil," April 2, 1946, *FRUS, 1946* 11:540–41; Department of State memorandum, "Petroleum Refinery Arrangements in Brazil," April 3, 1946, DS 832.6363/4-346, RG 59, NA. See also Daniels, dispatch to secretary of state, June 7, 1946, *FRUS, 1946* 11:546–47.

21. Report of Army-Navy Petroleum Board, "Petroleum Reserves in the Western Hemisphere," April 17, 1946, ABC, 463.8SA, RG 165, NA. See also JCS study, "Problems of Procurement of Oil for a Major War," February 1947, Records of the War Department General and Special Staffs, RG 218, NA; memorandum from Spruille Braden to Daniels, May 11, 1946, DS 832.6363/4-3046, RG 59, NA; memorandum from Acheson to diplomatic representatives in the American republics, "Consideration of Western Hemisphere Petroleum Supply Problem by the Inter-American Defense Board," April 14, 1948, *FRUS, 1948* 9:247; William Pawley, dispatch to secretary of state, December 20, 1946, *FRUS, 1946* 11:555–57; Pawley, dispatch to Will Clayton, January 29, 1947, DS 832.6363/1-2947, RG 59, NA; memorandum from Willard Thorp (assistant secretary for economic affairs) to Pawley, April 14, 1947, DS 832.6363/-1447, RG 59, NA; memorandum by John A. Loftus, *FRUS, 1947* 8:459; Allen Dawson to Pawley, February 25, 1947, *FRUS, 1947* 8:460–61; and Pawley, dispatch to secretary of state, March 7, 1947, *FRUS, 1947* 8:461.

22. See Wirth, *The Politics of Brazilian Development*, p. 160; and Smith, *Oil and Politics*, pp. 45–47.

23. See Flynn, *Brazil: A Political Analysis*, pp. 158–59; and Wirth, *The Politics of Brazilian Development*, p. 247.

24. For a discussion of the Peruvian oil industry and its development see Adalberto J. Pinelo, *The Multinational Corporation as a Force in Latin American Politics: A Case Study of the International Petroleum Company in Peru* (New York: Praeger, 1973).

25. Memorandum by Pawley, March 17, 1947, DS 832.6363/3-1747, RG 59, NA.

26. Smith, *Oil and Politics*, p. 5.

27. See Brown, "Possibilities for Mineral Development in Brazil by Private Enterprise," May 21, 1953, DS 832.25/5-2153, RG 59, NA. This memorandum contains a review of the efforts of the Truman administration.

28. Smith, *Oil and Politics*, p. 52.

29. Memorandum by Pawley, March 17, 1947, DS 832.6363/3-1747, RG 59, NA.

30. Smith, *Oil and Politics*, p. 52.

31. "Standard Oil Company's Review of Brazilian Legislation Affecting Petroleum," enclosure to DS 832.2553/4-1850, RG 59, NA.

32. Dickerson, "Rough Draft for a Communication to the Brazilian Government," enclosure to DS 832.2553/4-1850, RG 59, NA.

33. Smith, *Oil and Politics*, pp. 55–56; Flynn, *Brazil: A Political Analysis*, pp. 156–57; Wirth, *The Politics of Brazilian Development*, p. 172.

34. Smith, *Oil and Politics*, pp. 72–73. For a contrary view see Rabe, *The Road to OPEC*; Bryce Wood, *The Making of the Good Neighbor Policy* (New York: Columbia University Press, 1961); and Antonio J. Bermúdez, *The Mexican Petroleum Industry: A Case Study in Nationalism* (Stanford: Institute of Hispanic American and Luso-Brazilian Studies, 1963).

35. Memorandum by Daniels, "Brazilian Petroleum Development," February 14, 1948, DS 832.6363/2-1448, RG 59, NA. See also *Report of the Joint Brazil-United States Technical Commission*, Department of State Publication 3487 (Washington, DC: Government Printing Office, 1949).

36. Memorandum by DuWayne Clark, "Brazilian Petroleum Development," October 18, 1948, DS 832.6363/10-1848, RG 59, NA.

37. Department of State memorandum of conversation with officials from Standard Oil on oil development and refining in Brazil, May 16, 1949, DS 832.6363/10-1848, RG 59, NA.

38. Memorandum by Midriff, "Petroleum Development in Brazil," April 15, 1949, DS 832.6363/4-1549, RG 59, NA.

39. See dispatch from Rio #1296, Annual Economic Report, February 6, 1952, DS 832.00/2-552, RG 59, NA; and memorandum by Sterling Cottrell, "Petroleum Problem," October 27, 1954, Cottrell Files, Lot File 58D-42, RG 59, NA.

40. Memorandum by Dawson, "Proposed Petroleum Law in Brazil," August 21, 1947, *FRUS, 1947* 8:463–64; Clarence Brooks (chargé in Brazil), dispatch to secretary of state, June 26, 1947, *FRUS, 1947* 8:462; Clark, memorandum of conversation at the dinner given by Herbert Hoover, Jr., and John Curtis for Brazilian petroleum visitors, May 6, 1948, DS 832.6363/5-648, RG 59, NA. For the text of the revised draft petroleum law, see Brooks, dispatch to secretary of state, February 5, 1948, DS 832.6363/2-548, RG 59, NA. For Brazilian requests for Export-Import loans see memorandum by Dawson, July 15, 1947, DS 711-32/7-1547, RG 59, NA; memorandum by Dawson, May 10, 1947, DS 832.51/5-2647, RG 59, NA; and Petroleum Division memorandum, August 19, 1948, *FRUS, 1948* 9:362–63.

41. See Braden's comments on Dawson's memorandum, May 14, 1947, DS 832.51/5-2647, RG 59, NA; and Dawson, memorandum of conversation with Brazilian Ambassador Carlos Martin, July 15, 1947, DS 711.32/7-1547, RG 59, NA. See also the advertising campaign literature of the Standard Oil Company in Brazil attached to Robert T. Haslem to Thorp, October 18, 1949, DS 832.6363/10-1849, RG 59, NA.

42. Dispatch from Rio 1951 #1296, Annual Economic Report, February 6, 1952, DS 832.00/2-562, RG 59, NA.

43. See Smith, *Oil and Politics*, p. 80.

44. See ibid., pp. 55–58.

45. Cottrell (economic officer), interview with Herschel Johnson, May 8, 1951, DS 832.2553/5-851, RG 59, NA.

46. Eugene Holman to Edward Miller, April 10, 1952, DS 832.2553/4-1052, RG 59, NA.

47. See Miller to secretary of state, April 22, 1952, DS 832.2553/4-2252, RG 59, NA.

48. Ibid.

49. An *entreguista* is one willing to sell out the country's control of its own petroleum deposits to foreign trusts. See memorandum by Brown, "Political Aspects of the Petroleum Situation," May 21, 1952, DS 832.2553/5-2152, RG 59, NA.

50. R & A Report 8002, "Nationalism in Brazil," RG 59, NA; Sheldon Mills, dispatch to Randolph Kidder, May 21, 1951, *FRUS, 1951* 2:1198–99. Petrobrás had the support of the armed forces, the principal political parties, and most of the important economic groups, as well as student organizations and radicals. For a discussion of the Brazilian debate on the oil issue see Smith, *Oil and Politics*, pp. 90–98.

51. See Brandi, *Vargas*, p. 255; and Smith, *Oil and Politics*, pp. 44, 187.

52. "Brazil: The Crisis and the Promise," *Fortune* 50 (November 1954): 119–25. See also "What's Wrong in Brazil?" *U.S. News & World Report* 37 (September 3, 1954):2; and Skidmore, *Politics in Brazil*, p. 118.

53. Memorandum by Cottrell, "Petroleum Problem," Tab C, October 27, 1954, Cottrell Files, Lot File 58D-42, RG 59, NA.

54. José Viriato de Castro, *Liber Petri Espada x Vassoura: Marechal Lott* (Liberating the country, the sword against the broom: Marshal Lott) (São Paulo: Distribuidores Palácio do Livro 1959), pp. 218–19; Smith, *Oil and Politics*, p. 111.

55. Ibid., pp. 106, 186.

56. R & A Report 8002, "Nationalism in Brazil," RG 59, NA.

57. Ibid.

58. Brown, "Possibilities for Mineral Development in Brazil by Private Enterprise," DS 832.25/5-2153, RG 59, NA.

59. See James E. Webb to embassy, September 15, 1950, DS 832.2547/9-1150, RG 59, NA; memorandum by Clark of conversation between Miller (assistant secretary of state) and R. J. Wyson of United States Steel, February 7, 1950, DS 832.2547/2-750, RG 59, NA.

60. Report of task group on manganese and chrome procurement, April 7, 1948, *FRUS, 1948* 9:240; Department of State National Advisory Council Documents Action #452, February 8, 1951, Department of State, Records Relating to the National Advisory Council on International Monetary and Financial Problems (NAC), Lot File 60D-137, Washington National Records Center, Suitland, Maryland. See also the editorial note, *FRUS, 1951* 2:1188–89; Major General S. P. Spaulding, (director for Materials, Munitions Board) to Donald D. Kennedy (chief, International Resources Division, Department of State), DS 832.6359/12-1748, RG 59, NA; and Alfred E. Eckes, Jr., *The United States and the Global Struggle for Minerals* (Austin: University of Texas Press, 1979), pp. 150–62.

61. Department of State memorandum, "Brazilian Manganese Development," August 19, 1950, DS 832.2547/8-1850, RG 59, NA. See also Robert O'Toole, "U.S. Steel Corporation and Urucum Manganese Project," March 3, 1953, DS 832.2547/3-353, RG 59, NA.

62. Ibid.

63. W. Baner, "Brazilian Manganese Development," August 19, 1950, DS 832.2547/8-1850, RG 59, NA. See also memorandum by George F. Kennan, "U.S. Policy toward the American Republics"; position paper prepared in the Bureau of Inter-American Affairs, March 21, 1951, *FRUS, 1951* 2:949; NSC 68/3, December 8, 1950, and NSC 56/2, *FRUS, 1950* 1:628–38; and Department of State memorandum, "Justification for the Point Four Program in the Other American Republics," January 31, 1951, *FRUS, 1951* 2:1041–45.

64. Department of State memorandum, *FRUS, 1950* 1:663.

65. Memorandum by John C. Dreier, March 2, 1951, *FRUS, 1951* 2:941; Department of State, "Policy Statement for Brazil," December 18, 1940, DS 611.32/12-1850, RG 59, NA; telegram from Johnson to secretary, January 15, 1951, *FRUS, 1951* 2:1184–85; memorandum by Thorp, January 26, 1951, DS 832.00/1-2651, RG 59, NA; memorandum of discussions, March 6, 1951, DS 832.00/3-651, RG 59, NA. For the text of the agreement see *United States Treaties and Other International Agreements, 1951* (Washington, DC: Government Printing Office, 1952), 2:pt.2:1594. See also editorial note, *FRUS, 1951* 2:1195. During the war years 1942–1945 Brazil exported to the United States 45 percent of U.S. consumption of beryl, 43 percent of tantalite, 99.9 percent of quartz crystal, and 17 percent of magnesium. See General William H. H. Morris, Jr. (JBUSMC) to General Omar Bradley (chief of staff), June 28, 1948, PO 091 Brazil, RG 319, NA.

66. For the text of this agreement see March 25, 1952, Mutual Assistance Agreement, *U.S. Treaties and Other International Agreements, 1953* (Washington, DC: Government Printing Office, 1955), 4:pt.1:170–83.

67. Memorandum by E. R. Hamilton, January 19, 1950, DS 832.2546/1-1950, RG 59, NA; Miller to secretary of state, April 4, 1951, DS 832.2546/4-451, RG 59, NA. Monazite is a yellow, red, or brown mineral occurring often in sand and gravel deposits. It usually contains thorium, a radioactive element. Thorium oxide is a fissionable material.

68. Miller to secretary of state, April 4, 1951, DS 832.2546/4-45, RG 59, NA.

69. Telegram from Brown (minerals attaché, Rio de Janeiro) to Department of State, April 26, 1950, DS 832.2546/5-250, RG 59, NA. See also Acheson to American embassy, Rio de Janeiro, February 10, 1951, DS 832.2546/2-1051, RG 59, NA.

70. Johnson to secretary of state, February 17, 1951, DS 832.2546/2-1751, RG 59, NA. See also Acheson to Johnson, February 24, 1950, DS 832.2546/2-1150, RG 59, NA.

71. Johnson, dispatch to Acheson, February 17, 1951, DS 832.2546/2-1751, RG 59, NA; telegram from Acheson to Johnson, March 8, 1951, DS 832.2546/3-851, RG 59, NA.

72. James Douglas (acting administrator, Department of the Interior) to Miller, April 4, 1951, DS 832.2546/4-1851, RG 59, NA.

73. Memorandum by Brown, "Conclusion of Negotiations with Brazilian Government over U.S. Government Purchase of Monazite and Derivatives," January 8, 1953, DS 832.2546/1-853, RG 59, NA.

74. Cottrell to Robert P. Terrill (counselor, U.S. embassy, Rio de Janeiro), September 25, 1953, Cottrell Files, Lot File 58D-42, RG 59, NA; memorandum by Cottrell, December 1, 1954, Cottrell Files, Lot File 58D-42, RG 59, NA;

memorandum by Cottrell, September 25, 1953, Cottrell Files, Lot File 58D-42, RG 59, NA.

75. Memorandum by Cottrell, December 1, 1954, Cottrell Files, Lot File 58D-42, RG 59, NA.

76. Ibid.

77. Draft telegram by Cottrell for secretary of state, March 8, 1954, "Atomic Energy Problems—Department Report," Cottrell Files, Lot File 58D-42, RG 59, NA; secretary of state to embassy about text of draft note to Brazil, March 2, 1954, DS 832.2546/3-1254, RG 59, NA.

78. Memorandum from Clark to Miller, "Brazilian Quartz Crystal Purchase Program," January 25, 1950, DS 832.2546/1-2550, RG 59, NA.

79. Ibid.

80. Acheson to embassy, Rio de Janeiro, August 22, 1950, Miller Files, Lot File 53D-26, RG 59, NA.

81. Acheson to embassy, Rio de Janeiro, March 30, 1951, DS 832.2546/1-2451, RG 59, NA. The GATT agreements were designed to promote international trade by eliminating bilateral trade restrictions and special trade agreements. See Richard N. Gardner, *Sterling-Dollar Diplomacy in Current Perspective: The Origins and Prospects of Our International Economic Order*, rev. ed. (New York: McGraw-Hill, 1969).

82. Dickerson (counselor of embassy for economic affairs), dispatch to Department of State, September 25, 1950, DS 832.2546/9-2550, RG 59, NA.

83. Cottrell, dispatch to Department of State, "Industrial Diamonds," October 5, 1949, DS 832.2535/12-1250, RG 59, NA. See also Brown, "Comments by Diamond Dealer Re: Trade with USSR," October 12, 1950, DS 832.2535/10-1250, RG 59, NA.

84. The Mutual Defense Assistance Control Act (the Battle Act) of 1951 prohibited specific items of strategic value from being exported to the Soviet bloc. The act contained a list of such items to be embargoed effective January 24, 1952. See Public Law 213, 82d Cong., 1st sess., 65 *Statutes at Large* 644 (Washington, DC: Government Printing Office, 1952).

85. See memorandum by Cottrell for the files, "Iron Ore Exports from Brazil," DS 832.2541/6-454, RG 59, NA; memorandum by Cottrell, "Iron Ore: Brazil-Poland," May 11, 1954, DS 832.2541/5-1154, RG 59, NA; Harlan P. Bramble memorandum, "Sale of Iron Ore Produced by the Vale de Rio Doce Company," May 10, 1954, DS 832.2531/5-1054, RG 59, NA; and Cottrell, "Brazil's Iron Ore Trade with Sovbloc Countries," August 28, 1953, Cottrell Files, Lot File 58D-42, RG 59, NA. See also Hilton, "The United States, Brazil, and the Cold War."

86. See Smith, *Oil and Politics*, p. 1. For a Brazilian view see Juarez Távora, *O Petróleo do Brasil* (São Paulo: Editôra Fulgor, 1947).

Chapter Seven

Building an Infrastructure and Molding Industrial Development

Optimistic about building a postwar economic system based firmly on American ideals and expertise, most U.S. policymakers advocated a departure from the rather passive economic role the United States had followed after World War I to one of active participation in the development of a postwar world that would assure peace and prosperity for everyone. At the same time, American leaders, in general, opposed major industrialization plans of the Third World nations and rejected foreign aid programs based on public loans to promote economic growth. Instead they advocated careful planning and the application of American expertise and technology in a mercantilist approach to economic growth in these areas. They wanted to integrate these Third World economies into their U.S.-dominated free trade system. These foreign policy goals are readily apparent in U.S.-Brazilian negotiations about industrial development.

In general, Washington tried to guide and control Brazilian industrial development for the benefit of private U.S. corporations and to fit Brazil into its regional economic plans. They sincerely believed that the Brazilians would benefit most by using good old Yankee know-how and technical knowledge, not by requesting major government-to-government loans for ill-advised industrial development projects.

Unlike their Brazilian counterparts, who advocated a rapid industrialization program, U.S. officials preferred a cautious approach to industrial development. They did not believe that industrialization was the panacea for Brazil.[1] Instead they pushed Brazil toward creating industries complementary to U.S. business and toward expanding its exports of raw materials to the United States for processing. Ironically, despite such wide differences over ultimate development goals for Brazil, the two nations' leaders found themselves in close agreement about major infrastructure improvements. Experts in both countries accepted the need for massive projects to improve Brazil's transportation network and energy production. They did so, however, for radically different reasons. Washington wanted to facilitate the movement to and from the coast of export-bound strategic materials and imported U.S.-finished manufactured goods. A solid infrastructure would help speed Brazil into the U.S.-dominated, capitalistic, consumer-oriented world society. Brazilian leaders desired a strong infrastructure for internal security purposes: to aid their overall industrialization plans; to push forward their projects for creating domestic chemical, rubber, metal, cement, steel, and automobile industries; and to facilitate the necessary imports for manufacturing plants. This basic agreement on the need for infrastructure improvements helped paper over major disagreements over the direction of Brazilian industrial development and allowed both nations to claim that their economic policies were mutually acceptable and beneficial.

Despite the lack of any substantial government aid programs for Brazil, Washington continually pushed for a more direct involvement in Brazilian development planning. Accordingly, as early as 1942–43, U.S. experts were intimately involved in Brazilian economic development proposals. Under the Cooke mission, for example, they analyzed all factors in Brazil that inhibited rapid economic growth and identified "bottleneck" problems. Headed by Morris Llewellyn Cooke (a consulting engineer, past director of the Public Works Administration in Philadelphia, and a member of Roosevelt's National Resources Board), these experts outlined the pattern for postwar policy toward underdeveloped regions and their modernization plans. Pointing to an inadequate transportation system, lack of funds for industrial investments, restrictions on foreign capital, restrictions on immigration, low levels of technical training, a lack of large-scale production, investment policies based on excess profit considerations, and inadequate energy-producing facilities, the Cooke report asserted that the main task of industrialization should be left to private enterprise. The Brazilian government, the report reasoned, should concentrate its efforts on general industrial planning, facilitating industrial credit, and providing more technical education. In short, it should create a more "favorable climate" for private enterprise.[2]

Although the Cooke recommendations were well received by American officials, they were quickly forgotten as the Roosevelt administration pursued its war goals. They did, however, provide the basis for a new economic mission in 1948. Headed by John Abbink, director of McGraw-Hill and chairman of the National Foreign Trade Council, this mission stressed "balanced" development, "self-help," improving the Brazilian infrastructure, and the necessity and desirability of stimulating the flow of private capital into Brazil.[3]

Seeking to stimulate what it considered to be the mutually beneficial flow of private investment into Brazil, and to guide Brazilian industrial development into channels complementary to U.S. industry, the Abbink mission recommended that the Brazilian government end, as soon as possible, delays in remittance for imports and for the transmission of profits. American companies had experienced problems in getting state licenses to import manufactured products into Brazil and in getting their dollar profits out of the country. The mission also recommended that the Brazilians make tax concessions to attract direct private investment to the Brazilian economy and that they create a "receptive environment" for U.S. firms.[4]

Brazilian President Eurico Gaspar Dutra seemed to accept the American arguments that his government's role was to remove obstacles and to create conditions to attract foreign (American) firms to invest in Brazil. Not all Brazilians agreed with Dutra, however. The Communists were the most outspoken in their opposition. Styling the head of the mission as "Viceroy Abbink," they pictured the U.S. delegation as representatives of the monopolistic interests of Wall Street and of American economic imperialism who were attempting to hold Brazil in colonial bondage.[5]

Sensitive to such attacks the Truman administration tried to ward off any additional criticisms. When Abbink suggested that the Brazilian delegation to the mission visit the United States to give its members an opportunity "to witness our private enterprise development first hand," the Department of State rejected the idea. Not only would the Communists see it as American high-pressure sales technique, the department reasoned, but the delegation itself, seeing American industry, might project overambitious plans for Brazil's industrial development.[6]

Officials in the Truman administration viewed the Abbink report in a favorable light. The Brazilians, for their part, saw the mission as a stepping stone to increased American aid in their industrial development plans.[7] President Truman reflected the attitudes laid out by the Cooke and Abbink missions in his inaugural address in January 1949 when he announced a bold new program (Point Four) of technical assistance to underdeveloped areas. Stressing America's common interest in and concern for the economic and social progress of all peoples, Truman set forth as national goals the ideals of sharing American knowledge and skills and fostering the flow of private capital investment. Truman believed that this would assist the people of underdeveloped areas in improving their economic condition and in nourishing democracy.[8] The president made no mention of government-to-government loan programs to help finance industrial development. Implicit in Truman's Point Four proposal was the idea that America's scientific and technological assistance alone would provide sufficient incentive for economic growth.[9]

The White House put the Department of State in charge of creating a program to implement Point Four. It finally passed Congress in May 1950 as Title IV of the Foreign Economic Assistance Act, and Truman signed it on June 5, 1950. The act required that recipient nations "provide conditions under which such technical assistance and capital can effectively and constructively contribute to raising standards of living, creating new sources of wealth, increasing productivity, and expanding purchasing power."[10]

Although American policymakers sought to make the Point Four program in Brazil a model for all Latin America, they warned the embassy in Rio to be restrained in its publicity due to the "very modest amounts of aid actually available." Administration officials, concerned with the continuing crisis in Europe and the Far East, did not wish to arouse unduly high expectations among the Brazilians.[11] In fact, Congress appropriated only $34.5 million in 1950 for all technical assistance programs under the Act for International Development. Of this, only some $5 million was earmarked for Brazil.[12]

Outlining the objectives of the Point Four program in Brazil in 1951, Jonathan B. Bingham, acting administrator of the Technical Cooperation Administration, projected the basic purpose of the effort as "friendly assistance to develop its (Brazil's) resources, both material and human." The eventual objective of the program was to raise the standard of living and welfare of the Brazilian people, thereby strengthening democracy through increasing political and social stability. At the same time, according to Bingham, "quite aside from the general benefit to be derived by the United States from the promotion of sound and healthy economic and political growth among the other countries of the free world, the Point Four program could be expected to develop larger and more efficient sources of supply for the American economy, as well as create expanded markets for U.S. exports and expanded opportunities for the investment of private American capital."[13]

Meeting informally with Brazilian officials, American representatives attempted to crystallize a joint program on Point Four technical cooperation. The Brazilians made it abundantly clear in these discussions that they would welcome American technical aid and pushed hard for assistance in the fields of transportation, power, and agriculture, the bottleneck areas identified by the Cooke and Abbink missions. The U.S. delegation, headed by John Cady of the Office of Inter-American Affairs, basically agreed with its Brazilian counterpart but also stressed technical aid for the development of the production and exploration of strategic materials such as manganese and iron ore.[14] In the series of notes that established the Joint U.S.-Brazilian Economic Development Commission, the two sides gave the task of receiving and evaluating requests for technical assistance to the commission and agreed to place heavy emphasis on American technical aid for improving the Brazilian infrastructure.[15]

In the discussions that followed Brazilian planners emphasized their desire that the commission place great weight on specific projects rather than more general studies. They wanted the commission to initiate an "action program." According to the Brazilians, enough overall or general studies had already been undertaken with the Cooke and Abbink missions. What was urgently needed was immediate assistance in development projects in the fields of transportation, power, and agriculture.[16] The Brazilians wanted direct U.S. aid and loans for their industrial development program, not more rhetoric. The terms under which the commission was established, however, generally avoided the direct commitment of U.S. funds. The commission was to prepare studies and reports and make recommendations regarding "projects of great importance to the economic expansion of Brazil." It was also to examine how much technical assistance would be most appropriate for Brazil to expedite priority projects in transportation, power, and agriculture, to study opportunities for utilizing foreign technical knowledge, skills, and investment, and to examine the general and legal measures needed to remove hindrances to economic development.[17]

Formally established on July 17, 1951, the commission consisted of one American and one Brazilian member and each member's staff.[18] Ari Torres headed the Brazilian team, which included the cream of Brazil's financial, economic, and engineering personnel. Installed in the marble-walled Salao Nobre of the Brazilian Finance Ministry, the commission immediately began to address urgent bottleneck problems in transportation and power.[19]

Aside from its activities concerning transportation, power, and agriculture, the commission was called on to comment on various industrial projects. Reluctant to lay out any ambitious industrial program, Merwin L. Bohan (the interim U.S. commissioner) nevertheless was careful to feature industry in all of the commission's announcements. Bohan believed that Brazil, like several other Latin American countries, suffered from "a bad case of industrialitis." In discussions with the Brazilians, Bohan explained that "the phobia that the United States is opposed to industrial expansion pops up in the most unexpected places."[20]

Bohan was also careful when the commission came to promoting strategic minerals production. Despite the excellent opportunities for assisting Brazil in this area, Bohan was wary of helping to spread the idea that the exploitation of minerals for export did not benefit Brazil and that Washington's primary purpose in agreeing to establish the Joint Commission was to get more raw material exports from Brazil. In a like manner, Bohan steered the commission away from discussing petroleum matters. He warned all of his staff members to refrain from discussing the issue: "The less said about petroleum by foreigners the better." For Bohan, this was a Brazilian problem that only Brazil could solve. He did not want the commission to become bogged down discussing the merits of private petroleum development.[21] Nor did Bohan wish to see the commission remain active indefinitely. He reasoned that "in a proud and nationalistic country, such as Brazil, the United States cannot too long play the intimate role of economic doctor without unfortunate repercussions."[22] He envisioned permanent Brazilian organizations taking over the Joint Commission's functions. The commission would pass on the major portion of its transportation functions to a Brazilian railway authority, its functions in the fields of power, industry, and minerals to a Brazilian financial development organization, and its agricultural functions to a reorganized agricultural extension service of Brazil's Ministry of Agriculture and its "servicos" (agricultural field stations). The commission's recommendation of establishing a National Economic Development Bank (BNDE), however, raised Brazilian expectations for long-term financial cooperation and assistance.[23] In his report to the incoming permanent U.S. commissioner, J. Burke Knapp, Bohan concluded nevertheless that he hoped the commission could disappear "in a blaze of glory within a period of eighteen to twenty-four months."[24]

What Bohan and most American planners feared was that, having assisted the Brazilians in drawing up their economic development projects in "bankable" form, the Brazilians would use the commission to insist on U.S. financing for these projects.[25] Indeed, from the inception of the Joint Commission, the Brazilians repeatedly sought definite commitments from Washington to finance all projects prepared by the commission.[26]

Despite the firm Brazilian stand, the incoming Eisenhower administration was determined not to shift the financing of Brazilian development to the U.S. Treasury and therefore notified the Brazilian government of its intent to terminate the commission on June 30, 1953. Sterling Cottrell of the Department of State's Brazilian Affairs Office summed up department thinking: "As long as the Joint Commission stays in existence the Brazilians believe they have a chance of squeezing more loans out of the U.S."[27] Ambassador James Kemper explained to Brazilian Foreign Minister Vincente Rao and Finance Minister Oswaldo Aranha that a continuation of the commission would not improve prospects for financing the projects.[28] For the United States, the commission was part of a political and not an economic program. It was designed to play a major role in an effort to recapture the spirit of mutual confidence from the days of Franklin D. Roosevelt, not to provide massive government loans for financing Brazilian industrial development.[29]

In place of large loans and following Truman's Point Four proposals, officials in both the Truman and Eisenhower administrations continually emphasized the concept of the "technical solution" to Brazil's problems. Technically oriented experts such as engineers, economists, administrators, and managers would, according to these officials, produce rational, scientific plans that would shorten the road to Brazilian achievement of "status as a modern, powerful nation with a high standard of living."[30] Centralized, scientific planning became the panacea that would satisfy Brazil's "revolution of rising expectations." Apolitical technical specialists, armed with scientific data, would analyze the Brazilian economy and draw the road map for successful development.[31]

Utilizing private consulting companies, engineering firms, and research organizations, U.S. policymakers set about reshaping and remolding the Brazilian economy for the modern world. American technical experts invaded Brazil.[32] They saw Brazil as a testing area for modern scientific methods of industrial development.[33] Private capital and U.S. goods were emphasized, not government loans.[34] Naturally, funds available under Point Four would not be sufficient to carry out actual construction, but careful surveys, studies, and analyses by American experts would point the way for proper development.

At first, the Point Four effort focused on the bottleneck fields of transportation and power identified in the various economic mission reports. Viewing Brazil's transportation problem as urgent not only for the internal transfer of foodstuffs from production to consumption centers but also for the movement of exports such as coffee, cacao, manganese, and iron ore to foreign markets, the Department of State instituted a series of studies to survey the entire transportation network of Brazil. Concentrating on the rail and highway systems, the early surveys recommended an action program for the removal of the worst transportation bottlenecks.

Various American studies viewed the railroad problem as particularly alarming. At a time when Brazil had a rapidly expanding need for an improved transportation system to bring food and raw materials to industrial centers and to expand its exports, the system was falling apart.[35] American reports pointed to the 8 1/2-month delay for lumber shipments on the Nordeste Railroad in western São Paulo and southern Mato Grosso. While cattle herds had increased in Brazil by two million head from 1949 to 1952, the cattle-carrying capacity of the railroads had actually decreased by 15 percent during the same period. Cattle ranchers had to resort to cattle drives to get their herds to market. In the steel industry, the mill at Volta Redonda had to move raw materials such as iron ore, limestone, coal, and scrap iron by truck in order to maintain operations.[36] Even the movement of manganese, high on the critical list for export to the United States, had slowed to a trickle because of the rail problem, U.S. transportation experts reported.[37]

Reviewing the Brazilian railroad system, American experts identified two major problem areas: equipment and management. They found that 90 percent of all Brazilian rails had been laid prior to the 1900s, that (by 1953) 60 percent of all locomotives were over thirty years old and burned wood for fuel, and that fully one third of the freight cars were constructed entirely of wood, small in capacity, and unsuitable for heavy freight.[38] The Americans were amazed to find a multiplicity of Brazilian administrative agencies dealing with the railroads. The Brazilian National Railroad Department, established in 1941 as a part of the Ministry of Transportation and Public Works, directly regulated only 11 percent of the total system. Subject to a variety of regulatory, supervisory, or coordinating agencies of the federal government (including such offices as the Public Service Administration, the General Accounting Bureau, the SALTE Plan

Administration, and the Ministry of Transportation and Public Works), the railroads operated in a state of confusion. Because of the variety of federal, state, and private rail ownerships (there were forty-one separate companies in 1953) the railroads were reluctant to send their freight cars over another line lest they be "borrowed" for indefinite periods.[39] To further complicate the problem, various Brazilian railroads operated on different gauges, and their equipment came from not only the United States but also from Italy, France, Great Britain, and Germany. Brazil had only 30,000 miles of track in 1953, compared to 223,000 miles of track in the United States. To American experts the Brazilian railroads were a disaster.[40]

Discussing the managerial problem, the Americans recommended a central management organization. Such functions as purchases, budgets, accounting, and standards would in this way be centralized. Only a large, authoritative and efficient management organization, they argued, could possibly make the Brazilian rail system a modern, efficient transportation network and remove it from political interference. With barely a glance at the railroad operating system in the United States and its development, the Americans pushed a program that called for the United States to furnish the skills to deal with the immediate engineering requirements as well as the management and operation of the Brazilian railroads. American expertise in such areas as train operation and control, facility efficiency, maintenance and repair, safety, traffic development, labor relations, modern accounting practices, and cost analysis would put the Brazilian rail system on the right track.

Further studies recommended the standardization of equipment and the replacement of obsolete equipment with American diesel and electric locomotives, freight cars, rolling stock, track replacement, signaling systems, and maintenance facilities. Under various exchange programs Brazilian engineers and administrators trained in the United States and American engineers, mechanics, and specialists traveled to Brazil to help the Brazilians to determine not only what they should do but also how they should do it.[41] Training a number of young Brazilian railway engineers and other executive personnel in railway administrative practices and management in the United States would improve the Brazilian rail system and, U.S. officials believed, would expose the trainees to American methods, techniques, and equipment. Both nations would benefit. The Brazilians would gain much-needed training and experience in railway management. By inculcating the visiting Brazilians with American values and training them with American equipment the United States would gain valuable allies in its fight against communism as well as customers for American equipment.

The Brazilians thought that the American effort was unobjectionable, but what they really wanted were loans and credits to purchase modern rail equipment. Money was their pressing concern. President Getúlio Vargas complained that the United States gave grant aid to Italy to rebuild its railways while he could not even obtain loans to repair railways "which had worn out carrying strategic materials for the United States." State Department officials hurriedly reassured Vargas that they were doing everything possible to help Brazil. Privately, some of them saw Vargas's complaint as another attempt to get Brazil a seat on what Vargas saw as a gravy train that carried uncounted millions in grant aid to all quarters of the globe.[42]

Although both nations agreed on the need to improve Brazil's rail lines, sharp disagreements over financing the needed improvements surfaced. The question of loans for such infrastructure improvements also provoked major fissions in U.S. policymaking circles.

The Vargas administration regarded the upgrading of the Brazilian railroad system as a top priority in its industrial development scheme and attempted to gain U.S. backing for the work. Seeing the rehabilitation of the railroads as a major step toward alleviating the Brazilian transportation problem, the joint U.S.-Brazilian commission also approved several projects for improving the rail system. However, disagreement soon surfaced between the International Bank for Reconstruction and Development (IBRD) and the Department of State.[43] Picturing Brazil as vital to hemispheric stability and its support hinging on the form and extent of U.S. cooperation in its long-range economic development, State Department officials took the position that the IBRD should finance sound railway projects of approximately $140 million without insisting on major managerial reform first. The IBRD refused. The president of the bank, Eugene Black, announced that the IBRD would limit its loans for railroad improvement to $25 million until the Brazilian congress passed railroad reorganization legislation.[44]

According to Merwin Bohan, the IBRD was interfering once again in American foreign policy. The embassy and the Joint Commission, Bohan wrote Assistant Secretary of State for Inter-American Affairs Edward Miller, had been working quietly and effectively to convince the Brazilians of their responsibility in this area and the bank was "thoughtlessly" introducing an element of "coercion" into the situation.[45]

Upset with the bank's position, Brazilian Finance Minister Horácio Lafer threatened to take the railroad rehabilitation program "elsewhere" when he spoke with J. Burke Knapp about the IBRD during Knapp's visit to Brazil. Knapp responded that if Brazil adopted such a policy, the IBRD would have to revise its entire relationship with Brazil.[46] Lafer described the position of the bank as "impossible" and later complained to Ambassador Herschel Johnson that the IBRD was an inappropriate instrument to finance the major share of the Brazilian development program and suggested that the Export-Import Bank was a better vehicle.[47]

Although State Department officials were sympathetic to the Brazilian request and privately considered the bank's position to be detrimental to long-range U.S.-Brazilian relations, many department planners were also skeptical about Brazil's threat to go elsewhere. State officials were confident that a solution could be worked out. "The Brazilians will sulk," wrote Robert O'Toole of the South American Republics Division, "but they need us worse than we do them and they know it. They will get over it." Edward Miller saw "our heroine again tied to the railroad track," but he wrote Ambassador Johnson that he thought "she would be snatched from disaster next week."[48] Along these same lines, Sterling Cottrell recommended that the department again seek an agreement with the IBRD with specific reference to the railway program. If no solution was reached, Cottrell suggested, then State should recommend that the U.S. Treasury, through the Export-Import Bank, back up the commitment. But, Cottrell cautioned, "the Export-Import Bank was no bed of roses either."[49]

Meeting in April, representatives from the Treasury Department, the IBRD, and State attempted to iron out their differences. Arthur Garner of the IBRD set forth the bank's position. According to Garner, Brazil was at its borrowing capacity. Among all the countries of the world that had borrowed from the IBRD, Brazil had been lent the third highest amount. Its industrialization program was a major drain on its exchange position. It was in a poor economic position. Its exports were less in volume than they were in 1946. It had a major fuel problem and its new industries were dependent on imported goods. "Brazil has a great potential," Garner emphasized, "but had not cashed in on it for 300 years and may not in the future." Knapp from IBRD added that loans would not in themselves give Brazil good transportation or help the Brazilian economy unless they were accompanied by the necessary reforms. Nevertheless, the IBRD representatives concluded, the bank was willing to go ahead with a lending program in Brazil on a sound banking basis.[50]

Treasury representatives Andrew Overby (assistant secretary of the treasury) and Harold Linder supported the bank's position. It was in the interest of the U.S. government to refrain from taking action that would be prejudicial to the bank, they argued. Assistant Secretary of State Thomas Mann, while expressing general agreement, suggested that the problem was not whether or not the IBRD's position on a transaction was sound or unsound, but rather a question of tactics in dealing with the Latin Americans.[51]

The meeting broke up without a firm agreement, but the crisis passed as both the IBRD and the Export-Import Bank made loans available for the purchase of railroad equipment and the upgrading and expansion of the Brazilian rail lines.[52] The Brazilians moved ahead with the promised railway legislation.[53]

Viewing the rail system as only a part of Brazil's overall transportation crisis, American experts also analyzed, studied, and surveyed its highway, shipping, and aviation needs. They concluded that what the Brazilians needed was practical assistance in these areas. Studying their highway system, American experts found that although it had steadily improved since 1946, it still fell far short of the country's basic needs. A country larger than the United States, with 55 million people, had only 300,000 trucks and buses and a road system of only some 110,000 miles. According to the Americans, there was an urgent need for the development of a nationwide all-weather highway system similar to that being constructed in the United States, a federal system with state feeder lines. The creation of such a system would result in a greater flow of foodstuffs, more revenue for the railways and less waste in transporting resources to the industrial centers. It would also aid in the development, production, and flow of mineral resources and strategic materials to the ports for export—a goal U.S. planners always kept in mind but seldom stated publicly.[54]

In 1951 a major highway equipment show promoted by the Brazilian Highway Association and the National Highway Department opened in Rio de Janeiro. It was dominated by such U.S. firms as Caterpillar, Allis-Chalmers, and Ingersoll-Rand. The show featured graders, shovels, scrapers, road rollers, and other types of road-building equipment. According to U.S. Vice Consul William Rambo it was a fine show with great promotional value for American products. Most of the heavy equipment was already tagged "sold" before the opening, and the exhibitors could have sold many times more equipment if Brazilian credit and license restrictions had allowed.[55]

Rambo also noted that of the seventy-five exhibits, sixty-three were occupied entirely by American equipment and only twelve by European equipment manufacturers, mainly German and British. It was clearly an American show, although there was some concern about growing European competition.[56]

Nevertheless the completion of the President Dutra highway, consisting of 405 kilometers of paved road linking Rio de Janeiro and São Paulo and reducing the travel time between the two cities from eleven to six hours, strikingly illustrated American dominance and influence. U.S. engineers, methods, and equipment were prominent in the effort.[57] American advisers even suggested that Brazil adopt the U.S. toll road concept to help pay for the cost of construction.[58]

American experts realized that the emphasis on highway construction made the trucking industry uneconomical for the movement of bulky low-unit-cost materials and that this would place an increasing burden on Brazil's balance of payments. They justified the highway construction effort as essential for the ultimate development of Brazil, however, and as beneficial to their efforts to ensure the transportation of strategic materials to the coast. It also followed the U.S. plan for development by encouraging private investment.[59]

The status of Brazil's ports and its shipping fleet was also carefully studied by Americans. The Department of State brought in the New York engineering firm of Gibbs and Hill to evaluate Brazilian port operations with a view toward increasing capacity and efficiency. Gibbs and Hill found that although Brazil had over fifty ports only nineteen were organized on a commercial basis, and most of these were antiquated and had very limited capacity. They recommended a major port improvement program involving dredging and the construction of new warehouse space to relieve the congestion and called for improved management and the elimination of preferential berthing privileges for the Brazilian carrier Lloyd Brasileiro. The Gibbs and Hill report deplored the condition of Brazil's foreign trade fleet noting that, even using Brazil's notoriously poor data, the tonnage of native flag ships' entries into Rio de Janeiro and Santos constituted less than 6 percent for Rio and 4 percent for Santos of the tonnage of foreign vessel entries. Most of the Brazilian fleet was over thirty years old and had a small carrying capacity. In response, the Brazilians noted rather caustically that they understood the problem. What they needed was money to begin improvements.[60]

Although the Eisenhower administration merged much of the Technical Cooperation Administration (TCA) program into the Mutual Security Agency (MSA) in 1953, it continued to focus on the shipment of strategic raw materials to the United States.[61] In addition, American shipping firms pressed the Eisenhower administration to eliminate discriminatory privileges for Lloyd Brasileiro, and U.S. exporters, especially the automobile companies, pushed for modern port facilities to increase their market shares in Brazil. In response the Eisenhower administration dangled before the Brazilians Export-Import Bank loans, the possibility of obtaining surplus American ships, and the partial waiving of regulations that required freight delivery from Export-Import loans to be carried in American flag ships as bait for the Brazilians to remove their discriminatory practices. Anxious to obtain the loans, the Brazilians dropped their preferential treatment and exclusive use laws, justifying their actions as "politically necessary." In response the Export-Import Bank waived its standard clause concerning the shipment of goods and granted additional credits to Brazil for port improvements.[62] This quid pro quo deal seemed satisfactory to both parties, although the Economics Division of the Department of State opposed it as rewarding Brazil for discriminating against U.S. ships and setting a dangerous precedent for other countries.[63]

American representatives also closely examined Brazilian aviation. Using the Civil Aeronautics Board (CAB), its technical assistance missions, and International Field Offices, Washington encouraged Brazil to expand and improve its airway facilities. American officials reasoned that improved facilities would not only benefit the commercial airlines, both Brazilian and foreign, but the U.S. military would also receive considerable benefits in case of an emergency. Improved airfields would provide access to large areas containing strategic materials. Technical assistance and training were again stressed, rather than loans for such improvements. For example, while denying loans to Brazil for the purchase of major modern aircraft (which would enable the Brazilians to expand their civil aviation services), the Americans were more than happy to assist with technical training. When the Brazilian Institute of Aeronautical Technology sought to establish a technical aeronautical training center at São José dos Campos in the state of São Paulo to train mechanics and engineers, the United States volunteered to provide training equipment and twenty-eight aeronautical engineers and technicians to organize the school and to serve as instructors.

Washington believed that the installation of American equipment and the assignment of American instructors to teach in such centers would have a measurable effect on the use of U.S.-manufactured products in Brazil in years to come. Only when the Brazilians hinted, however, that they would turn to other specialists, such as the Germans, for help did the United States provide enough money to cover the expenses of its specialists. Even then, U.S. officials were little concerned with foreign competition. They argued that Brazilian aviation had a firm American orientation and that U.S. leadership in this field would continue for a long time to come. The close relationship between the two nations' military establishments in this area was an additional guarantee, according to Washington.[64]

This did not prevent bickering between CAB officials and members of the State Department over how to handle the aviation problem, however. CAB officials at times accused the department of meddling in affairs it knew nothing about, and at other times it chastised the embassy for not taking a strong enough stand against arbitrary Brazilian air rate hikes. Despite such disputes, the U.S. agencies closed ranks over providing aircraft equipment and spare parts to the Brazilians. When they learned that Great Britain was attempting to sell de Haviland Mark II Comets to Panair for international jet service, the two agencies agreed that it would be "regrettable to see British equipment get a foothold" in the Brazilian market. The Brazilian civil air fleet consisted mainly of U.S.-manufactured DC-3s, and the Eisenhower administration wanted to retain this market for American companies.[65]

It was not only aircraft sales that concerned American policymakers. They also wanted Brazil to buy standardized U.S. communications equipment, safety equipment, and spare parts. The Korean crisis, however, put a strain on the ability of U.S. firms to supply the growing Brazilian demand.

Despite the desire to promote U.S. goods, officials of the Eisenhower administration agreed that the Export-Import Bank should not make loans to the Brazilian airline Varig if Brazil persisted in having one fare rate for domestic carriers such as Varig and another for competing foreign carriers such as Pan-American Airways. They further justified their opposition to loans for Varig's proposed service expansion by picturing it as a luxury Brazil could do without, since U.S. carriers could offer all the services needed.[66] Implicit in the American reaction was the concept that Brazilian development was all right as long as it did not interfere with American profits and dominance.[67]

U.S. recommendations for the development of the Brazilian power industry followed a similar pattern. Industrial development was severely hampered by Brazil's inability to generate sufficient power. Increasing demands of expanding industry and urban development created a serious power shortage in Brazil, despite the fact that by 1950 energy output in Brazil had grown by 150 percent compared with that of 1939. Rapid urbanization brought new public and private demands. The population of the city of São Paulo, for example, grew from 1.3 million in 1940 to over 2.6 million in 1953. This growth was accompanied by the introduction of electrical appliances and cooking, elevators, air conditioning, street lighting, sanitation facilities, and public transportation. The accelerated rate of industrialization with its heavy demands for energy in the new chemical, rubber, metal, and cement industries also pushed the demand for power far beyond Brazil's ability to provide it. By 1946, for the first time, the peak electric power load had reached the level of installed capacity. For the next twenty years the system was never able to satisfy the demand.[68] American engineers estimated that even with a 10 percent increase per year the power industry would not be able to fully satisfy the projected demand until well into the 1960s. Further complicating the problem was Brazil's lack of energy resources such as coal, petroleum, and natural gas. Brazil had to rely on hydroelectric energy for its major source of power.[69]

To the Brazilians, as well as to the Americans, the consumption of energy was a decisive index of the standard of living, the comfort, and the well-being of a nation. Increased energy consumption marked the progress of a nation.[70] Viewed in this light, Brazil had a long way to go. In 1950 power was available to only 3,771 out of 5,436 organized municipalities. Comparing the power supply per capita in selected countries, Brazil was far down on the list.[71] In the area served by São Paulo Light and Power Company in 1952 some 30,000 residences awaited electrical connections, and there was at least one year's delay for industrial hookups. The demands for power created major shortages, rationing, brownouts, and reductions in the level of industrial operations and schedules. For example, some plants in São Paulo worked only at night or on weekends as this was the only time sufficient power was available. In 1953–54 power was cut off five to seven hours a day in Rio de Janeiro and São Paulo.[72]

Viewing the energy crisis as a major bottleneck for Brazil's development, American experts set about analyzing the Brazilian power industry.[73] They discovered that two predominantly foreign-owned companies, the Canadian Brazilian Tractor Light and Power Company and the largely American Empresar Eléctricios Brasileiras, provided nearly two thirds of Brazil's power supply. The Americans found these companies, in general, to be well run, efficient, and effective. According to the experts, by organizing large engineering and design staffs, procurement services, shipping agencies, and financial disbursing service companies in North America, these companies were able to provide economical service. They recommended that the remainder of the Brazilian power companies, which were predominantly small-scale and locally owned, be merged and integrated to restore the power industry's profitability and provide economies of scale for large energy development projects such as dams, reservoirs, and transmission lines.[74]

While recognizing the regulatory functions of the public authorities as necessary and often beneficial, the Americans cautioned against the state becoming too active and too dominant in this area. They were unanimous in their recommendation that state and federal governments should not assume direct responsibility for the construction and operation of power facilities. According to these experts, private enterprise had proven its administrative and technical competence in this area. What was needed was for government to make the industry attractive to private capital. It seemed much wiser to rely on the American model of effective public regulation to ensure that the power industry fulfilled its role as a basic public utility rather than to make the state itself responsible. Government action should remain regulatory and promotional. Given incentives, the experts argued, Brazilian and foreign private capital could produce the desired results.[75]

Ironically, at the same time, U.S. advisers were promoting private development in the energy field, the Truman administration showed off the Tennessee Valley Authority to President Dutra during his tour of the United States.[76] Disregarding this contradiction, Washington continued to work out a new plan for Brazil's power industry. They pointed out the need for Brazil to develop engineers, technicians, and specialists to maintain such a highly technical industry. The ratio of engineers to industrial workers in Brazil in 1953, the Americans discovered, was similar to that of the United States in 1910. To speed up the training process the policymakers offered American educational opportunities for specialists in engineering, construction, and administration. U.S. specialists moved into Brazil not only to assist in the development of new generating facilities, but also into management and administrative positions. For example, they served as advisers to the Brazilian Federal Power Commission, which developed the power rate structure for the energy industry.[77]

The Brazilians accepted the technical assistance but continued to push for financial aid to undertake major power projects. Privately they complained that they knew what the problems were, but what they needed was the money to carry out costly expansion operations.[78]

They quite frankly desired expert guidance from the United States in the preparation of applications for loans from the IBRD and the Export-Import Bank.[79]

Both nations also recognized that the Brazilian power industry depended upon the importation of equipment and capital, and this put a serious drain on Brazil's finances. Encouraged by Washington, American manufacturing companies such as Westinghouse proposed as early as 1943 to produce a complete line of electrical equipment in Brazil if they were granted monopoly licenses. Because of nationalist sensitivities, however, nothing came of these proposals until 1952, and it was not until 1960 that Brazil was capable of producing most of the materials used in the power industry internally.[80]

Although Washington was wary of promoting a Brazilian industry that might in the future compete with American firms, they were not above encouraging Brazilian-owned and Brazilian-supplied concerns if they squeezed out foreign competitors. For example, the United States promoted a plan for Brazilians to take over the Canadian-owned Brazilian Light and Traction Company, which also controlled the Brazilian Telephone Company. Picturing a new corporation modeled on the AT&T-Bell Telephone System as the ideal, American officials envisioned a predominantly Brazilian-owned firm with American managerial direction. Such a company not only would be efficient and profitable but also would cut the dollar drain on Brazil. U.S. advisers pointed out that Brazilian Light and Traction's finances and equipment purchases primarily benefited Canada and Great Britain, not Brazilian industry. Although nothing came of the proposal it clearly illustrates the American desire to eliminate all foreign competition from Brazil and the overwhelming self-confidence American leaders had in their industry and its organizational ability and efficiency. Brazil needed only to follow the American example to have a modern, effective power industry.[81]

Under both the Truman and Eisenhower administrations, technical assistance poured into Brazil. American engineers, technicians, experts, and specialists from the private and public sectors became part of the effort to remake the Brazilian economy. At first, the technical cooperation programs they established were favorably received and achieved, in general, positive results. Both nations praised the effort.[82] By late 1952, however, some criticism of the overall program began to surface. The Department of State was "shocked and alarmed at the cancerous growth of the TCA and FOA [Foreign Operations Administration] bureaucracy." According to the department, too many Americans were centered in Rio, and, although the programs enjoyed great prestige among "the important and forward-looking elements among the professional, business, and military classes," few Brazilians among the general population were even aware of the effort. According to Walter Walmsley, the American chargé in Brazil, the program was in danger of being overwhelmed with professional civil servants rather than with outstanding specialists who had demonstrated proficiency in private pursuits. Walmsley pointed to the fact that, of 144 U.S. officials assigned to current projects in Brazil, only 23 were located outside of Rio.[83]

Moreover, whereas during the establishment of the Point Four effort most of the successful technical cooperation programs came from Brazilian initiatives and were truly joint programs, the entire effort under first the Technical Cooperation Administration (Truman) and then the Foreign Operations Administration (Eisenhower) was beginning to acquire a connotation of paternalism and condescension on the part of the more fortunate toward the less fortunate partner. Herschel Johnson, the U.S. ambassador in Brazil, even questioned Brazil's ability to utilize technical aid effectively given its limitations in the fields of decision making and public administration. Johnson suggested the United States return, at least psychologically, to the concept of "the good neighbor" or "mutual cooperation."[84]

Although confident in the ability of American industry to maintain its competitive advantage and aware of the tremendous increase in the power of the United States and the concurrent decline in the power of such competitors as Germany, France, Great Britain, Japan, and Italy, both the Truman and Eisenhower administrations maintained a close watch over the resurgence of foreign commercial interests in Latin America, and especially in Brazil. They closely monitored all Brazilian exchange and financial agreements with other nations and noted Great Britain's attempts to increase its share of the Brazilian market by sterling devaluation, French interest in providing funds and equipment for petroleum refineries and industrial production, and Italian, Portuguese, Austrian, Czechoslovakian, and Yugoslavian bilateral agreements for barter transactions.[85] The Americans protested these agreements as discriminatory and unhealthy. These barter deals were not only unfavorable to the United States, they were not in the best interests of Brazil. They were but "two small jumps away from the pre-war German system of compensation trading."[86]

American officials reported in 1951 that the United States continued to be Brazil's principal supplier, accounting for 47 percent of its total imports. They noted, however, a noticeable shift in Brazil's import trade pattern toward Western Europe, especially West

Germany.[87] Making a strong bid for Brazil's trade, West German officials in 1953 signed a trade agreement that called for German sales of capital equipment to be financed by long-term credits to Brazil. They set up a Volkswagen factory in São Paulo and a Kloechmer steel mill in Victoria, and they established a joint German-Brazilian commission to supervise additional projects. They also signed a treaty of friendship, commerce, and navigation.[88] Although concerned with the aggressiveness of the Germans, the Eisenhower administration rationalized that Germany, as well as France and Great Britain, labored under the handicap of their weakened political and economic position in the world.[89] The U.S. position seemed safe for the present.

The Brazilians showed increasing interest in reestablishing and developing trade relations with the Western European countries and even the Soviet bloc countries. In 1952 they sent an economic delegation to Europe. Headed by João Alberto, chief of the Economic Department of the Brazilian Foreign Office, most members of the commission were convinced that Brazil had to expand trade rapidly with Europe so as not to be too dependent on the United States. Increased trade with Europe would also strengthen Brazil's bargaining position vis-à-vis the United States, some officials argued.[90] Again, the Americans were not overly alarmed. Ambassador Johnson noted that the Brazilians, "for all their occasional high-flown Latin apostrophes to idealism," were exceedingly realistic when it came to appraising trade opportunities and the essentials of political and economic power.[91] Even Brazil's closer trade contacts with Soviet bloc states did not really upset U.S. officials. When João Alberto announced trade agreements with Hungary, Romania, and Bulgaria, Economic Affairs Counselor Robert Terrill sniffed "that except for cotton such trade will be more a diversion from existing markets than any net increase." Washington believed that the Brazilians were grasping at straws and that only the United States could provide the quality and quantity of trade, technical assistance, and goods to drive the Brazilian economy forward.[92]

Confident of their own abilities, American business interests held similar views. American goods and know-how would transform Brazil into a modern twentieth-century industrial state. Despite growing competition and the chronically troublesome petroleum situation, U.S. business saw Brazil as a land of opportunity. Especially after the suicide of President Vargas, American business pictured the government of João Café Filho as a government of businesslike technicians, friendly to free enterprise and foreign capital.

The American automotive industry, for example, saw a huge potential market in Brazil in the early 1950s. Observing that the average Brazilian-owned car was approximately ten to twelve years old, that highway improvements were on the way, and that there was an increased demand for private automobiles, the American firms foresaw a wide-open market in Brazil. All of the major car makers— General Motors, Chrysler, Ford, Studebaker, Packard, Hudson, Nash, Willy, and Kaiser/Frazer—entered the Brazilian market and quickly dominated it. Of 238,474 passenger cars registered in Brazil as of January 1, 1951, 186,010 were American made. Ninety-five percent of the taxicabs and 90 percent of the trucks were of American origin. U.S. manufacturers believed that this preponderance of American cars was due to their easy availability and superior performance. Besides, according to the Americans, there was an overwhelming preference for American cars. They were superior in appearance, and the U.S. system for stocking and distributing replacement parts was unsurpassed.[93]

During the late 1940s and early 1950s there were no motor vehicle factories in Brazil, however. Ford and General Motors refused, at first, to set up manufacturing plants in Brazil. Their executives argued that there was not a sufficiently large market for automobile production in Brazil.[94] Every automobile was imported, and the major U.S. firms all had assembly plants in Brazil. Only the restriction of import licenses prohibited an explosion of demand. Most American firms advertised only to keep their brand names before the Brazilian public. There were no major sales campaigns and no exhibitions. Even the introductions of new makes and models seldom were accompanied by promotional campaigns.[95] It was a seller's market.

Only two developments clouded the horizon for U.S. manufacturers—foreign competition and Brazilian desires for a domestic manufacturing capability. Foreign, mostly German-made vehicles continued to increase their share of the local market with lower prices and smaller cars, and this worried the Americans. By 1951, Germany, eager to increase its presence in Brazil, had advanced to third place as a supplier of all types of vehicles in Brazil and was pressing the British for second place. Germany was emerging as a strong competitor. Although concerned, U.S. officials attributed the improved market share of the European manufacturers primarily to the availability of their nations' currencies and the shortage of dollar exchange. Surely if given a choice most Brazilians would still prefer an American product.[96]

Of more concern to the Eisenhower administration and industry officials were the Brazilian attempts to create a domestic automotive industry, including the manufacture and production of automotive parts and accessories. With President Vargas's approval, the Brazilian Industrial Development Commission (CDI) recommended that importation of assembled automobiles for resale be prohibited beginning July 1, 1953, and that the importation of knocked down motor vehicles be limited beginning January 1, 1954, in order to encourage domestic manufacture. Vargas praised the work of the commission and approved its recommendation in October 1953.[97]

Convinced that in order to protect their large and expanding market in Brazil they would have to install full manufacturing facilities, the major U.S. automakers now pushed ahead with large-scale plans for the expansion of their plants. Under American management, company officials reasoned, these plants would be modern and efficient. Both Brazil and the U.S. automotive industry would benefit.[98] Employees trained by the American companies would be skilled and knowledgeable and would become the economic leaders of the future.[99]

The American business press showered these efforts with praise. American management, and not just in the automotive industry, would lead Brazil into the modern, industrial future. *Fortune*, for example, lauded Sears, Roebuck for pioneering new market techniques in Brazil that rescued customers from "dilatory European-style salesclerk-cashier-wrapper run around" and "provided them with modern, quick, efficient service." Sears's insistence on large volume, large turnover, and low prices instead of tall per-unit profits based on undersupply was revolutionizing the Brazilian consumer market, according to *Fortune*.[100] American business was providing what Brazil needed most: management and administrative skills, up-to-date business practices and organization, modern technology, specialized training, and scientific methods. Boasting about American contributions to Brazilian development, the business press urged the adoption of the "American way" to ensure success. All the Brazilian government had to do was increase business incentives and provide training for the necessary engineers, managers, and technicians. Emerging entrepreneurs would provide the driving force for Brazilian development.[101]

The optimism of the American business community about Brazilian economic development was, in general, shared by Washington. The basic goal of the cooperative technical assistance program was to help Brazil to develop the skills and techniques of its people so that it would become an economically strong and politically stable ally of the United States. Specifically this included helping Brazil to improve its infrastructure including transportation and distribution facilities, aiding the Brazilian development of energy resources, and encouraging the expansion of industries that did not compete with U.S. businesses. The beneficial effects of these efforts would be enjoyed not only by the Brazilian people but also by the United States. They would produce closer relations and dilute Brazilian suspicions of U.S. motives. In the long run American industry and trade also would benefit as Brazil developed into a major modern market for consumer goods and private investment. Confident that American industry could compete with anyone, Washington monitored the growth of foreign competitors in the Brazilian marketplace but, in general, took no drastic actions to curtail it.[102]

The Brazilians welcomed the technical aid and assistance. But, unlike their American counterparts who viewed technical cooperation as the primary focus of their aid, the Brazilian policymakers saw such technical assistance as secondary to the main objective of obtaining the necessary funds for major economic improvement projects, especially the creation of domestic industries. They attempted to use growing European and Soviet bloc interest in trade to pressure the Americans into increasing their monetary aid.[103] As the two countries argued over the proper way to encourage development and the type of development best suited for Brazil, a mixed package emerged that incorporated centralized planning concepts, government control, and free-enterprise, private capital expansion. Both nations encouraged the expanding Brazilian economy for their own reasons, and both took credit for the economic success that followed.

Notes

1. Charles S. Maier, "The Politics of Productivity: Foundations of American International Economic Policy after World War II," *International Organization* 31:4 (1977): 607–33. See also Randall, *A Foreign Economic Policy*; and Acheson, "Waging Peace in the Americas."

2. See Morris Llewellyn Cooke, *Brazil on the March, A Study in International Cooperation: Reflecting on the Report of the American Technical Mission to Brazil* (New York: Whittlesey House, 1944), pp. 1–3. See also Baer, *Economic Development in Brazil*, pp. 32–33; and McCann, *Brazilian-American Alliance*, p. 387.

3. U.S. Department of State, *Report of the Joint Brazil-United States Technical Commission* (Publication 3487, Washington, DC: Government Printing Office, 1949), pp. 1–10.

4. Herschel Johnson, dispatch to secretary of state, October 8, 1948, *FRUS, 1948* 9:561. See also Silva and Carneiro, *Dutra*, pp. 137–38.

5. Baer, *Economic Development in Brazil*, pp. 34–36.

6. Memorandum from Johnson to secretary of state, November 18, 1948, *FRUS, 1948* 9:368; George C. Marshall to Johnson, November 24, 1948, DS 832.50 JTC/11-1848, RG 59, NA. Marshall proposed that select members of the delegation be invited individually to tour the United States.

7. Memorandum by Harold Midriff, December 22, 1949, DS 832.51/12-2249, RG 59, NA.

8. Paterson, "Foreign Aid under Wraps," p. 120.

9. Truman, *Memoirs*, 2:229–39. See also Ben Hardy, "Use of U.S. Technological Resources as a Weapon in the Struggle with International Communism," December 15, 1948, in George Elsey Papers, Harry S. Truman Presidential Library, Independence, Missouri; and Rabe, *Eisenhower and Latin America*, p. 17.

10. For the text of the act see 64 *Statutes at Large*, pt.1:198–207.

11. See Department of State memorandum, "Legislative Background of Point Four Program," June 20, 1950, *FRUS, 1950* 1:846–52; and *FRUS, 1950* 1:866.

12. Editorial note, Point Four Assistance, *FRUS, 1950* 1:846–52; Department of State memorandum, "Economic and Technical Cooperation Program in the Other American Republics," March 7, 1951, *FRUS, 1950* 1:1048. In contrast, by the end of 1952, Marshall Plan aid to European Recovery Plan countries amounted to $13 billion. Occupied Germany alone received $342 million. See Paterson, "Foreign Aid under Wraps," pp. 101, 122.

13. Jonathan B. Bingham to Johnson, December 29, 1951, DS 832.00-TA/12-2951, RG 59, NA. See also memorandum by Charles E. Dickerson (counselor of embassy for economic affairs), "Brazilian Request under Technical Assistance Programs (Point Four)," October 24, 1950, DS 832.00TA/10-2450, RG 59, NA.

14. Dickerson, dispatch to Department of State, October 3, 1950, DS 832.99-TA/10-2450, RG 59, NA; memorandum by Dickerson, "Brazilian Request under Technical Assistance Programs (Point Four)," October 24, 1950, DS 832.00-TA/10-2450, RG 59, NA.

15. See notes by James E. Webb attached to Dickerson, DS 832.00-TA/10-2450, RG 59, NA. See also memorandum by Webb to embassy, DS 832.00TA/12-2050, RG 59, NA.

16. Webb to U.S. embassy, Rio de Janeiro, December 20, 1950, DS 832.00TA/12-3050, RG 59, NA; Osmar Salles de Figueiredo, *Brasil, Passado e Presente* (Brazil, past and present) (São Paulo: Editôra Pedagógica e Universitária, 1979), p. 248.

17. Memorandum by Dickerson, October 3, 1951, DS 832.00TA/10-2450, RG 59, NA.

18. See Dickerson memorandum, "Activities of Joint Brazil-U.S. Economic Development Commission," DS 832.00/11-551, RG 59, NA.

19. John W. Dulles, *Vargas of Brazil: A Political Biography* (Austin: University of Texas Press, 1967), p. 311.

20. President Truman appointed Francis Adams Truslow, a New York lawyer and former director of the Rubber Development Corporation, as the U.S. commissioner with the personal rank of minister. Ari Frederico Torres, a prominent São Paulo businessman, served as the initial Brazilian member.

Truslow died en route to Rio, and Truman chose J. Burke Knapp, a foreign services reserve officer and former assistant director of the Economic Department of the IBRD, as the new U.S. commissioner. Merwin L. Bohan served as interim U.S. commissioner until Burke arrived in Rio in late 1951. See memorandum by Edward Miller, August 9, 1951, DS 832.00TA/8-951, RG 59, NA; Dean Acheson to Rio, July 10, 1951, DS 832.00TA/7-1851, RG 59, NA; memorandum by Miller, "Joint Brazil-U.S. Economic Development Commission," October 9, 1951, DS 832.00TA/10-951, RG 59, NA; and Acheson to Rio, July 11, 1951, DS 832.00TA/7-1151, RG 59, NA.

21. Memorandum from Bohan to Knapp, "Resume of Activities and Programs of the Joint Commission," October 11, 1951, DS 832.00TA/10-1151, RG 59, NA.

22. Ibid.

23. See McCann, "Brazilian Foreign Relations," p. 16; Rogério Pinto, *The Political Ecology of the Brazilian National Bank for Development (BNDE)* (Washington, DC: Organization of American States, 1969); Dulles, "Post-Dictatorship Brazil," pp. 22–23; and Daland, *Brazilian Planning*, pp. 35–37.

24. Memorandum by Bohan, "Resume of Activities and Programs of the Joint Commission," October 11, 1951, DS 832.00TA/10-1151, RG 59, NA.

25. See memorandum from Henry Holland to acting secretary of state, April 16, 1954, Holland File, Lot File 57D-295, RG 59, NA.

26. Bohan, "Commitments Covering Financing Joint Commission Program," May 20, 1953, DS 832.00TA/5-2053, RG 59, NA. See also D'Araujo, *O Segundo Governo Vargas* (The second government of Vargas), pp. 138–41.

27. Memorandum by Sterling Cottrell, "Joint Brazil-U.S. Economic Development Commission," May 6, 1953, DS 732.5/5-653, RG 59, NA. See also the foreword by Ronald M. Schneider in Selcher, ed., *Brazil in the International System*, p. xv; Henriques, *Ascensão e Queda de Getúlio Vargas* (The rise and fall of Getúlio Vargas), 3:285; and Caido Prado, *História econômica do Brasil* (Economic history of Brazil), 12th ed. (São Paulo: Editora Brasiliense, 1969), pp. 307–14.

28. Cottrell, "Termination of the Joint Brazil-U.S. Economic Development Commission," March 9, 1953, DS 732.5/3-953, RG 59, NA; Cottrell, "Termination of the Joint Brazil-U.S. Economic Development Commission," March 12, 1953, DS 732.5/3-1253, RG 59, NA; Cottrell, "Joint Brazil-U.S. Economic Development Commission," May 6, 1953, DS 732.5/5-653, RG 59, NA; John W. F. Dulles to U.S. embassy, May 8, 1953, DS 832.00TA/5-653, RG 59, NA.

29. Bohan, final report on the Joint Brazil-U.S. Economic Development Commission, May 22, 1953, DS 832.00TA/5-2053, RG 59, NA. See also Joint Brazil-United States Economic Development Commission, *The Development of Brazil*.

30. Daland, *Brazilian Planning*, pp. 1–12. See also Leff, *Economic Policy Making and Development in Brazil*, p. 143.

31. Leff, *Economic Policy Making and Development in Brazil*, pp. 144–47; Daland, *Brazilian Planning*, p. 214. Daland argues convincingly that the Brazilian economy expanded at a rapid rate during this period despite the failure of major planning efforts. The economic development of the Western nations, including the United States, were hardly examples of central, specialized planning, Daland argues, yet most Brazilians bought the "myth of the technical solution and centralized planning" for Brazilian development. See Daland,

Brazilian Planning, especially pp. 12, 214; and Albert Waterston, *Development Planning: Lessons of Experience* (Baltimore: Johns Hopkins University Press, 1979), p. 6.

32. See U.S. Department of State, *Technical Cooperation: The Dramatic Story of Helping Others to Help Themselves* (Washington, DC: Government Printing Office, 1959).

33. See Daland, *Brazilian Planning*, p. 27.

34. Ray M. Hill, Institute of Inter-American Affairs (IIAA), "Preliminary Views on Comprehensive Point Four Program for Brazil," October 10, 1950, DS 832.00-TA/10-1050, RG 59, NA.

35. Bohan, "Resume of Activities and Programs of the Joint Commission," October 11, 1951, DS 832.00-TA/10-1151, RG 59, NA.

36. Baily, *Development of Brazil*, pp. 34–35.

37. See Dickerson, dispatch to Department of State, Brazilian Railroad Problem, Annex 1, October 24, 1950, DS 832.00TA/10-2450, RG 59, NA; and Baily, *Development of Brazil*, pp. 34–35.

38. Ibid., pp. 83–85.

39. Ibid., p. 99.

40. Ralph Budd, "The Improvement of the Railways of Brazil," in Institute of Inter-American Affairs, *Brazilian Technical Studies Prepared for the Joint Brazil-United States Economic Development Commission* (Washington, DC: Government Printing Office, 1955), p. 14.

41. Hill, "Some Thoughts on the TA Program for Brazil," October 10, 1950, DS 832.00-TA/10-1050, RG 59, NA.

42. Memorandum by Bohan, October 24, 1950, Cottrell Files, Lot File 58D-42, RG 59, NA. Upon Department of State urging, the United States did grant some loans to Brazil for rail development. In 1951, for example, the Export-Import Bank announced a $4.5-million credit to Brazil to help finance the purchase of forty Pullman-Standard passenger train cars. In 1952 and 1953 the bank made additional funds available for the purchase of U.S. railway equipment, particularly diesel engines. See Marie Richardson to R. S. Atwood, "Credit Application for Expansion Programs in Brazil," August 30, 1951, DS 832.00TA/8-3051, RG 59, NA; and Export-Import Bank of Washington, *Fourteenth Semiannual Report to Congress*, pp. 15–18.

43. Thomas C. Mann to Ambassador Johnson, January 16, 1953, DS 932.512/1-1653, RG 59, NA.

44. For a summary of the IBRD argument see Bohan to Miller, "Brazil," Miller Files, Lot File 53D-26, RG 59, NA.

45. Bohan to Miller (assistant secretary of state), October 6, 1952, Cottrell Files, Lot File 58D-42, RG 59, NA; memorandum by Bohan, October 15, 1952, DS 732.5/10-152, RG 59, NA. See also memorandum, "General Comments on Mr. Knapp's Presentation of the International Bank's Position," February 3, 1953, Cottrell Files, Lot File 58D-42, RG 59, NA.

46. "Causes for Present Deadlock between Brazilians and IBRD," January 29, 1953, Miller Files, Lot File 53D-26, RG 59, NA.

47. Johnson, dispatch 1056 to Assistant Secretary of State Mann, January 26, 1953, DS 932.512/1-2653, RG 59, NA.

48. Memorandum from Robert O'Toole to Cottrell, "Railroad Financing," January 30, 1953, DS 932.512/1-3053, RG 59, NA; Miller to Johnson, May 31, 1952, *FRUS, 1952–1954* 4:580–81.

49. Cottrell to Atwood, March 9, 1953, Cottrell Files, Lot File 58D-42, RG 59, NA.

50. See memorandum by Mann of conversation, April 15, 1953, DS 832.10/4-1553, RG 59, NA.

51. Ibid.

52. See editorial note, *FRUS, 1952–1954* 4:584–86 for samples of these loans.

53. For railroad reforms see Bohan, Report on Joint Brazil-U.S. Economic Development Commission, May 22, 1953, DS 832.00TA/5-2053, RG 59, NA.

54. See Dickerson, dispatch to Department of State, Annual Economic Report, 1951, February 6, 1952, DS 832.00/2-652, RG 59, NA.

55. Memorandum by William P. Rambo, American vice consul, "Highway Equipment Show," DS 832.191-RI/3-2851, RG 59, NA.

56. Ibid.

57. See Dickerson, dispatch to Department of State, October 24, 1950, DS 832.00TA/10-2450, RG 59, NA; Dickerson, dispatch to Department of State, Annual Economic Report, 1951, February 6, 1952, DS 832.00/2-652, RG 59, NA; and Dickerson, dispatch to Department of State, Quarterly Economic Review, September 3, 1952, DS 832.00/9-352, RG 59, NA.

58. Dickerson, dispatch, October 24, 1950, DS 832.00TA/10-2450, RG 59, NA.

59. Dickerson, dispatch to Department of State, Annual Economic Report, 1951, February 6, 1952, DS 832.00/2-653, RG 59, NA.

60. Dickerson, dispatch, September 3, 1952, DS 832.00/9-352, RG 59, NA. Even some U.S. loans were forthcoming. The Export-Import Bank and the IBRD authorized major loans to finance the purchase of U.S. equipment required for maintenance and construction of highways. For additional information regarding these loans see IBRD, *Eighth Annual Report to the Board of Governors, 1952–1953* (Washington, DC: Government Printing Office, 1953), p. 8; and Export-Import Bank, *Sixteenth Semiannual Report to Congress*, pp. 8–12.

61. "Brazil—Program of Economic Reforms," September 13, 1955, Cottrell File, Lot File 58D-42, RG 59, NA; Bohan, "Resume of Activities and Programs of the Joint Commission," October 11, 1950, DS 832.00TA/10-1151, RG 59, NA; Paterson, "Foreign Aid under Wraps," p. 124. See also Tarun C. Rose, "The Point Four Programme: A Critical Study," *International Studies* 7:1 (1965): 66–97.

62. See memorandum by Cottrell of conversation, "Waiver for Lloyd Brasileiro," March 6, 1953, DS 932.53/3-653, RG 59, NA; Warren H. McKenney (maritime attaché), dispatch, "Brazil Removes Shipping Discrimination," January 9, 1953, DS 932.53/1-953, RG 59, NA; McKenney, report, "Registered Tonnage of Vessels by Flag Entering Major Brazilian Ports," February 24, 1954, DS 932.53/2-2454, RG 59, NA; and Bohan, "Resume of Activities and Programs of the Joint Commission," October 11, 1951, DS 832.00TA/10-1151, RG 59, NA.

63. Memorandum by Harold Linder to secretary of state, October 10, 1952, Miller Files, Lot File 53D-26, RG 59, NA. See also *FRUS, 1952–1954* 4:623.

64. Embassy dispatch, Annual Economic Report, 1952, DS 832.00/1-31-53, RG 59, NA.

65. Memorandum from J. Paul Barringer to Walter A. Radius, "Aviation Aid to Brazil," December 20, 1954, DS 932.52/12-2054, RG 59, NA. See also

memorandum by McKenney (transportation officer), "Jet Planes for Panair Do Brazil," January 10, 1953, DS 932.526/1-1053, RG 59, NA; and Cottrell to Robert P. Terrill (counselor of embassy), November 13, 1953, DS 932.52/11-1353, RG 59, NA.

66. Cottrell to Walter Walmsley, August 25, 1953, Cottrell Files, Lot File 58D-42, RG 59, NA; memorandum from Ivan White to Miller, January 31, 1951, Miller Files, Lot File 53D-26, RG 59, NA.

67. Embassy dispatch, Annual Economic Report, 1952, DS 832.00/1-31-53, RG 59, NA.

68. Judith Tendler, *Electric Power in Brazil: Entrepreneurship in the Public Sector* (Cambridge: Harvard University Press, 1968), p. 9.

69. Raouf Kahil, *Inflation and Economic Development in Brazil, 1946–1963* (Oxford: Clarendon Press, 1973), p. 164; White to Miller, "Brazil-Economic Development," January 31, 1951, Miller Files, Lot File 53D-26, RG 59, NA.

70. Lucan Lopes, "Electric Energy in Brazil," in Institute of Inter-American Affairs, *Brazilian Technical Studies*, p. 273.

71. Tendler, *Electric Power in Brazil*, p. 14.

72. Ibid. Rather ironically the São Paulo-Rio de Janeiro region's great surge of development occurred not when power was in ample supply but during a period when facilities were inadequate. See Tendler, *Electric Power in Brazil*, p. 17.

73. Bohan, "Resume of Activities and Programs of the Joint Commission," October 11, 1951, DS 832.00TA/10-1151, RG 59, NA.

74. Lopes, "Electric Energy in Brazil," in Institute of Inter-American Affairs, *Brazilian Technical Studies*, pp. 275–76.

75. Ibid.

76. Department of State memorandum, "Visit of President Dutra to the United States," May 17, 1949, DS 832.00/Dutra, Gaspar/5-1749, RG 59, NA.

77. Lopes, "Electric Energy in Brazil," in Institute of Inter-American Affairs, *Brazilian Technical Studies*, pp. 280–85.

78. Dickerson, dispatch to Department of State, October 24, 1950, DS 832.00TA/10-2450, RG 59, NA. See also Kahil, *Inflation and Economic Development in Brazil*, pp. 303, 174; Bohan, "Resume of Activities and Programs of the Joint Commission," October 11, 1951, DS 832.00TA/10-1151, RG 59, NA; and Tendler, *Electric Power in Brazil*, p. 55.

79. Dickerson, dispatch to Department of State, October 24, 1950, DS 832.00TA/10-2450, RG 59, NA.

80. Lopes, "Electric Energy in Brazil," in Institute of Inter-American Affairs, *Brazilian Technical Studies*, p. 290; Tendler, *Electric Power in Brazil*, p. 280.

81. Terrill (counselor of embassy) to Cottrell (officer in charge of Brazilian affairs), July 2, 1954, Cottrell Files, Lot File 58D-42, RG 59, NA.

82. See "There Is Money to be Made in Brazil," *Business Week* (December 29, 1951): 97–98. See also D'Araujo, *O Segundo Governo Vargas* (The second government of Vargas), pp. 138–41.

83. Telegram from Walmsley to Department of State, July 16, 1953, DS 732.5MSP/7-1653, *FRUS, 1952–1954* 4:626. See also memorandum from Marion N. Hardesty (acting regional director of the Office of Latin American Operations) to Harold Stassen (director of FOA), November 15, 1954, *FRUS, 1952–1954* 4:258–59; memorandum of conversation, "Question of Changing the Nature of the Technical Assistance Program in Latin America," April 9,

1954, *FRUS, 1952–1954* 4:221–22; and memorandum from Norman M. Pearson (Bureau of Inter-American Affairs) to John Cabot (assistant secretary of state for inter-American affairs), "A More Positive Policy of Assistance," March 13, 1953, *FRUS, 1952–1954* 4:187–89.

84. See Bohan to Miller, November 28, 1952, Miller Files, Lot File 53D-26, RG 59, NA; and Johnson, summary report, January 8, 1953, DS 732.5-MSP/1-853, RG 59, NA.

85. See Rudolf E. Cahn (American vice consul), dispatch, "Discrimination against Imports from U.S.," September 23, 1950, DS 832.131/11-2150, RG 59, NA; DuWayne Clark to Ambassador Johnson, May 23, 1950, DS 832.2422/5-1550, RG 59, NA; John Logan Hagan (economic officer), "Financing by French Banks Arranged for National Alkaki Co.," September 3, 1952, DS 832.2422/3-1053, RG 59, NA; Kathryn R. Dillabough, "Foreign Trade of Brazil, 1953," June 10, 1953, DS 832.00/6-1053, RG 59, NA; and embassy dispatch, Annual Economic Report 1951, DS 832.00/2-652, RG 59, NA.

86. See Webb (acting secretary of state) to embassy, DS 832.131/8-150, RG 59, NA; and Clark to Johnson, May 22, 1950, DS 832.2422/5-1550, RG 59, NA. See also Gardner, *Sterling-Dollar Diplomacy.*

87. Annual Economic Report for 1951, DS 832.00/2-652, RG 59, NA; Quarterly Economic Review, September 3, 1952, DS 832.00/1-552, RG 59, NA.

88. Terrill (counselor of embassy), dispatch, "Joint Weeks," September 4, 1953, DS 732.00(W)/9-1153, RG 59, NA; "Germany Invests Overseas," *Economist* 24 (September 26, 1953): 119–32.

89. Miller to Johnson, December 6, 1951, Miller Files, Lot File 53D-26, RG 59, NA.

90. See NIE, December 4, 1953, *FRUS, 1952–1954* 4:642–43; Hilton, "The United States, Brazil, and the Cold War," p. 616; memorandum by Randolph Kidder, April 2, 1952, DS 832.00/4-252, RG 59, NA; and Edward N. McCully (second secretary of embassy), "Indication of Brazilian Attitude toward Foreign Investments," April 8, 1952, DS 832.10/4-452, RG 59, NA. See also John W. Bailer, Jr. (American consul general, Zurich), "Brazilian Attempt to Obtain Swiss Bank Loan," DS 832.10/11-1052, RG 59, NA; and McCully, "UK-Brazilian Debt Agreement," September 3, 1952, DS 832.10/10-2953, RG 59, NA.

91. Johnson to Miller, November 30, 1951, Miller Files, Lot File 53D-26, RG 59, NA.

92. Terrill, dispatch, "Economic Report," November 13, 1952, DS 732.00(W)/11-2053, RG 59, NA. See also Arthur M. Hartman (economic assistant to Terrill), "Brazilian Trade with the Soviet Bloc, January-March 1954," August 20, 1954, DS 832.60/8-2054, RG 59, NA.

93. See annual automotive report, Brazil, December 11, 1950, DS 932.51/3-2751, RG 59, NA; and August 20, 1953, DS 932.51/8-2053, RG 59, NA.

94. McCann, "Brazilian Foreign Relations," p. 15.

95. Annual automotive report, Brazil, August 20, 1953, DS 932.51/8-2053, RG 59, NA.

96. Annual economic report, Brazil, 1951, August 20, 1952, DS 932.51/8-2052, RG 59, NA.

97. Orlando Soares, *Desenvolvimento econômico-social do Brasil e Eua* (The socioeconomic development of Brazil and the United States) (São Paulo: Coleĉao Nôvos Tempes, 1976), p. 145.

98. See John G. Gossett (American vice consul, São Paulo), report of dedication of new Ford plant, April 22, 1953, DS 832.3331/4-2253, RG 59, NA; industries report, January 28, 1954, DS 832.19/1-2854, RG 59, NA; and "Brazilian Automotive Industry," September 18, 1953, DS 832.3331/9-1853, RG 59, NA.

99. Memorandum by J. C. Corliss, "Financial Assistance to Latin America" [n.d.], Miller Files, Lot File 53D-26, RG 59, NA.

100. "Sears, Roebuck in Rio," *Fortune* 41 (February 1950): 78; "Letter from Brazil," *Fortune* 35 (February 1947): 207–8.

101. Ibid.

102. Description of Latin American technical assistance programs, FY 1954 budget narrative for Brazil, April 1, 1953, DS 832.00-TA/4-153, RG 59, NA. See also summary report on mutual security program, Brazil, January 8, 1953, DS 732.5-MSP/1-853, RG 59, NA.

103. Henriques, *Ascensão e Queda de Getúlio Vargas* (Rise and fall of Getúlio Vargas), 3:205; Brandi, *Vargas*, pp. 233–85.

Chapter Eight

Americanizing Brazilian Agriculture

Just as Washington sought to mold the industrial development of Brazil by applying American techniques, ideas, and expertise, they also attempted to change Brazilian farming practices, methods, and ways of thinking. Sincere and well-meaning agricultural experts in both the Truman and Eisenhower administrations tried to create a family-oriented, productive, successful agricultural sector in Brazil that reflected basic rural American values and agricultural standards. With American farming methods as the goal and the technical assistance program as the means, they set about restructuring Brazilian agriculture to reflect American thinking. Stressing increased productivity, mechanization, efficiency, training, and scientific management, the American experts instituted an intensive program to restructure Brazilian agriculture from its traditional nomadic, slash-and-burn exploitative practices into a modern, commercially viable, market-oriented system.[1]

What was needed, according to the Americans, was the development of a new Brazilian agricultural mentality—one that stressed price consciousness, large-scale entrepreneurship, and modern methods of cultivation. Viewing agricultural efficiency as the key to general economic progress, the experts saw at the heart of the Brazilian agricultural problem a need to increase productivity. The Americans estimated that it took eight to ten times as many man hours in Brazil to raise an acre of corn, beans, or other major crop as it did on commercial farms in the United States. They pointed out that the United States produced 2.8 metric tons of rice per hectare while Brazil produced 1.7 tons, and that the United States produced 2.3 tons per hectare of corn while the Brazilians produced 1.3 tons. According to American studies, Brazil was using 65 to 70 percent of its labor force to produce the agricultural products it needed. The United States used only 18 percent of its total labor force for food production. Brazilian methods were inefficient and unproductive.[2]

Increased productivity and efficiency, according to the specialists, would result not only in increased production but also in a general increase in the buying power of the agricultural population. It would release labor for employment in nonagricultural industries, thus further fueling Brazilian development and reducing the Communist threat.[3]

Increased productivity became the key to the agricultural program in both the Truman and the Eisenhower administrations. Working within the framework of the Point Four technical cooperation effort, agencies such as the U.S. Department of Agriculture, the Institute of Inter-American Affairs, and the Department of State, and private entities such as the Rockefeller Corporation and the Carnegie Foundation all offered a stream of advice on improving Brazilian agriculture.[4] All urged increased mechanization, especially the use of tractors, combines, and harvesting equipment, as part of the solution. In a nation with 2 million farmers there were only 15,000 farm tractors in 1951, U.S. Agricultural Attaché C. A. Boonstra pointed out. Most of Brazilian agriculture was still unmechanized.[5] As late as 1950, 73 percent of all Brazilian farms employed only human labor using hoe and other hand tools. Steel plows were unknown on three fourths of the farms.[6]

Although the governments of Eurico Gaspar Dutra and Getúlio Vargas officially recognized that greater and more efficient agricultural production was essential for feeding Brazil's growing population, paying for necessary imports, supporting continued industrial growth, and producing a sound, stable economic basis for development, they remained oriented toward rapid industrial expansion and large urban public works projects. Agricultural concerns took a backseat to industrial expansion. According to data from *Conjuntura Economica* of the Getúlio Vargas Foundation, industry in Brazil from 1931 to 1951 showed a real expansion of 140 percent, whereas agriculture showed only a 25 percent increase. Budget support through the Ministry of Agriculture was only 2 to 4 percent of the total national budget during the early 1950s. Only 4 percent of the Brazilian Development Bank loans went to the agricultural sector.[7] Despite the Vargas government's emphasis on mechanization in the early 1950s, actual imports of farm machinery fell in 1952 and 1953 because of a critical shortage of dollar exchange and lack of available credit.

Ignoring the problems associated with the dollar shortage, U.S. farm specialists continued to argue that the farm equipment suited for Brazilian needs was best obtained in the United States, not Europe. These products, despite pressures from European manufacturers for a share of the market, were preferable, the Americans reasoned, because there was no spare parts problem and the equipment was better adapted to large-scale commercial farming.[8] To help Brazil obtain farm equipment the Eisenhower administration, through the Export-Import Bank, granted an $18-million credit to Brazil in late 1953. U.S. manufacturers also provided private credits to the individual Brazilian states for purchases of their equipment.[9]

American advisers praised mechanized farming methods at every opportunity. For example, they looked upon the introduction of modern sugar mill equipment and harvesting techniques in the sugar zone of Campos as a major revolution. The purchase of U.S.-manufactured cane harvesters, cultivators, and power-operated loading equipment would substantially increase production and the standard of living of the workers, according to Economic Assistant Herbert K. Ferguson, who also predicted that the lead the Campos producers had taken in field mechanization would quickly spread, ending the antiquated planting and harvesting methods in Brazil.[10] In their enthusiasm for mechanization, the advisers gave little thought to what would happen to displaced workers except for the vague notion that they would somehow find work in the growing urban industrial sector.

American experts realized that mechanization was only a part of the overall solution to Brazil's agricultural problems. They also promoted agricultural training and scientific farming methods as well as the development of an agricultural extension service. On June 26, 1953, for example, the Eisenhower administration and Brazil signed an agreement establishing a continuing program whereby U.S. technicians were assigned to work in agriculture with various Brazilian agencies. This officially extended the work in Brazilian agriculture that the Department of State, the Department of Agriculture, and the Foreign Operations Administration (FOA) had begun during the Truman era.[11]

Training personnel in modern agricultural methods and the use of mechanical equipment was a high priority, according to the American technicians, if Brazil was to move ahead. Careful not to offend the Brazilians by too direct control of the program, the United States attempted to work through specific Brazilian agencies and to have their specialists work under the supervision of Brazilian officials. This was not always easy, as the Americans found a maze of government organizations involved in agriculture. The Ministry of Agriculture was theoretically the major organization; it supervised various experimental stations and agricultural schools throughout the country. But there were also state agricultural agencies (many with their own experimental stations and extension services), seed farms, demonstration farms, animal breeding stations, twelve colleges or universities of agriculture or agronomy, six colleges of veterinary science, as well as semiofficial and semi-independent institutes for coffee, cacao, and sugar.

Although this was an extensive and complex hierarchy, the Americans soon found that it reached only a very small portion of Brazil's farmers. There was a large gap between theory and practice. For example, in surveying the graduates of the agricultural schools, the U.S. experts discovered that they seldom returned to occupations in practical agriculture, but more often found employment in the bureaucracy. This puzzled and perplexed the Americans. U.S. officials assumed that the Brazilians accepted the classical concept of a rationalistic bureaucracy with its hierarchy of authority, its achievement orientation, and its emphasis on trained, dedicated professionalism. The function of the Brazilian bureaucracy was quite different: it provided an upwardly mobile channel for the urban, educated middle class. It provided a permanent income as well as opportunities for private entrepreneurship based on the powers attached to certain government offices.[12] Most trainees were from urban areas, not farming communities. Moreover, the curriculum of the agricultural schools stressed "theoretical subjects rather than practical applications." There were few courses actually geared to practicing farmers.[13]

Attempting to correct this situation, U.S. officials encouraged agricultural schools such as Purdue University and Michigan State University to advise Brazilian colleges on expanding their courses and teaching advanced, practical agricultural methods. Brazilians were also brought to the United States for training. American officials believed that this program provided dual benefits. Not only would these trainees take home current farming technical knowledge, but they would also return with a respect for democracy and a better understanding of the American way of life.[14]

In an attempt to improve the work of the extension services and the experimental stations, both the Truman and Eisenhower administrations sent a variety of personnel to Brazil. Utilizing American technology and the American agricultural extension service as a model, the objective was to assist Brazil in developing programs to meet the needs of its farm families. The scope of the program was enormous. It included instruction in the latest methods of soil conservation, erosion control, crop rotation, contour farming, irrigation, seed improvement, livestock breeding and the use of insecticides, fungicides, and fertilizers as well as the proper use and maintenance of mechanized equipment. It also provided instructions for dairy, hog, and poultry production, the use of medicines and mineral supplements for livestock, pasture improvement, and farm management. All was done to recreate, in effect, the American farm in Brazil and to make the Brazilian farmer into a modern market-oriented businessman.[15]

Tackling the age-old problem of land abuse and the ingrained Brazilian attitude that there was an abundance of good land in the west, the Americans stressed soil conservation techniques, irrigation, and the application of fertilizers. They tried to prevent the increasing abandonment of older lands and the shifting of coffee production to newly cleared land. They soon discovered, however, that the Brazilians preferred their old methods. New land was cheaper, more productive, and readily available, and imported fertilizer was expensive, so the Brazilian farmer was reluctant to implement the American suggestions.[16]

The Americans encountered similar problems with the Brazilian cattle industry. Their pasture improvement techniques, pest and disease control methods, mineral supplements, and selective breeding programs were not readily adopted by the Brazilians. Even when they were tried, unforeseen problems often arose. Attempting to upgrade his herd, a Brazilian cattle breeder in Minas Gerais, for example, proposed to purchase forty head of red sindhi cattle from Pakistan. U.S. agricultural experts, upon hearing of the transaction, were deeply concerned. These cattle would probably bring into Brazil Rhinderpest and other Asiatic exotic diseases. Although Rhinderpest was unknown in the Western Hemisphere, in Asia it was one of the most destructive of all livestock diseases. In the opinion of the U.S. Department of Agriculture the danger far outweighed any advantage to the breeding program of Brazil.[17] Cattle productivity remained low. Brazilian cattle consistently had a low carcass yield per animal compared with other cattle producing areas. In the period 1954–1959 Brazilian cattle averaged 164 kilograms, Argentine cattle 207 kilograms, and U.S. cattle 249 kilograms.[18]

Undeterred by these setbacks, however, the U.S. specialists pushed ahead on recommendations for improving experimental model farms such as the one established by the federal Ministry of Agriculture at Fazerola Ipanema in the state of São Paulo. Providing Fazerola Ipanema with a number of experts, the United States hoped to train personnel from all over Brazil in modern agricultural methods and in the operation of modern farm equipment. These newly educated farmers would then return to their local communities and speed the adoption of modern agricultural techniques. Again, the results disappointed the Americans, as few trainees returned to their local communities. They preferred to work for the government on large-scale, relatively modern farms in São Paulo.[19]

Although proclaimed as a major success by both governments, these agricultural efforts received only a mixed review from some of the American experts. J. Burke Knapp, the director of technical cooperation for Brazil, for example, believed there was a general overoptimism regarding the accomplishments of these agricultural programs. The impact upon Brazil was negligible. According to Knapp, the United States had only "scratched the surface" of the problem. The most that could be hoped for was that the Brazilians would follow the examples set and apply them to other areas.[20] Knapp was closer to the truth than most American planners cared to admit. A high proportion of Brazil's agricultural population was made up of landless laborers with poor health, a high illiteracy rate, and an inadequate diet. There was little capital available for agricultural improvements and little professional management of Brazil's agricultural resources. Moreover, much of the land was held by large ranching and mining interests, both foreign and domestic, so there was little chance of major land reforms.[21]

Although they strongly advocated the creation of medium-sized and small diversified family farming units that would produce food supplies for the growing urban population, policymakers in both Truman and Eisenhower administrations realized that the large landowning sector, which produced for the export market and had a great deal of political influence, was not likely to support a drastic land reform program. Rural labor and tenant farms had little clout, politically or economically. C. A. Boonstra, the U.S. agricultural attaché, concluded upon surveying the situation that, in general, whatever government credits were available went mostly to large-scale producers and exporters. Small growers, particularly those producing food for local markets, according to Boonstra's report, had great difficulty in obtaining any government funds for improvements. Boonstra pointed out that in 1953 the crops that received most of the bank credits were sugarcane, coffee, rice, and cotton. All were crops produced for export and all were produced on large land holdings. Large cattle ranches also obtained substantial bank credits. Contrary to the often-stated policy of the Vargas government of support for the small farmer, most Brazilian farmers received little government financial support, and there was little movement for major land reform.[22]

Neither the Truman administration nor the Eisenhower administration, despite the best of intentions, was about to make land reform a major issue or to antagonize the important landowning sector of the Brazilian population. Both desired stability and a strong anti-Communist stance by Brazil, not social revolution.[23] Nevertheless, the Americans pushed ahead. They applied their expertise in attempts to discover ways to eliminate the sauva ant (an insect that destroyed young trees and crops) and citrus diseases such as tristeza. They tried to improve rubber and coffee production. U.S. planners saw these efforts to implement increasingly efficient agricultural methods as not only helping the Brazilians but also lowering the cost and improving the quality of agricultural products that the United States imported from Brazil and, indirectly, aiding in the struggle against communism by creating a more prosperous, healthy Brazil.[24]

The American effort also affected the Brazilian diet. U.S. experts fostered dairy and vegetable truck farming techniques and pushed wheat production in an effort to feed the growing urban population. This brought about notable changes in the food consumption habits of Brazilians, especially those living in cities. Whereas in the interior rice and manioc flour constituted the most important source of carbohydrates in the diet, in the urban centers wheat bread increasingly dominated. This was, in part, a reflection of the fact that southern European immigrants made up a large proportion of the population in the urban centers, and wheat bread had always been a staple food for them. However, increased emphasis by the Americans on the Brazilian domestic wheat and wheat flour processing and distribution system pushed wheat consumption even higher. Despite annual wheat production increases, by 1951 local wheat production was able to meet only 20 percent of the consumption demand. Wheat had to be imported, and this placed additional pressures on the Brazilian economy. When drought reduced the wheat crop in Argentina, Brazil's traditional supplier, Brazil was forced to use its precious foreign exchange to purchase wheat from the United States and Canada. Moreover, increasing the amount of land devoted to wheat in the areas of Rio Grande do Sul, the western Santos, Paraná, and Goiás cut into cash-producing export crops such as coffee and cotton and into cattle pasture lands. As administration officials under both Truman and Eisenhower discovered, there were no simple solutions to Brazil's agricultural problems.[25]

The Americans did encourage the Brazilian government's attempts to attract Europeans and Japanese to colonize the interior as positive steps toward solving the agricultural problem. According to U.S. estimates, Brazil cultivated only 4 percent of its arable land. The influx of Italians, Yugoslavs, Poles, and Japanese would not only provide skilled farmers to develop the interior, but they would also bring along farming know-how and European methods of production.[26] With this in mind, U.S. officials encouraged the development of the Amazon region under the Vargas government's Plan of Economic Valuation of the Amazon (SPVEA), established in 1953. Still, little government money was spared for this project. Neither the Brazilians nor their American advisers foresaw the problems Amazon development would later create.[27]

Yet another problem singled out by U.S. experts was the heavy reliance by the Brazilian government on export crops such as coffee, cotton, and cacao. These crops furnished Brazil with most of its foreign exchange. Complicating this issue, from the American point of view, was the elaborate system of exchange and trade controls imposed on export products by the Brazilian bureaucracy. According to the Americans, these controls placed on agriculture the burden of providing exchange at a relatively low rate for imports of fuel, machinery, wheat, and consumer goods. These policies benefited the industrial and urban groups far more than the farm producers, as farmers were forced to pay high prices for manufactured goods and imports such as tractors while their major products sold at low government-fixed rates.[28] This problem was examined repeatedly in Brazilian government surveys and reports. In a profusion of statements and planning projects the Dutra, Vargas, and João Café Filho governments announced their concern for the agricultural sector. The rhetoric had little effect on actual policy, however, as the main focus of these governments remained on massive industrial development projects, not on agricultural problems.[29]

Examining the major cash crops of Brazil, U.S. technicians found that coffee, cotton, and cacao furnished 90 percent of Brazil's foreign exchange. Because of its financial difficulties these export crops were closely regulated by the government. The U.S. experts were astonished to learn that the Ministry of Finance, not the Ministry of Agriculture, determined agricultural policy. The Ministry of Agriculture served only in an advisory capacity. In addition, industrial groups and state governments influenced decisions. The Americans had little respect for this bureaucratic maze and even less respect for what they perceived as the poor management skills of the Brazilians. What was needed were American management and administrative skills, U.S. experts claimed, otherwise Brazil's agriculture would continue to flounder and its farmers would continue to suffer.[30] U.S. officials tried to solve this problem by establishing business and administrative courses in the universities that would make the Brazilians into good administrators and managers.

Attacking still another part of the agricultural problem, the Americans pointed to inadequate transportation and storage facilities as contributing directly to low productivity and higher prices. Over 11 percent of the cereal crop, for example, was lost because of poor or nonexistent storage facilities. Looking at the Brazilian cattle industry, U.S. officials were again perplexed. In a country with one of the largest cattle populations in the world, the major cities suffered from a lack of fresh, quality meat. Brazil sadly lacked meat packing and cold storage plants as well as silos and warehouses with cleaning, drying, and disinfection facilities. Transportation facilities to get the cattle to market also needed to be vastly improved, the Americans asserted. If only the Brazilians would follow the example set by U.S. agribusiness in producing, transporting, and marketing its products.[31]

The U.S. model for marketing agricultural products became a key point. Americans urged their Brazilian counterparts to establish networks of large, modern supermarkets throughout Brazil. Such a program of large volume, low markup sales of prepackaged foodstuffs would compel Brazilian middlemen in food distributing to accept a lower margin of profit and would result in lowering the retail price of foodstuffs.[32] It would also foster private industry. The American food industry was again held up as an example. If the Brazilians would adopt American methods they could solve their processing and distribution problems and raise their standard of living.[33]

Americans also set to work raising the standard of living of the rural population of Brazil, convinced that this would not only aid farm production but would also be effective in fighting the encroachment of communism. Concentrating on health and sanitation projects, American engineers and technical specialists helped plan and develop water supply systems and sewage disposal programs. The Institute of Inter-American Affairs (IIAA), for example, provided public health and nursing consultants for training Brazilians in modern vaccination techniques, nutrition, communicable disease control, and general hygiene. U.S. specialists helped establish rural medical services, and

Brazilians came to the United States to study basic health and sanitation facilities and to train in nursing and medical science. The United States also instituted a DDT-spraying program for malaria-carrying mosquitoes. In addition, the IIAA set up training programs in home care, child welfare and development, and home economics. The Brazilian housewife in the Amazon valley and in Marachad and Ceará received the latest American information on child rearing, food preparation, sewing, and general hygiene.[34]

Rural illiteracy was yet another problem attacked by the Americans. In 1952, Brazil and the United States signed an agreement for rural education (CABER). This agreement provided for the training of teachers and the preparation of instructional materials for rural primary schools. Education, in general, was a low priority for Brazilian governments in the early 1950s. With a population growth of 3.1 percent per year, the yearly increase in the rate of students finishing elementary schools stood at only 2.6 percent.[35]

Both the Truman and Eisenhower administrations considered their effort in these areas to be a major success story. Not only did the Brazilians benefit directly through low-cost, highly visible, efficient, and effective health and education programs, but indirectly the programs also solidified U.S.-Brazilian ties and fortified the hemisphere against Communist exploitation.[36]

In summary the American effort, although geared to helping the Brazilians alleviate their critical agricultural problems, was intended to aid in developing new markets for U.S. agricultural commodities in Brazil, such as dairy products and wheat, and to foster commodities that complemented U.S. production, such as coffee, cacao, rubber, and jute. What the Americans did not want to see happen was the development of commodities that competed with U.S. agricultural products or the displacement of American markets.[37] Brazilian agricultural development would be beneficial to both nations as long as it followed the path set out for it by American advisers.

The Brazilians readily accepted U.S. technical assistance in the agricultural area, just as they had in the industrial sector, in the hopes that it would lead to substantial loans and credit. Their major concern was building the infrastructure to support an expanding agricultural base. For that they required U.S. government funds. Privately, although the Brazilians believed the American advice was beneficial and would help their farm production in the long run, they generally believed that what was needed was not more advice. Brazil needed major loans and credits to purchase the farm machinery for modernizing the agricultural sector, to construct the vitally needed warehouses and storage units, to improve the socioeconomic conditions of rural Brazil, and to improve rural education.[38]

Although both the Truman and the Eisenhower administrations made a limited number of loans available to Brazil for the purchase of U.S.-manufactured farm machinery, Washington never considered massive amounts of credits and aid for Brazilian agriculture. Even the Brazilians concentrated their own efforts on urban/industrial development rather than on agriculture, which was neglected. The American consultants and agricultural experts sent to Brazil, along with their Brazilian counterparts, made do with limited resources in their efforts to improve the rural standard of living. Although agricultural production did increase during the early 1950s as major Brazilian landowners adopted modern farming practices, in the absence of land reform most of the peasant poor continued to practice slash-and-burn agriculture.

Notes

1. Kahil, *Inflation and Economic Development in Brazil*, p. 3; Werner Baer, "Socio-Economic Imbalances in Brazil," in Baklanoff, ed., *The Shaping of Modern Brazil*, pp. 137–54.

2. See John Logan Hagan (embassy economic officer), "Industries Report," February 20, 1953, DS 832.19/2-2053, RG 59, NA; and C. A. Boonstra (agricultural attaché), dispatch, "Recent Developments in Brazilian Agricultural Policy," July 10, 1953, DS 832.20/7-1653, RG 59, NA.

3. Ibid.

4. In addition, the Food and Agricultural Organization of the UN and the Organization of American States had programs and technical specialists in Brazil. See Boonstra, "Brazilian Agricultural Policy in 1953–1954," June 1, 1954, DS 832.20/6-154, RG 59, NA.

5. Ibid.

6. See G. Edward Schuh, *The Agricultural Development of Brazil* (New York: Praeger, 1970), pp. 153–54.

7. See Boonstra, "Recent Developments of Brazilian Agricultural Policy," DS 832.20/7-1653, RG 59, NA; and Schuh, *Agricultural Development of Brazil*, p. 286. Nevertheless, according to Schuh, the agricultural sector performed reasonably well during this period. See Schuh, *Agricultural Development of Brazil*, p. 70.

8. See telegram from Herschel Johnson to Edward Miller, June 24, 1952, DS 832.00-TA/6-2452, RG 59, NA.

9. Boonstra, "Brazilian Agricultural Policy," DS 832.20/6-154, RG 59, NA; "Brazilian Importation of Farm Machinery," September 3, 1953, DS 832.3312/9-35, RG 59, NA.

10. Allan Ferguson, "Mechanization of Field Operations in Brazil's Sugar Industry," August 22, 1951, DS 832.2351/8-2251, RG 59, NA.

11. For the text of the agreement see *U.S. Treaties and Other International Agreements, 1953* (Washington, DC: Government Printing Office, 1957), 9:1357.

12. See Daland, *Brazilian Planning*, p. 210.

13. John A. Hopkins (agriculture attaché), "Notes on Agricultural Schools, Experiment Stations, and Extension Services in Eastern Brazil," February 8, 1951, DS 832.20/2-851, RG 59, NA.

14. See Robert G. Groves (acting director of technical cooperation), "Descriptions of Latin American Technical Assistance Program—Budget Narrative for Brazil," April 1, 1953, DS 832.00-TA/4-153, RG 59, NA.

15. Ibid.

16. Eric N. Baklanoff, "Foreign Private Investment and Industrialization in Brazil," in Baklanoff, ed., *The Shaping of Modern Brazil*, pp. 101–36. This was not the case everywhere in Brazil. The state of São Paulo had a relatively modern agricultural sector, including an efficient, intensive Japanese tomato-growing section. See Schuh, *Agricultural Development of Brazil*, p. 336.

17. Telegram from Dean Acheson to U.S. embassy, Rio de Janeiro, October 10, 1952, DS 832.24221/10-1052, RG 59, NA.

18. Schuh, *Agricultural Development of Brazil*, pp. 180–81. The Americans remained frustrated.

19. Charles Dickerson, dispatch to Department of State, October 24, 1950, DS 832.00TA/10-2450, RG 59, NA; Knapp, "Analysis of Narrative Justification for FY 1953 Budget," June 4, 1952, DS 832.00TA/6-452, RG 59, NA.

20. J. Burke Knapp, "Analysis of Narrative Justification for FY 1953 Budget," June 4, 1952, DS 832.00TA/6-452, RG 59, NA.

21. See Kahil, *Inflation and Economic Development in Brazil*, pp. 35–84; and Bourne, *Getúlio Vargas of Brazil*, p. 164.

22. See Boonstra, "Brazilian Agricultural Policy in 1953–1954," June 1, 1954, DS 832.20/6-154, RG 59, NA; and Boonstra, "Recent Developments in Brazilian Agricultural Policy," DS 832.20/7-1053, RG 59, NA.

23. Ibid.

24. Ibid.

25. For a discussion of the wheat problem see Institute of Inter-American Affairs, *Brazilian Technical Studies*, pp. 397–406. See also Gordon W. Smith, "Agricultural Marketing and Economic Development: A Brazilian Case Study" (Ph.D. diss., Harvard University, 1965); and Henriques, *Ascensão e Queda de Getúlio Vargas* (The rise and fall of Getúlio Vargas), 3:491–95.

26. Hopkins (agriculture attaché), "Notes," February 8, 1951, DS 832.20/2-851, RG 59, NA.

27. See Schuh, *Agricultural Development of Brazil*, pp. 271–72. On the destruction of the Amazon basin see Sylvia Ann Hewlett, *Cruel Dilemmas of Development: Twentieth-Century Brazil* (New York: Basic Books, 1980).

28. Boonstra, "Recent Developments in Brazilian Agricultural Policy," July 10, 1953, DS 832.20/7-1053, RG 59, NA.

29. See Kahil, *Inflation and Economic Development in Brazil*, pp. 85–126; Schuh, *Agricultural Development of Brazil*, p. 286; Baer, "Socio-Economic Imbalances in Brazil"; and J. Petrelli Gastaldi, *A Economia Brasileira e Os Problemas do Desenvolvimento* (The Brazilian economy and the problems of development) (São Paulo: Edicão Saraiva, 1968), p. 135.

30. Boonstra, "Recent Developments in Brazilian Agricultural Policy," July 10, 1953, DS 832.20/7-1053, RG 59, NA.

31. Quarterly economic review, September 3, 1952, DS 832.00/1-552, RG 59, NA.

32. "Supermarket Sponsored by SAPS (Popular Food Distribution and Workers Restaurant Service)," August 18, 1954, DS 832.055/8-1854, RG 59, NA.

33. See "Brazil Begins Campaign to Lure Investments by U.S. Food Industry," *Wall Street Journal*, July 7, 1953.

34. See IIAA monthly operations reports on Brazil, DS 832.00TA/various dates, RG 59, NA; IIAA, "Health and Sanitation Program in Brazil," January 31, 1950, DS 832.00-TA/1-2750, RG 59, NA; joint State/FOA message, "Agreement for Contributions to the Health Services in Brazil for 1954," March 19, 1954, DS 732.5MSP/3-1954, RG 59, NA; and Portuguese translation of *Your Child from One to Six*, March 10, 1950, DS 511.3221/3-1050, RG 59, NA.

35. See Baer, "Socio-Economic Imbalances in Brazil," p. 145.

36. See IIAA monthly operations reports on Brazil, DS 832.00TA/various dates, RG 59, NA; IIAA, "Health and Sanitation Programs in Brazil," January 27, 1950, DS 832.00TA/1-2750, RG 59, NA; and joint State/FOA message, "Agreement for Contribution to the Health Services in Brazil for 1954," March 19, 1954, DS 732.5MSP/3-1954, RG 59, NA.

37. See telegram from John W. F. Dulles to U.S. embassy, Rio de Janeiro, "Sale of U.S. Agricultural Commodities under PL480," December 28, 1954, DS 732.5-MSP/12-2854, RG 59, NA.

38. Boonstra, "Recent Developments in Brazilian Agricultural Policy," July 10, 1953, DS 832.20/7-1053, RG 59, NA.

Chapter Nine

Cultural Relations and Projecting a Favorable American Image

American decision makers in the postwar era sincerely believed in the exceptional superiority of the United States not only politically and economically but also culturally. They accepted the notion that the center of world culture had shifted, with World War II, to the United States. Firm believers in peace, prosperity, and progress as the inevitable blessings of Western civilization, they saw the United States as the ordained instrument of providence, civilization, and progress. Many held to the traditional view that culture evolved from primitive, irrational forms into modern liberal-rational entities. They believed that American cultural values and assumptions reflected the ultimate triumph of rationality and progress.[1] Viewing much of their relations with Latin America, indeed with the entire Third World, as a problem in the dynamics of cultural lag, they had little doubt as to the desirability of spreading American ideals and values abroad.[2]

With the advent of the Cold War, policymakers in both the Truman and Eisenhower administrations adopted cultural diplomacy as an explicit weapon in their arsenal to fight communism. Cultural policy became inextricably linked to foreign policy objectives. By the 1950s, national security justifications came to dominate all cultural programs. During this period the U.S. cultural program greatly expanded and emerged as a combination of national interest, anticommunism, and bureaucratic activism.[3] Secretary of State John Foster Dulles put the U.S. position succinctly in a telephone conversation with President Eisenhower: "Cultural affairs [were] a very good way of doing things

[for] you have to pat them a little bit and make them think that you are fond of them."⁴

This was a major change from earlier policy. Traditionally, U.S. cultural relations were primarily in the hands of private interests. The government played little or no role in the process. Cultural relations were to sensitize the elite sectors of other nations to similarities and differences between peoples in order to promote understanding, trade, and international peace. World War II and the Soviet-U.S. confrontation that followed concentrated power in the cultural field in the government.⁵

With the conclusion of World War II, President Truman transferred the informational and cultural programs of the Office of War Information (OWI) and the Office of the Coordinator of Inter-American Affairs (OCIAA) to the Department of State. These programs had been largely liquidated by 1946.⁶ The department continued, however, a greatly reduced effort to present "a full and fair picture of the United States" to the rest of the world under its International Information and Educational Exchange program and later under the United States Information Service (USIS). In December 1947 the new National Security Council (NSC) called for a carefully coordinated cultural and informational program "to influence foreign opinion in a direction favorable to United States interests and to counteract the effects of anti-United States propaganda." Convinced that the Soviet Union had declared psychological war on the United States, the NSC ordered the Department of State "to develop a vigorous and effective ideological campaign."⁷

In 1948, Congress enacted the Smith-Mundt Act to counteract Soviet propaganda and to sell America to the world. In response to growing Cold War tensions, President Truman directed Secretary of State Acheson in the spring of 1950 to prepare a vigorous "Campaign of Truth" as a U.S. offensive in response to Communist lies.⁸ Department of State planners had already designed and implemented a multifaceted program of cultural, educational, and informational persuasion for the worldwide struggle between democracy and communism. Drawing on the experience of the OCIAA and the OWI, which during World War II had managed an extensive and successful propaganda program, the Department of State used traditional cultural interchange methods such as the exchange of persons, books, art, and music and the new mass media approach to cultural relations to get the U.S. message across and to strengthen the international bonds against communism. The mass media approach, using the press, radio, television, and motion pictures, meshed perfectly with American predilections for technological solutions to political and economic problems. It held unprecedented possibilities for mass education and, given its populist, mass audience approach, was attuned to immediately altering opinions and attitudes.[9]

In response to its increasing responsibilities in the area of psychological warfare and to Congressional urging to expand overseas information services and programs, the Department of State established the International Information Administration (IIA) in 1952. Now the United States had a full-fledged propaganda program.[10] Responsibility for the effort, however, was still split between the Department of State, the Technical Cooperation Administration, and the Mutual Security Agency. President Eisenhower's Advisory Committee on Government Organization, headed by former OCIAA Coordinator Nelson Rockefeller, recommended in April 1953 the consolidation of the information programs under a new foreign information agency.[11] It also pleaded for the commitment of greater financial resources to take on the Communists in the battle for minds.[12]

Another Eisenhower committee, the President's Committee on International Information Activities, also argued that the information program lacked funds and central direction and recommended that the United States take the offensive in a global propaganda campaign. The committee reflected the prominent American belief that the Communist movement was a tool of Soviet power bent on world domination. The United States had to respond to Communist propaganda with the "dissemination of truth."[13]

Following the advice of his committees Eisenhower created the United States Information Agency (USIA) on July 31, 1953. The USIA was to be an instrument of foreign policy employed in combination with diplomatic, military, and economic policy. The new agency's primary purpose was to persuade foreign peoples that it was in their own interest to follow the lead of the United States in opposing Communist expansion and promoting peace and prosperity. While it was to avoid a propagandistic tone and present a straightforward picture of the life and culture of the people of the United States, including not only scholarly and artistic fields but also "the spirit of America" from athletics to political oratory, it was not required to present all facets of American life. In short, it was to present an appealing picture of the United States and to interpret and explain American objectives and policies in a favorable light.[14] Its job was to sell the United States to the world just as a salesman's job was to sell a Buick or a Cadillac or a radio or television set.[15]

Because of Brazil's strategic importance and dominant position in Latin America, it became a focal point for U.S. cultural and informational programs. U.S. planners concentrated on "the traditional spirit of friendship between Brazil and the United States." With an almost missionary zeal USIS officials attempted to develop individualistic and democratic traits in the Brazilians, to get them to "think things through in patterns similar to our own in politics, economics, and social welfare."[16]

In general, U.S. planners sought to increase the general knowledge and appreciation by Brazilians of the United States, its culture and foreign and domestic policy. Convinced that intellectual and cultural understanding were the handmaidens of economic and political cooperation, policymakers in both the Truman and Eisenhower administrations set about cultivating the cultural goodwill of the Brazilian people. Furthermore, they tried to persuade Brazil to follow the lead of the United States in its opposition to communism and to counter Communist propaganda with an "instructive, enlightened information program." Both Truman and Eisenhower tried to demonstrate the mutual interests of Brazil and the United States in democratic institutions and to spur the Brazilians to protect their freedom by "cleansing their system of Soviet-controlled or influenced communist and peronist elements." All was to be done without giving the impression that the United States was interfering in any way with the internal affairs of Brazil.[17]

In addition, Washington continually stressed its concern for Brazilian development and attempted to persuade the Brazilians that they could best ensure the success of their economic development proposals through close cooperation with the United States and with private enterprise. The U.S. government should not attempt to force America's culture or its economic system on Brazil, the planners maintained, but it was essential to tell the Brazilian leaders and mass audience the story of how free enterprise and the American way of life had been successful in contrast to what prevailed behind the Iron Curtain. By the time of the Korean War, U.S. objectives in Brazil had expanded to include combating neutralism and stressing the value of playing an active role in the conflict between the "free and slave world." Strong support for American and UN efforts to organize the world for peace was the "only hope for survival of Western Christian civilization."[18]

Calling for the aggressive promotion of this program and an expanded effort to meet the Communist threat, USIS officials in Brazil in 1950 pictured the possible activities of an effective cultural and information program as almost limitless. According to Sheldon Thomas, the public affairs officer in Brazil, "vast areas remain to be explored; large segments of the population should be reached much more frequently; media actively should be supplemented with personal contacts; and the emotional reflex of the average citizen should be conditioned to a fine degree." Thomas felt certain that by employing the best techniques of American advertising, ingenuity, originality, and persistence, all the American goals in this area could be met with "spectacular results." He warned, however, that the U.S. reservoir of goodwill in Brazil was only half full. They would have to act quickly to preserve and expand pro-American feelings.[19]

Analyzing Brazilian attitudes toward the United States, the planners generalized that the two nations had a long history of friendly relations, that most middle-class Brazilians had a traditional and deep-rooted liking for Yankees, and that since World Wars I and II Brazil had drifted away from France and the rest of Europe toward a closer association with the United States. Other favorable factors affecting relations, according to these American analysts, included Brazil's recognition of the United States as the leading world power; its admiration for American achievements in the fields of industry, science, agriculture, and medicine; common Western traditions and democratic ideals; the influence of the Catholic church; and close business associations. The United States was Brazil's best customer, it supplied Brazil with many basic materials and equipment, and the Rotary Club and American Chamber of Commerce were very active in Brazil.[20]

However, on the negative side of the ledger was the fact that a large percentage of the Brazilian population was illiterate, undernourished, and socially submerged. Coupled with a provincial suspicion of foreigners was a degree of envy, resentment, and bitterness toward Americans and toward the United States as an exploiter nation. Widespread ignorance of American cultural achievements and the feeling that the United States was essentially materialistic and lacking in culture, general apathy toward world events, growing nationalism, and general corruption, demagogy, and incompetence all contributed to an atmosphere, according to the USIS report, that promoted instability, anti-Americanism, and a receptive ground for Communist propaganda.[21]

Moreover, U.S. officials believed that Brazil was dangerously apathetic toward the Soviet Union and its satellites. According to American embassy officials in Brazil, the government there displayed a remarkable tolerance toward Communists entrenched in strategic positions and generally saw no real or immediate danger in Soviet Russia. Anti-American forces would grow and conditions worsen, the embassy warned, unless the program in Brazil was considerably strengthened. Any curtailment of the U.S. cultural and informational programs would necessitate additional expenditures at a later date in an effort to regain the ground that would be lost. For USIS planners, the United States was in a life-and-death struggle against the advancing adversaries of democracy.[22]

Attempting to counter the reportedly growing anti-American trend and expanding on Truman's information program, policymakers in the Eisenhower administration stepped up the American cultural and propaganda effort in Brazil. Various sectors of Brazilian society, such as the media, the military, government workers, business and political leaders, the literate middle class, labor, the church, and educators, were singled out for special attention and identified as target groups.[23] To get the American message across to these target groups and to stimulate pro-American sentiment in Brazil, both the Truman and Eisenhower administrations initiated a vast array of traditional cultural exchange programs and new mass media informational programs. They believed that they were contesting for the very souls of the Brazilians.

As early as 1950 the two nations signed a bilateral cultural convention that allowed each country to establish in the other's territory cultural institutes, information offices, libraries, and film centers and to increase its educational exchange programs and exhibits. Using this convention as well as the education exchanges authorized under the Smith-Mundt Act of 1948 as a legal basis, the United States greatly increased its cultural activities in Brazil.[24] For example, officials of the United States Information and Education Service (USIE, another State Department program) established a variety of exchange programs including a foreign leader program to bring future Brazilian leaders to the United States. Concentrating on educators, working journalists, artists, intellectuals, scholars, and students since, according to U.S. reports, they frequently harbored anti-American prejudice, U.S. policymakers hoped to win them over by "providing a genuine understanding of the United States and its people, its democratic form of government, and its social and political institutions." This could best be accomplished by visits, training grants, and scholarships for study and travel in the United States. These elites would, as a result of their stay, be imbued with a politically helpful pro-American orientation and would take back to Brazil a favorable image of the United States.[25]

U.S. officials wanted not only to promote American culture and values and anti-Communist attitudes but also to wean the Brazilians away from the "European influence," notably French, that dominated Brazilian culture. According to Deputy Public Affairs Officer Francis J. McArdle, Brazilians were well aware of the technical competence of the United States but distressingly unaware of American activities in and contributions to the theater, music, literature, and art.[26] The exchange programs were acclaimed a major success by U.S. officials as Brazilians visited and studied in the United States. It seemed a splendid investment, as the Brazilians developed a deep appreciation for the United States and its institutions.[27] William A. Wieland, the public affairs officer in Brazil, observed that the returning Brazilians were, in most cases, ardent champions of American democracy.[28]

Despite such laudatory statements the exchange program encountered a number of problems. Many American academicians complained that the long-term educational and informational benefits of such a program were being subordinated to short-range propaganda objectives. Even programs such as the Fulbright scholarships were designed to indoctrinate as well as educate. Educators were uneasy about "the propaganda motives" behind these programs. Education was now part of a "total American effort to build a free world."[29] Returning Brazilians also expressed their shock at the widespread ignorance they had encountered regarding Brazil. Upon arriving in the United States one Brazilian student was asked such questions as "How many revolutions do you have in Brazil per year? Do you like being governed by Perón?" and told "I must learn Spanish and visit Brazil." The high cost of travel and the expensive living standard in the United States also caused problems. U.S. officials in Brazil constantly complained that only rich Brazilians could really afford to go to the United States and that people from the arts were usually excluded.[30]

Although both the Truman and Eisenhower administrations continued to build an official cultural and information program, they also paid homage to the ongoing tradition of private initiative in the cultural area and public-private cooperation.[31] For example, when the USIS learned of a visit of Leonard Bernstein to Brazil it not only advertised his appearance as guest conductor with the Symphony Orchestra of Rio de Janeiro but also arranged to distribute copies of his recordings to various Brazilian radio stations and featured him in an issue of its publication *Em Marcha*. Similar arrangements were made when the distinguished American poet Robert Frost attended a writer's congress in São Paulo in 1954. American officials were especially delighted when the black U.S. labor leader Hilton E. Hanna visited Brazil. Not only did he read his speech in Portuguese, but he also "answered questions about racial prejudice in the United States with ease," citing the activities of other black leaders throughout the United States.[32]

U.S. officials in Brazil were acutely sensitive to Brazilian racial attitudes. Although they realized that racial discrimination existed in Brazil, they played up its reputation for racial tolerance and suppressed publicity regarding the refusal of well-known hotels in Rio de Janeiro and São Paulo to admit Joe Louis and Katherine Dunham during their tours of Brazil.[33]

Despite such problems, the United States continued its cultural offensive. To counter Soviet attempts to picture the United States as a nation of materialists interested primarily in industrial rather than cultural riches, the Department of State encouraged American businessmen, university professors and students, labor groups, and private organizations to take part in cultural and artistic achievements. Although the U.S. government did not directly finance projects such as the exchange of paintings between the Museum of Modern Art in New York and the Museum de Arte Moderna in São Paulo or the performance of the American National Ballet company in Rio, or American theatrical companies performing "Porgy and Bess" at the São Paulo Exposition, U.S. officials promoted such activities at every opportunity. Such events illustrated the high achievement of cultural life in the United States, they argued. Even the search for American basketball coaches by the Brazilian Basketball Confederation caught the attention of USIS planners. Encouraging this purely American sport in Brazil would help to improve relations, reasoned William V. Denning of the International Educational Exchange Service.[34]

U.S. officials even sent Mother Goose pinups to cement relations between the two nations. These cardboard cutouts of Mother Goose characters the cynical American vice counsel at Bahia, Robert S. Henderson, wrote "would undoubtedly impress Brazilian children with a sustaining faith in the principles of democracy through the examination of Little Bo Peep." Henderson questioned, however, their value in influencing the opinion makers of Brazil.[35] By 1953, nineteen different federal agencies and numerous private groups engaged in exchange programs in Brazil.

Cultural exchange programs were only part of the overall U.S. effort to promote mutual understanding and to get the American message across. Under its USIS program the Department of State established a number of cultural and information centers and libraries and attempted to alter radically the nature of Brazilian education. The centers conducted seminars for teachers of English, supplied popular U.S. magazines, organized lectures, passed out pamphlets on such subjects as "Communism," "How to Run a Union Meeting," "Organizing a Democratic Trade Union," "First Aid," and "Personal Hygiene," and in general promoted American culture.[36]

The binational centers and information libraries also organized discussions relating to American literature, history, music, and art. Under a book translation program the U.S. government encouraged commercial publishers to translate appropriate American books into Portuguese. Such books as Eleanor Roosevelt's *This I Remember*, George Orwell's *Animal Farm*, Lewis Mumford's *Condition of Man*, Henry David Thoreau's *Walden*, Margery Miller's *Joe Louis: American*, Catherine Owens Pearce's *Mary McLeod Bethune*, Herman Melville's *Moby Dick*, and Dorothy Thompson's *The Truth about Communism* soon appeared at U.S. information centers throughout Brazil.[37] To ensure that U.S. publishers were able to recover the proceeds of their sales in Brazil, since the Getúlio Vargas government restricted foreign exchange transactions, the Eisenhower administration also guaranteed convertibility and negotiated an Informational Media Guaranty Agreement with Brazil.[38]

Despite careful review of the types of material included in the libraries, the Department of State's book program came under increasing domestic attack during the 1950s, as Senator Joseph R. McCarthy accused the department of promoting Communist propaganda. Although McCarthy's attack was rambling and never specific, the International Information Agency (IIA) reacted quickly by issuing a policy directive in early 1953 that "no materials by any Communists, fellow-travelers, etc., will be used under any circumstances by an IIA media or mission."[39]

The IIA directed its libraries to withdraw any material detrimental to American objectives. Assistant Secretary of State for Public Affairs Carl McArdle wrote that any materials "which are receptive to international communist propaganda have no place in the program." IIA libraries were not reference libraries but rather were intended to disseminate favorable information about the United States.[40]

In Brazil this resulted in the removal of such books from the shelves as I. F. Stone's *Secret History of the Korean War*, Shirley Graham's *Paul Robeson, Citizen of the World*, and Howard Fast's *The American* and *Patrick Henry and the Frigate's Keel*. The U.S. embassy in Rio also temporarily removed the books of Gilberto Freire, the noted Brazilian sociologist from its libraries but quickly restored them to the shelves because of possible adverse comment.[41] Despite McCarthy's attack, U.S. publications flooded Brazil.[42]

Books were only part of the program. In addition to helping establish university chairs in American studies in São Paulo and Rio de Janeiro and promoting the use of American textbooks in classrooms throughout Brazil, U.S. educational experts sought to change the old attitudes and habits of the entire Brazilian education system. Attempting to wean the Brazilians from their long-established traditional European system, which stressed a classical education for the elite in the social sciences, humanities, and law, the American educators emphasized the need for professional training in such fields as engineering, agricultural science, medicine, physics, and chemistry. What was needed, according to these educators, was more practical education—technical training in industrial arts programs, vocational courses, management, and business administration. These courses would create both a trained labor force and a new managerial class. This American concept of practical education, the experts stressed publicly, would greatly benefit Brazilian development. Privately, they believed that the adoption of the American system would also greatly aid U.S. businesses operating in Brazil and help the anti-Communist campaign.[43]

Sensitive to criticism that they were "soft on communism," Department of State officials pointed proudly to their activities abroad that effectively countered the Soviet "hate America" propaganda effort. In Brazil the anti-Communist campaign focused on influencing the mass media—newspapers, magazines, radio, television, motion pictures—as well as the government information agency, Agencia Nacional.[44] Here was a chance to achieve immediate positive results by putting to use the burgeoning U.S. communications technology.[45]

Viewing the Brazilian press as the major molder of public opinion, U.S. policymakers wooed local publishers, editors, columnists, and reporters. USIS personnel and embassy officials provided the Brazilian press with personal copies of the department's wireless file, books, periodicals, and other background materials in an attempt to influence the content of Brazilian newspapers and magazines. Seeing each newspaper as a potential outlet for "our cause" U.S. officials distributed materials to over five hundred Brazilian newspapers and magazines. Concentrating on the major newspapers in the Assis Chateaubriand chain (which owned twenty-nine dailies, five magazines, twenty radio stations, and two television stations), the papers controlled by pro-American publishers such as Carlos Lacerda, Pereira Carneiro, and Paulo Bittencourt, and the Agencia Nacional, the

USIS provided background materials, wire service information, photographs, and cartoons depicting the United States in a favorable light. In addition, the embassy press office wrote and distributed under pseudonyms a variety of anti-Soviet and anti-Communist articles. Reasoning that USIS material would be received more favorably and avoid cries of "Yankee propaganda" if it was not attributed to the U.S. government, the embassy press office wrote newspaper columns and series under the pseudonyms Claude McKnight, Barry W. Richards, Walter J. Taylor, and George Dexter. These columns were designed to unmask the true nature of communism and Soviet expansionism. Exercising extreme caution in the distribution of these series, the embassy forwarded copies to the various consulates as classified matter. U.S. consuls then placed them personally with key Brazilian reporters and publishers. All was done without any attribution to USIS. Such articles as "The Sinking of a Nation," which described the various steps the Communists and Soviets used in seizing Hungary; "Nations that Disappear," which portrayed Soviet expansionism; and "The Press in the Satellite Countries," which showed the absolute domination of information media by the Comiform ran as featured articles in such papers as *O Globo* and in such popular magazines as *O Cruzeiro*.[46]

The Korean War brought an increased effort to sway the Brazilian press. Numerous articles promoting international cooperation to stop aggression and peace through strengthening the free world were placed with key newsmen. The Americans expanded their efforts to reach the Brazilian masses with photographs of the U.S. actions in Korea (especially of attempts to care for Korean children war victims), cartoons depicting Stalin helping to crush South Korea, comic strips promoting American heroes such as Superman and Captain Marvel rescuing everyday citizens from the Communist menace, and serialized books such as *Death Comes from the Kremlin* and *One Who Survived*.[47]

Treating the case of Julius and Ethel Rosenberg, public information officials carefully followed Washington guidelines to provide a matter-of-fact treatment of the case and to stress the scrupulously fair process of the trial. The USIS-inspired editorial that ran in *O Globo, Jornal Do Brasil*, and *Última Hora* condemned the death penalty but argued:

> If North American justice is criminal for condemning to death convicted and confessed spies—of most important atomic papers— tried under free procedures before a large public and with the participation of several defense lawyers, some of whom were

designated by the North American Communist Party itself, what is communist justice, which sends citizens to their deaths because of simple party quarrels, in secret trials, under accusations of merely subjective and strictly political value?[48]

The embassy press section followed up this editorial by providing the Brazilian press with a series of articles entitled "Watch Out for Spies." Written by U.S. Press Section Chief Robert Gonzaga, the series was based on the House Committee on Un-American Activities document "100 Things You Should Know about Communism" and focused on the infiltration of Communist spies into both public and private organizations. Gonzaga placed the articles by direct arrangements with Chateaubriand, and they bore no attribution to the USIS when *O Globo* featured them on its front page.[49]

To counteract magazines perceived as Communist such as *Para Todos, Orientacāo, Horizonte*, and *Emancipacāo*, which were geared to the Brazilian middle class and intellectuals and railed against "America's decadent imperialism, war mongering, and rotten capitalistic society," the USIS in Brazil began producing the monthly magazine *Em Marcha*. Patterned after the old OCIAA publication *Em Guardia*, the elaborately illustrated, sleek new magazine was edited primarily to interest opinion-forming groups and through them to reach the broader public. It emphasized the traditional friendship between the United States and Brazil, promoted mutual interests, and attempted to allay Brazilian fears of economic exploitation. It combated the Soviet line by exposing "communist lies with factual material representing the American point-of-view."

As envisioned by USIS representatives in Brazil, *Em Marcha* was to present an overall picture of American concepts, institutions, culture, and "the democratic way of life." Carrying such features as "Figuras da America" (which profiled Brazilian leaders one month and U.S. leaders the next), "Elections in a Democracy," "Partners in Progress," "Brazilians in the United States," and columns on U.S.-Brazilian military cooperation and free enterprise, the magazine, according to U.S. officials, was a positive approach in the propaganda war for freedom and democracy.[50] First published in February 1952, *Em Marcha* received a number of glowing reviews from Brazilian critics. Embassy officials considered the new venture a major success, for it got the American message across to leader groups who would, in general, not be receptive to the more blatant approach carried out by the embassy in newspapers.[51]

The Brazilian press was not the only concern of American officials. U.S. policymakers viewed Brazilian radio and television as extremely important elements in their information program, since more than 60 percent of the nation's population were illiterate. The Brazilian Institute of Public Opinion estimated that there were over 3.5 million radios in the country and that an average of four people listened to each radio set. This put the audience at 14 million listeners. In addition, in rural areas and in the *favela* (urban slum) sections a loudspeaker system was employed to broadcast programs. Radio was thus the only mass media capable of reaching all the identified target groups.[52]

As for television, it was in its infancy but growing rapidly. The embassy estimated that there were fewer than twenty-five thousand sets in Rio de Janeiro and twenty thousand in São Paulo in 1952. Nevertheless, seeing television's potential, American officials encouraged their Brazilian counterparts to adopt the regulations and standards used by the U.S. Federal Communications Commission. This would not only facilitate the export of television equipment to Brazil by such U.S. firms as RCA, GE, Zenith, and Philco but, with American technical help and training in this new media, it also would promote U.S. methods and the American message.[53]

Using techniques similar to those developed to influence Brazilian newspapers and magazines, U.S. embassy personnel produced radio and television scripts and even complete programs for broadcast in Brazil as part of their "Campaign of Truth." Concerned that if the origins of the programs were known they would be labeled propaganda and immediately suspected, the embassy made every effort to avoid any such identification. Approaching Assis Chateaubriand, U.S. officials made arrangements for the programs to be sponsored as a public service by Emissoras Associadas (the radio station chain owned by Chateaubriand) in its "desire to contribute to Brazilian progress and the strengthening of freedom and democracy."[54] They used local writers and actors to provide "a sensitivity to local political and social trends" and the correct accents, and employed Brazilian production techniques, "although inferior to U.S. methods," to earmark the shows as a local product and thus help remove any taint of "foreign propaganda."

U.S. planners, however, controlled every script. Over 60 percent dealt with anticommunism and were specifically tailored for the Brazilian market. For example, the radio program "Nos Bastidores do Mundo" (Our World behind the Scenes) was a daily five-minute news commentary that explained to the people of Brazil the meaning of world events seen in the light of U.S. foreign policy. Written in the vernacular of the man-in-the-street, the program was aimed primarily at the lower middle class and laboring groups. Its objectives included presenting the United States favorably, countering misconceptions deliberately spread by the local Communist party, and exposing Communist falsehoods and Kremlin claims to the allegiance of Brazilian workers. It also strove to create a climate of confidence in the free world and to encourage a spirit of self-help and self-reliance. The commentary was written daily by the U.S. embassy radio editor, a Brazilian citizen, Al Neto, who soon became one of the most popular people in Brazil. More than three quarters of all Brazilian stations carried his daily broadcast.[55] Another program, "O Destino e a Esperanca" (Destiny and Hope), was a fifteen-minute thrice-weekly dramatic serial centering around a São Paulo factory worker who goes to the United States in an exchange program to work in a New Jersey plant. A Brazilian veteran of World War II, he is married to an American girl. The hero tells the story of his life among American working men. Thus the hero, a Brazilian, tells of the common experiences and concerns of the American and Brazilian working classes.[56]

Concerned about Communist propaganda that focused not only on Yankee imperialism and the exploitation of Brazil but also on U.S. racial prejudice, embassy officials attempted to design and produce programs dramatizing the life, struggle, and success of American blacks such as Marian Anderson, Joe Louis, Jackie Robinson, Ralph Bunche, and Mary McLeod Bethune. U.S. writers provided scripts for local productions that portrayed blacks in sympathetic roles and made Negro spirituals and American jazz recordings available to Brazilian radio stations. The embassy also attempted to eliminate phrases such as "for the first time" from news releases when American blacks performed or appeared at cultural events in the United States. For example, in describing combat activities of the U.S. 25th Division in Korea, the embassy commented on its heroism and efficiency and then, toward the end of the news item, simply stated that the division was composed of both black and white troops. No mention was made of the fact that this was the first integrated division in the U.S. Army. Carried by many Brazilian newscasts, the embassy considered this item very successful.[57]

Embassy officials believed that the shortwave Voice of America programs were far less effective. Not only had local stations greatly improved their own news presentations, but Brazilians preferred the BBC (British Broadcasting Corporation). Its signal was cleaner, and many Brazilians believed that the BBC presented better balanced, more varied, and less biased programs. One typical Brazilian critic said: "Last night I heard a BBC broadcast in which the English government policy in Tehran was severely criticized. I never hear anything of the sort from the Voice of America. According to the VOA the United States has never erred in its foreign policy or anything else." Furthermore, VOA broadcasts came during an hour of a popular Brazilian soap opera.[58]

Despite such criticism, U.S. officials in Brazil as well as in the United States considered Voice of America as presenting "the truth" and looked upon it as "insurance" against Communist propaganda. They reasoned that it had influence among the leadership classes even if it was not a popular mass program.[59] In fact, an embassy radio survey of 1952 found that the most listened to American programs were privately sponsored shows such as "Hit Parade" and "Jack Benny." In the long run these programs probably had a more lasting effect on the Brazilian people than any of the USIS-produced programming.[60]

Efforts "to get the American message across" in the motion picture field suffered a similar fate. Despite the wide distribution of well-intended, well-produced films and film strips on communism, health, travel, science, the arts, and the Korean War, films produced by the major American studios gained the most attention and popularity in Brazil. "Twelve O'Clock High," "Sands of Iwo Jima," "Neptune's Daughter," "Donald Duck," and "Tom and Jerry" filled Brazilian theaters. Twentieth Century Fox, MGM, Paramount, Universal, Warner Brothers, and Walt Disney dominated the Brazilian motion picture market. Still, U.S. officials quietly attempted to prevent distribution in Brazil of films considered harmful to the American image. Of special concern were films portraying American gangsters or showing racial discrimination in the States.[61] U.S. officials in Brazil complained that Hollywood films were often harmful, wiped out much of USIA's effectiveness, and presented a distorted picture of the United States. All Americans were gangsters, millionaires, or cowboys. Bedroom farces distorted American values, and American women were portrayed either as gold diggers or career women.[62] Nonetheless, over 70 percent of all films shown in Brazil in 1952 were American.[63]

Although both the Dutra and the Vargas governments attempted to stem the flow of American films into Brazil, and there was the usual criticism that Yankee films were corrupting the youth of Brazil, the public continued to flock to see American pictures. Reluctantly, U.S. information officials sought to capitalize on the success of the American motion picture industry by running documentaries in the major theaters along with the feature attractions.

They also cautioned that popularity was not the only standard for judging the success of their information programs. The films shown at military barracks and public schools were effective, USIS officials claimed, in implanting the idea in youthful minds of Brazilian-U.S. collaboration, friendship, and anticommunism.[64]

In 1950 the American anti-Communist campaign received a boost when the Brazilian National Defense Council made a secret decision to intensify its anti-Communist efforts and ordered the Agencia Nacional to approach USIE officials for help. The U.S. embassy was only too eager to assist. It supplied Portuguese-language pamphlets, books, film strips, and motion pictures to the official government propaganda agency. When the Agencia Nacional launched the strongly anti-Communist radio programs "Agencia Informative Europa Livre" (Information Agency for Free Europe) and "Paisagens de Vila" (The Villagers) under direct orders from the Vargas government, the USIE radio unit systematically supplied the programs with material. U.S. Counselor for Public Affairs Herbert Cerwin evaluated the programs as "rather amateurish by American standards" and not truly effective as a propaganda vehicle. They were, however, according to Cerwin, "a welcome initiative and indicated that the Brazilian Government is conscious of the Communist threat."[65]

In addition to promoting American culture, the American way of life, and anticommunism, U.S. officials in Brazil carefully monitored the cultural efforts of other nations. The Soviet Union and its satellite states received the most attention. Embassy officials such as the counselor for public affairs, the cultural attaché, the information officers, the legal attaché, the labor attaché, and the motion picture, press, and radio officers all reported on newspapers, pamphlets, books, and trips suspected of being subsidized by the USSR and its satellites. Although releases from the Soviet news agency Tass were not distributed in Brazil after the Dutra administration broke diplomatic relations with the Soviet Union in 1947, embassy officials noted that Radio Moscow was still clearly heard in most of Brazil. They also believed that the Czechoslovakian and Polish legations distributed large quantities of Soviet-sponsored Communist propaganda in an attempt to influence Brazilian students, industrial and rural workers, and intellectuals.[66]

The Soviet Union and the Communist bloc states were not the only countries monitored by the U.S. embassy. It carefully noted and analyzed the activities of all foreign nations in Brazil. The embassy reported to Washington that the French, for example, set up an information service in Brazil that distributed press materials and supplied publishers such as Diarios Associados with newsreels and photographs and maintained a strong cultural exchange program with Brazil. Great Britain not only beamed BBC broadcasts into Brazil but also signed a long-term cultural agreement with the Vargas government in 1950, the British News Service actively promoted BBC film, radio materials, newsreels, and the distribution of its wire service, and Britain also established cultural institutions in Brazil and promoted Brazilian-British friendship and cooperation.

Analyzing these efforts, U.S. embassy officials believed that, although the Brazilian elite considered France as the natural spiritual and cultural mentor of Brazil and French cultural influence was still present, younger Brazilians no longer had such strong attachments. They were more American-oriented. As for the British, according to the embassy, although the Brazilians respected them for their honesty and reporting abilities, England was now looked upon as a faded symbol of an empire in decline.[67] Although U.S. policymakers were primarily concerned with the Soviets and their propaganda campaign, they did not want to see any foreign power become too influential in Brazil, politically, economically, or culturally. They desired a cultural Monroe Doctrine.[68]

In comparing the cultural and informational programs of the other countries in Brazil, Ambassador Herschel Johnson, writing in 1952, stated that the United States was far ahead and, except possibly for BBC radio broadcasts, provided by far the most balanced, most effective information and cultural programs. This effort was extremely valuable in getting the American message across and counterbalancing not only Soviet but also other foreign power propaganda programs, according to Ambassador Johnson. Most American policy leaders agreed with Johnson's assessment.[69]

In summary, during the early Cold War period, policymakers in both the Truman and Eisenhower administrations believed that a Soviet-directed global Communist movement that spread anti-American sentiments and suspicion was undermining U.S. influence not only in Brazil but also in Latin America and the rest of the world. Viewing the Communist propaganda program as a major threat to the United States, both administrations developed and promoted a vast, hard-hitting, anti-Communist, and pro-democracy "Campaign of Truth." Drawing on the World War II experience of the OCIAA and the OWI, policymakers instituted a massive cultural and informational program designed to win over the Brazilian populace. They used both traditional cultural interchange methods and, increasingly, the mass media to influence the Brazilians. A steady flow of U.S. visitors, information, and educational materials flooded Brazil. All proclaimed the advantages of a free way of life, of the American way. By the 1950s, U.S. policymakers viewed their cultural and informational programs in Brazil as important tools in the ideological confrontation between the United States and the Soviet Union. Ironically, just as in the economic arena, despite continuing rhetoric encouraging private initiative and private action, the U.S. government increasingly came to dominate all aspects of this cultural and informational program.

Viewed as a major success in fostering closer Brazilian-U.S. relations, feelings of cooperation and mutuality, and a better understanding of U.S. society and values, the cultural and information program in Brazil grew quickly in size during the early 1950s. Begun under the auspices of the Department of State in 1947, by 1952 it threatened to overwhelm the American embassy in Rio de Janeiro, and by 1954 it became a totally separate agency, the United States Information Agency, committed to persuading the Brazilians that it was in their interest to follow the lead of the United States in world affairs and in economic, political, social, and cultural development. While attempting to win the psychological battle with the Soviet Union, U.S. officials also sought to displace traditional European influence throughout Brazil with American values, trends, and standards.

Avoiding a propagandistic tone, this informational program attempted to portray U.S. objectives and policies in a favorable light and to counter false Communist charges. In the final analysis, however, although the official U.S. cultural and information programs in Brazil were widespread, targeted to numerous Brazilian groups, and undoubtedly effective, they constituted only a very small part of the total impact the United States had on Brazilian society. U.S. private corporations advertising for popular consumer products and American films, fashion, architecture, music, sports, and life-style inundated Brazil. Brazilians thirsted after things American. Adopting the American model of consumption, they wanted consumer items ranging from blue jeans to soft drinks, from rock and roll to automobiles and televisions. The Brazilian language reflected this growing unofficial American presence. Brazilian Portuguese, like American English, has an enormous ability to absorb vocabulary from almost any source. Slang from American movies and comic strips merged with English terms in sports, science, technology, and the press to provide Brazilians with terms such as *sex appeal, show, far west, films, bar, nylon, shorts, gangsters, duplex, DJ,* and *rock and roll.* For better or for worse, by accident or by design, the North American presence in Brazil grew in intensity and sophistication in the early 1950s.[70]

Notes

1. Frank A. Ninkovich, *The Diplomacy of Ideas: United States Foreign Policy and Cultural Relations, 1938–1950* (Cambridge: Cambridge University Press, 1981), pp. 70–72.

2. See Ninkovich, *Diplomacy of Ideas*, p. 30; and Manuel J. Espinosa, *Inter-American Beginnings of U.S. Cultural Diplomacy 1936–1948*, Department of State Publication 8854, International Information and Cultural Series 110 (Washington, DC: Government Printing Office, 1976).

3. See Charles A. Thompson and Walter H. C. Laves, *Cultural Relations and U.S. Foreign Policy* (Bloomington: Indiana University Press, 1971); and Morrell Heald and Lawrence S. Kaplan, *Culture and Diplomacy: The American Experience* (Westport: Greenwood Press, 1977).

4. John Foster Dulles to Eisenhower, February 26, 1953, Telephone Series. John Foster Dulles Papers, Dwight D. Eisenhower Library, Abilene, Kansas.

5. See Ninkovich, *Diplomacy of Ideas*, p. 176.

6. For a description of the OCIAA see Donald W. Rowland, *History of the Office of the Coordinator of Inter-American Affairs* (Washington, DC: Government Printing Office, 1947). For a review of the effectiveness of this early U.S. program in Latin America, see Gerald K. Haines, "Under the Eagle's Wing: The Franklin D. Roosevelt Administration Forges an American Hemisphere," *Diplomatic History* 1:4 (Fall 1977): 373–88. The OCIAA was abolished in 1947.

7. See NSC 4, December 9, 1947, RG 273, NA; NSC 7, March 30, 1947, RG 273, NA; and NSC 20/1, August 18, 1948, RG 273, NA.

8. See "Program for Strengthening U.S. International Information," *FRUS, 1952–1954* 2:2, 1600. See also Howland Sargeant, "Helping the World to Know Us Better," Department of State *Bulletin* 19 (November 28, 1948): 672; U.S. Congress, House, Hearings on HR 3342, *U.S. Information and Educational Exchange Act of 1947*, 80th Cong., 1st sess., 1947, and U.S. Congress, Senate, Hearings on Senate Resolution 243, *Expanded International Information and Education Program*, 81st Cong., 2d sess., 1950.

9. Ninkovich, *Diplomacy of Ideas*, pp. 116–19; Jeremy Tunstall, *The Media Are American* (New York: Columbia University Press, 1977), p. 9.

10. See Department of State, Departmental Announcement No. 4, "Establishment of the U.S. International Information Administration (IIA)," January 16, 1952, *FRUS, 1952–1954* 2:2, 1591–95, 1627.

11. See memorandum for the president by the president's Advisory Committee on Government Organization, April 7, 1953, *FRUS, 1952–1954* 2:2, 1691–97.

12. Ninkovich, *Diplomacy of Ideas*, p. 132.

13. "Report to the President by the President's Committee on International Informational Activities," June 30, 1953, *FRUS, 1952–1954* 2:2, 1795–1899. See also Edward Barrett, *Truth Is Our Weapon* (New York: Funk and Wagnalls, 1953), p. 9; and U.S. Department of State, Office of Intelligence and Research,

Communist Offenses against the Integrity of Education, Sciences, and Culture (Washington, DC: Government Printing Office, 1951).

14. Theodore C. Streibert was the first director of USIA. For an outline of the USIA program and goals see memorandum from Streibert to Eisenhower, October 27, 1953, *FRUS, 1952–1954* 2:2, 1754–55, 1765. See also "Summary of USIA Operations, January 1, 1954–June 30, 1954," Report of NSC, August 18, *FRUS, 1952–1954* 2:2, 1777–79.

15. See Leo Bogart, *Premises for Propaganda* (New York: Free Press, 1976), p. xv. See also Barrett, *Truth Is Our Weapon*, pp. 8–10; and Robert E. Elder, *Information Machine: The United States Information Agency and American Foreign Policy* (Syracuse: Syracuse University Press, 1968), p. 4.

16. See Ninkovich, *Diplomacy of Ideas*, p. 53; and Espinosa, *Inter-American Beginnings of U.S. Cultural Diplomacy*, pp. 15–23.

17. Sheldon Thomas, draft report to Joseph B. Tisinger, February 1, 1950, DS 511.32/2-150, RG 59, NA; "Country Plan for Brazil," March 20, 1953, DS 511.32/3-2053, RG 59, NA.

18. See the "Country Plan for Brazil," March 20, 1952, DS 511.32/3-2052, RG 59, NA; and "Country Plan for Brazil," April 28, 1953, DS 511.32/4-2853, RG 59, NA. For earlier plans see dispatch 1217 of December 22, 1949, DS 511.32/439, RG 59, NA; and Thomas, draft report to Tisinger, February 1, 1950, DS 511.32/2-150, RG 59, NA.

19. Thomas, "USIE Psychological Offensive in Brazil," November 8, 1950, DS 511.32/11-850, RG 59, NA. See also William A. Wieland, "USIS Program in Brazil," March 19, 1953, DS 511.32/3-1953, RG 59, NA.

20. Ibid.

21. Ibid.

22. Ibid.

23. Ibid.; "Country Plan for Brazil," March 20, 1953, DS 511.32/3-2052, RG 59, NA; F. R. Lineaweaver (U.S. consul, Recife), "USIE Semi-Annual Evaluation Report," May 31, 1950, DS 511.32/8-350, RG 59, NA.

24. See Dean Acheson to U.S. embassy in Rio, October 17, 1950, DS 511.32/10-1750, RG 59, NA. For the text of the Smith-Mundt Act see PL 402, 80th Cong., 2d sess. 64 *Statutes at Large* 987.

25. Ninkovich, *Diplomacy of Ideas*, p. 43.

26. Francis J. McArdle, dispatch to the Department of State, June 10, 1953, DS 511.32/6-1053, RG 59, NA.

27. See, for example, U.S. Consul George T. Colman, "Brief Report on Returned Leader Grant," May 29, 1954, DS 511.323/5-2954, RG 59, NA.

28. Wieland, "IIA Prospectus for Brazil," April 30, 1953, DS 511.32/4-3053, RG 59, NA.

29. See Welson S. Compton, Administrator of IIA, extract from "Report on International Information Administration—1952" to the secretary of state, December 31, 1952, *FRUS, 1952–1954* 1:2, 1648; and Ninkovich, *Diplomacy of Ideas*, pp. 148–49.

30. See Thomas (public affairs officer), "Comments on the Department's Exchange of Persons Program," January 18, 1950, DS 511.323/1-1850, RG 59, NA; and Colman, "Educational Exchange: Evaluation Report," August 31, 1954, DS 511.323/11-1254, RG 59, NA. See also Raymond C. Smith to embassy, "Student Grants in Artistic Fields," September 3, 1954, DS 511.323/9-354, RG 59, NA.

31. Ninkovich, *Diplomacy of Ideas*, p. 168.

32. See Wieland, "Exchange of Persons Program," October 13, 1953, DS 511.32/10-1353, RG 59, NA; Dulles to American embassy, "Frost Visit," June 30, 1954, DS 932.119-SA/6-3054, RG 59, NA; and Colman, "Visit of Hilton E. Hanna," December 1, 1953, DS 511.323/12-153, RG 59, NA. During World War II the OCIAA had actually sponsored the visits of many American artists and film stars to Brazil. See Haines, "Under the Eagles' Wing," p. 386.

33. See Henry S. Hammond (labor attaché), "Anti-Racial Discrimination Law," July 13, 1951, DS 832.411/7-1351, RG 59, NA. See also Soares, *Desenvolvimento econômico-social do Brasil e Eua* (The socioeconomic development of Brazil and the United States), pp. 24–53.

34. See William V. Denning to Edward Krause (director of athletics, University of Notre Dame), December 16, 1953, DS 511.32/12-1653, RG 59, NA. On the museum exchanges see Nelson Rockefeller to Acheson, November 2, 1950, DS 511.32/11-250, RG 59, NA; and Acheson to Rockefeller, January 18, 1950, DS 511.32/1-1850, RG 59, NA. See also Edward W. Barrett to Herschel Johnson, April 28, 1951, DS 511.32/4-2851, RG 59, NA; and Tapley Bennett to John Cabot, "São Paulo Exposition," May 15, 1953, DS 832.191/SA/5-1553, RG 59, NA.

35. Robert S. Henderson, "Mother Goose Pinups," July 17, 1953, DS 511.32/7-1753, RG 59, NA.

36. The U.S. libraries and binational centers often complained that many of these popular magazines were stolen from the mail and requested diplomatic pouch service for delivery. They also requested that subscriptions to such scholarly journals as *Saturday Review of Literature, Harper's, Music Educator's Journal*, and the *NEA Journal* be canceled as nobody read them. See Andy G. Wilkison (director of library services), "Magazine Distribution Plan," June 5, 1950, DS 511.32/6-550, RG 59, NA; Robert C. Johnson, Jr. (American consul, Bahia), "Cultural Center Request for Changes in Subscriptions to Magazines," October 10, 1950, DS 511.3221/10-1050, RG 59, NA; and Robert C. Johnson, "Bi-National Centers: Transmission of Magazine List," January 31, 1952, DS 511.32/1-3152, RG 59, NA. For a list of the pamphlets see *FRUS, 1952–1954* 2:2, 1620–28. See also Dorothy Greene, *Cultural Centers in the Other American Republics*, (Department of State Publication 2503, Washington, DC: Government Printing Office, 1946).

37. See Alan K. Manchester (cultural affairs officer), "Request for Books under Book Translation Program," January 3, 1952, DS 511.3221/1-352, RG 59, NA; Herbert Cerwin (counselor of embassy for public affairs), "Division of Overseas Information Centers: Book Translation Program Plans for Brazil," March 13, 1952, DS 511.3221/3-1352, RG 59, NA; and Acheson to embassy, June 25, 1951, DS 511.3221/6-2551, RG 59, NA.

38. See Ellis M. Goodwin (first secretary of embassy), "Effects of the Dollar Shortage on Commercial Imports of American Publications," September 5, 1952, DS 511.32/8-552, RG 59, NA; memorandum by Sterling Cottrell, "Informational Media Guaranty Program, November 22, 1954, DS 511.11-2254, RG 59, NA; and Streibert, "Informational Media Guaranty Program," November 16, 1954, DS 511.32/11-1654, RG 59, NA.

39. See memorandum from Bradley W. Connors (assistant administrator for policy and plans of the U.S. International Information Agency) to Walter K. Scott (deputy assistant secretary of state for administration), February 20, 1953, *FRUS, 1952–1954* 2:2, 1671–73. See also Joseph R. McCarthy to Dulles, April 7, 1953, *FRUS, 1952–1954* 2:2, 1697–98. McCarthy never produced a

detailed list of which publications he considered to be written by Communists. See Bogart, *Premises for Propaganda*, pp. xvi–xvii.

40. McArdle to Herschel Johnson, March 17, 1953, *FRUS, 1952–1954* 2:2, 1685–86.

41. See memorandum by Wieland, May 22, 1953, DS 511.32/5-2253, RG 59, NA. See also "Bookburning" folder, John Foster Dulles papers, Dwight D. Eisenhower Library, Abilene, Kansas.

42. For a sample of this propaganda material and a listing of a variety of leaflets, pamphlets, books, and posters, see Dulles, circular to certain diplomatic and consular offices, and bulky file, February 15, 1952, DS 511.00/2-1552, RG 59, NA. See also U.S. Consul V. Lansing Collins, Jr., "Annual Review of USIE Activities, Distribution of Publications in Pôrto Alegre," January 14, 1950, DS 511.32/1-2650, RG 59, NA.

43. See Adolf Berle, "Mission of American Professors and Specialists to Brazil," May 18, 1945, DS 832.017/5-1845, RG 59, NA; Brazilian Division memorandum, "Activities in Brazil," May 8, 1946, records of the Office of American Republics Affairs, Brazil, RG 59, NA; William Pawley, dispatch to secretary of state, June 25, 1947, DS 832.12/6-2547, RG 59, NA; Allen Dawson, "Activities to Be Carried on by the Inter-Departmental Committee on Scientific and Cultural Cooperation in Brazil," May 8, 1947, records of the Office of American Republics Affairs, Brazil, RG 59, NA; McArdle (deputy public affairs officer), "Educational Exchange Programs," June 8, 1954, DS 511.323/6-854, RG 59, NA; and "IIA Prospectus for Brazil," various dates, DS 411.323, RG 59, NA. See also John V. D. Saunders, "Education and Modernization in Brazil," in Baklanoff, ed., *New Perspectives of Brazil*, pp. 109–41; and Robert J. Havighurst and J. Roberto Moreira, *Society and Education in Brazil* (Pittsburgh: University of Pittsburgh Press, 1965).

44. See "Positive Content in IIA Programming to the Other American Republics," January 26, 1953, DS 511.00/1-2653, RG 59, NA.

45. Ninkovich, *Diplomacy of Ideas*, p. 116.

46. See Edward Miller to Herschel V. Johnson, January 19, 1951, Miller Files, Lot File 53D-26, RG 59, NA; Cerwin (public affairs officer), "USIE Press Operations in Brazil," May 25, 1951, DS 511.32/5-2551, RG 59, NA; Thomas (public affairs officer), "New Series of Feature Articles," March 16, 1950, DS 511.3221/3-1650, RG 59, NA; Thomas "Articles in Brazilian Publications," August 21, 1950, DS 511.322/8-2150, RG 59, NA; Thomas, "Pamphlet Series Entitled *Countering Soviet Propaganda*," November 29, 1950, DS 511.3221/11-2950, RG 59, NA; Thomas, "USIS Press Campaign," November 10, 1950, DS 511.32/11-1050, RG 59, NA; and Cerwin, "Placement of Material on World Peace Council," July 16, 1951, DS 511.32/7-1651, RG 59, NA.

47. Wieland, "Comic Strips," February 13, 1953, DS 511.3221/2-1353, RG 59, NA; and Wieland, "Embassy Operations Memorandum," January 27, 1953, DS 511.322/1-2753, RG 59, NA.

48. See Dulles, circular to certain diplomatic posts, December 11, 1953, 511.00/2-1153, *FRUS, 1952–1954* 2:2, 1668–70; and Wieland, "Rosenberg Case," December 11, 1952, DS 511.322/1-653, RG 59, NA.

49. See Cerwin, "Three Articles Entitled 'Watch Out for Spies' Frontpaged by *O Globo*," October 8, 1952, DS 511.322/10-852, RG 59, NA. The Brazilian armed forces picked up the articles and reprinted them as a pamphlet, much to the delight of the U.S. press section. See Cerwin, "Publication by Brazilian Armed

Forces of Watch Out for Spies," October 14, 1952, DS 511.322/10-1452, RG 59, NA.

50. See Cerwin, "Production of *Em Marcha*," July 3, 1952, DS 511.32/7-352, RG 59, NA; and Cerwin, "Embassy's Magazine *Em Marcha*," July 10, 1952, DS 511.32/7-1052, RG 59, NA.

51. Cerwin, "Production of *Em Marcha*," July 3, 1952, DS 511.32/7-352, RG 59, NA; Cerwin, "Reviews of Magazine *Em Marcha*, June 30, 1952, DS 511.322/6-3052, RG 59, NA; Cerwin to Howland Sargeant (assistant secretary of state), February 11, 1952, DS 511.3221/2-1152, RG 59, NA.

52. See Cerwin, "Brazilian Potential Market (Radio, Newspapers and Magazines)," June 26, 1951, DS 511.32/6-2651, RG 59, NA; Wieland, "USIS Program in Brazil," March 19, 1953, DS 511.32/3-1953, RG 59, NA; and Cerwin, "Radio," May 15, 1951, DS 511.324/5-1551, RG 59, NA.

53. See John Logan Hagan (economic officer), "Standardization of Television in Brazil," January 28, 1953, DS 932.44/1-2853, RG 59, NA; Thomas, "Policy Guidance on Use of Television in USIE Programs," March 27, 1950, DS 511.324/3-2750, RG 59, NA; Charles K. Ludewig (American consul, São Paulo), "Status of Television in São Paulo," August 31, 1950, DS 932.44/8-3150, RG 59, NA; William P. Rambo (American vice consul, Rio), "Television Development in Brazil," June 16, 1950, DS 932.44/6-1650, RG 59, NA; Acheson to embassy, August 30, 1950, DS 932.44/8-3040, RG 59, NA; Cerwin, "Television," June 16, 1952, DS 511.32/6-1652, RG 59, NA; and Cerwin, "Television," September 3, 1952, DS 511.324/9-352, RG 59, NA.

54. Cerwin, "Radio," October 15, 1952, DS 511.324/10-1551, RG 59, NA.

55. See James Scott Kemper (U.S. ambassador to Brazil), "Evaluation of the Program Effectiveness of United States International Broadcasting," April 7, 1954, DS 511.324/4-754, RG 59, NA; Cerwin, "USIE Semi-Annual Evaluation Report," August 23, 1951, DS 511.32/8-2351, RG 59, NA; Cerwin, "USIE Radio Programs," July 16, 1951, DS 511.324/7-324 through 7-1651, RG 59, NA; and Cerwin, "Local Radio Operations," May 15, 1951, DS 511.324/5-1551, RG 59, NA.

56. See Cerwin, "Radio," October 15, 1951, DS 511.324/10-1551, RG 59, NA.

57. See Cerwin, "Packaged Radio and Television Programs Dealing with the American Negro," February 27, 1952, DS 511.324/2-2952, RG 59, NA; Lee M. Hunsaker (assistant public affairs officer), "Projected Transcribed Radio and Television Series," March 4, 1952, DS 511.324/3-452, RG 59, NA; and Robert Johnson, Jr. (American consul, Bahia), "USIE Semi-Annual Evaluation Report, December 1, 1950, to May 31, 1952," June 27, 1951, DS 511.32/6-2751, RG 59, NA.

58. Cerwin, radio survey on the Voice of America, the Al Neto program and "A Vida Que O Mondo Leva" (The life that the world leads), November 20, 1952, DS 511.324/11-2052, RG 59, NA. See also Cerwin, "Report on Field Trip through Northern Brazil," July 25, 1951, DS 511.32/7-2551, RG 59, NA.

59. See "IIA Prospectus for Brazil," April 30, 1953, DS 511.32/4-3053, RG 59, NA. See also Bogart, *Premises for Propaganda*, p. xii.

60. For the survey see Cerwin, "Radio Survey," November 20, 1952, DS 511.324/11-2052, RG 59, NA.

61. See *FRUS, 1952–1954* 2:2, 1625–26.

62. Bogart, *Premises for Propaganda*, p. 90; William J. Bushwaller (assistant cultural attaché), "Recent Motion Picture Developments," April 17, 1953, DS 832.452/4-1753, RG 59, NA.

63. See Robert Lobel, "Motion Pictures—Current Developments," May 19, 1950, DS 832.452/5-1950, RG 59, NA.

64. See Thomas (public affairs officer), "USIE: Effectiveness of Program," December 29, 1950, DS 511.32/12-2950, RG 59, NA; Stewart Anderson, "Motion Pictures—Current Developments," January 27, 1950, DS 832.452/1-2750, RG 59, NA; Acheson to embassy, April 29, 1950, DS 511.325/4-2750, RG 59, NA; Thomas, "Special Showing of USIS Films," May 29, 1950, DS 511.325/5-1950, RG 59, NA; and Lineaweaver (U.S. consul, Recife), dispatch, August 3, 1950, DS 511.32/8-350, RG 59, NA. For Brazilian attempts to limit U.S. film imports see Bushwaller, "Recent Motion Picture Developments," April 17, 1953, DS 832.452/4-1753, RG 59, NA; Bushwaller, "Motion Picture Developments," May 20, 1952, DS 832.452/5-2052, RG 59, NA; and John G. McCarthy (president, Motion Picture Association of America) to Miller, September 30, 1952, DS 832.452/9-3052, RG 59, NA. Brazil provided U.S. filmmakers with their largest market in Latin America and was second in importance out of all the countries in the world, according to McCarthy. See also "Brazilian Restrictions on Motion Pictures," February 15, 1952, DS 832.452/2-1552, RG 59, NA; and Bushwaller, "Developments since Signing of Motion Picture Decree," December 11, 1952, DS 832.452/12-1151, RG 59, NA. With regard to U.S. government sponsored films see Cerwin, "Film *With These Hands*," October 30, 1952, DS 511.325/10-3052, RG 59, NA. (This film was designed specifically for Brazilian labor leaders and showed the Communist party destroying free labor unionism in Brazil.) Cerwin, "Film *The Impressionable Years*," June 9, 1952, DS 511.325/6-952, RG 59, NA. (This film portrayed U.S. family life and attempted to show how Americans, like Brazilians, had great affection for children and family. It was designed especially to appeal to Brazilian women.) Cerwin, "*Soldiers of Freedom*," April 24, 1952, DS 511.325/5-2252, RG 59, NA. (The Portuguese version of this film showed the destructive work of communism and the community of interest of free people.)

65. Cerwin, "Anti-Communist Programs," October 8, 1951, DS 732.001/10-851, RG 59, NA; Cerwin, "Anti-Communist Radio Programs," October 11, 1951, DS 732.001/10-1151, RG 59, NA; telegram from Herschel Johnson to Acheson, December 14, 1950, DS 511.325/12-1450, RG 59, NA.

66. See Cerwin, "Country Plan for Brazil," March 20, 1952, DS 511.32/3-2052, RG 59, NA for a summary of Communist activities.

67. See Wieland, "USIS Country Plan for Brazil," April 28, 1953, DS 51.32/4-2853, RG 59, NA; Thomas, "USIE Films for Television," August 9, 1950, DS 511.325/8-950, RG 59, NA; George E. Miller (American consul, Recife), "Monthly Report on Information and Cultural Activities," January 13, 1950, DS 511.32/1-1350, RG 59, NA; William A. Krauss (public affairs officer, São Paulo), "Exposition Commemorating the Centenary of the English Public Library," September 29, 1950, DS 832.19 1-SA/9-2950, RG 59, NA; and telegram from Herschel Johnson to Acheson, September 12, 1952, DS 511.32/9-1252, RG 59, NA.

68. See Ninkovich, *Diplomacy of Ideas*, p. 89.

69. See Herschel Johnson to Acheson, September 12, 1952, DS 511.32/9-1252, RG 59, NA.

70. See Santos, "A Psychologist Reflects on Brazil and Brazilians"; and Earl Thomas, "Emerging Patterns of the Brazilian Language," in Baklanoff, ed., *The Shaping of Modern Brazil*, pp. 264–300. See also Wesson, *Limits of Influence*, p. 145.

Chapter Ten

Conclusion: The American Way

During the early postwar era, 1945 to 1954, U.S. officials attempted to control, influence, and direct Brazil's political, economic, and cultural development in order to preserve U.S. power and influence in the Western Hemisphere, to eliminate foreign, particularly Communist, influence from the region, and to integrate Brazil into the U.S.-dominated, capitalist, worldwide trading system. Despite the Europe-first orientation of a whole generation of American leaders, neither the Truman nor the Eisenhower administration neglected Latin America, especially Brazil, during this period. Although the major decision makers in both administrations focused most of their attention on Europe, Asia, and the Middle East and only occasionally discussed Brazil, their subordinates concerned with Third World development saw Brazil as the key not only to creating a solid regional program to counter global communism but also to shaping a successful U.S. response to Third World demands and to molding a capitalist prototype for Third World development.

Based on ingrained images, values, stereotypes, and myths that distorted reality, U.S. policy toward Brazil was a combination of political calculation, self-interest, benevolent paternalism, and evangelism. Nevertheless, it succeeded.

Both administrations worked to make Brazil an integral part of the U.S. sphere of influence. Both tried to eliminate competing foreign powers and competing economic, political, and cultural ideologies from Brazil. In short, they sought to mold Brazil into their perceived image of the United States. Brazil was to be a strong, stable, democratic, capitalist ally. It was to be modeled on American principles, values, and ideals. Brazil was to be made over in the American image—to be Americanized.

Politically, the planners encouraged the Brazilians to follow the U.S.-directed path to democracy. They pushed them to emulate the American political system and stressed a basic common heritage shared by the two nations. Following World War II, U.S. officials vigorously promoted the development of democratic institutions and concepts in Brazil. They regarded Brazil as a fledgling democracy, especially after the overthrow of Getúlio Vargas in 1945. Even the return of Vargas to the presidency in 1950 did not dampen U.S. enthusiasm. Vargas had been democratically elected, and he followed a pro-U.S. foreign policy.

Dominated by Cold War thinking and fearing the spread of communism into the hemisphere, U.S. officials increasingly turned their attention to making Brazil into a bulwark against communism rather than a functioning democracy. They now sought stability, law, and order in Brazil as well as solid support for the United States against the Communist menace. In their eagerness to eliminate Communist influence in Brazil, U.S. planners, often confused communism with nationalism and at times worked to defeat legitimate democratic dissent. In the long run this produced some major problems, but in the short run it produced a solid American ally.[1]

Cultivating the Brazilian military, U.S. officials promoted it as the protector of democracy and tried to use it as a tool in their worldwide struggle against Bolshevism. Imbued with the U.S. tradition of military noninvolvement in domestic affairs, these officials eagerly sought to train and equip the Brazilian military to be an active partner in the war against communism. They believed that exposing Brazilian military leaders to American ways and equipment would show them democracy at work. Unfortunately, U.S. planners ignored or overlooked the long-standing position of the military as the final arbiter of power in Brazil. American technology, training, and support only encouraged the Brazilian armed forces to assume a more active role in domestic affairs. It did not lead to the adoption of the U.S. military traditions of submission to civilian authority and adherence to democratic procedures. The U.S. view of the Cold War world also encouraged Brazilian officers to see their own role as encompassing the control and direction of all aspects of national life. The Brazilian military establishment felt obliged to maintain this control in order to ensure national security.

With the coming of the Korean War, U.S. planners increasingly, but unsuccessfully, sought the commitment of Brazilian troops to the conflict. Nevertheless, the Brazilian armed forces maintained close ties with their U.S. counterparts and generally supported the United States in its opposition to communism in the hemisphere and around the globe. It also agreed with many of the American concepts and proposals regarding Brazilian economic development.

Economically, U.S. policymakers urged the Brazilians to adopt American practices and duplicate the American success story. Convinced that the blueprint for successful economic development lay in this direction, these policymakers generally credited private enterprise free of government restraints with producing rapid industrial growth, greater abundance, and a modern progressive state. Focusing on classic liberal trade principals such as private capital investment, open access to markets, and free trade, and emphasizing the American predilection for technological solutions to all problems, U.S. planners promoted a mythical yet often self-validating concept of economic development for Brazil.

In advocating this model economic development program for Brazil, U.S. policymakers ignored or distorted the historical development of the United States as an industrial power. U.S. development had followed an expedient mix of individual initiatives and government policies that promoted growth, not laissez-faire economics. Thus, U.S. officials prescribed a development process for the Brazilians quite unlike America's own. At the same time, American leaders took it for granted that their assistance in the form of advice and technical knowledge would automatically nurture democratic government in Brazil and prevent the expansion of world communism by increasing Brazilian prosperity.

Despite bureaucratic infighting, U.S. policymakers concerned with Brazil generally exhibited continuity in their approach to Brazilian economic development. Although primarily concerned with the reconstruction of Europe and events outside the Western Hemisphere, these officials nevertheless promoted a far-reaching program for Brazil that proposed to influence its development dramatically. With unctuous prose declaring American devotion to Brazil and concern for its development, U.S. officials confidently pointed out the American way to economic prosperity.

Certain that the adoption of the American system would bring peace, stability, and prosperity, U.S. planners tried to direct all aspects of Brazilian economic development. They advocated private development and exploitation of Brazil's strategic raw materials and petroleum resources, for example. They argued that only U.S. companies had the technical knowledge, expertise, and capital to develop these resources. U.S. officials considered the 1954 creation of the state monopoly, Petrobrás, to develop Brazil's oil reserves a major setback not only for U.S. policy but also for Brazilian development. Nevertheless, private industry and capitalism continued to flourish in Brazil. Major U.S. companies invested heavily in the "new" Brazil, and Brazilian officials continued to embrace western capitalism.

In their development proposals, U.S. officials attempted to avoid the commitment of any major U.S. government funds for Brazilian development. They relied instead on American expertise and technical assistance programs to guide the Brazilians along the right path to development. These officials sincerely believed that U.S. technical assistance alone was sufficient. Only as a last resort did Truman and Eisenhower consider the use of public funds for Brazilian development, and then they demanded that Brazil follow a strict U.S.-directed financial course designed to benefit U.S. corporations and private investors as much as the Brazilian government. This policy often involved major bureaucratic disputes within Washington. State Department officials constantly complained that the IBRD and the Treasury and Commerce departments were interfering in American foreign policy decisions. Despite such bureaucratic bickering, the United States usually denied major government loans to Brazil.

U.S. planners also opposed Brazilian construction of its own processing industries or other economic projects that would allow Brazil to compete directly with American firms. They constantly advocated the export of unfinished raw materials and the development of industries that would not compete with U.S. corporations. What they envisioned, but seldom stated, was a neocolonial relationship, with Brazil furnishing the raw materials for American industry and the United States supplying Brazil with manufactured goods. Only when pressed by the Brazilians or by outside competition did the Americans agree to aid Brazil in developing its industrial and manufacturing potential.

What was needed above all, U.S. policymakers proclaimed, for Brazil to move ahead was Yankee know-how and technical assistance. In 1949, Truman announced his Point Four program designed to help nations such as Brazil to help themselves by providing American technical aid. Eisenhower continued and expanded Truman's initiative. Brazil became a pilot area for testing the modern, scientific methods and theories of U.S. experts concerning development and modernization. The technical assistance programs also came to be used as an effective tool against communism.

Convinced that apolitical technical specialists, engineers, economists, administrators, and managers armed with scientific data and centralized model economic development plans would provide the road map for successful development, U.S. policymakers advocated technical solutions for all of Brazil's problems. The experts swarmed into Brazil. They focused their attention on Brazil's infrastructure and economic bottlenecks. For example, they studied and analyzed Brazil's transportation network in detail and recommended major changes. U.S. officials promoted development of a railway, highway, and coastal shipping system that would, in addition to promoting Brazilian modernization, facilitate the movement of critical resources to the coast for export and aid in the import of U.S.-finished

Both public and private American leaders promoted U.S. goods in the Brazilian market. Both believed sincerely that, given an equal opportunity, U.S. business could compete successfully with anyone. As a precaution, however, embassy officials carefully monitored the activities of foreign competitors in Brazil. At every opportunity they tried to drive not only Soviet and Eastern bloc countries from the Brazilian market but also Western European and Japanese competitors. During the early 1950s they were highly successful: U.S. products dominated the Brazilian market.

In agriculture, U.S. specialists attempted to create a family-oriented, productive, business-minded, and market-sensitive agricultural sector in Brazil. They tried to change long-standing Brazilian farming methods and practices by introducing modern scientific techniques. For example, they heavily promoted mechanization and modern fertilizers. They urged the adoption of not only American farming methods but also rural American values. The major concern of officials in the Truman and Eisenhower administrations, however, was stability and the creation of a strong anti-Communist government in Brazil, not social revolution. Without significant land reform legislation, it was unlikely that U.S. farming suggestions would lead to the creation of a progressive, middle class farming sector in Brazil. Nevertheless, Brazilian agricultural production did increase significantly during the early 1950s.

Culturally, using traditional exchange programs, education, and the mass media, the United States countered Communist propaganda in Brazil with a "campaign of American truth." Increasingly convinced that cultural and informational efforts were an integral part of American foreign policy goals and objectives, U.S. officials actively spread American culture and ideas in Brazil. Adopting a multifaceted program of cultural, educational, and informational persuasion, they tried to "get the Brazilians to think as we do."

Ingrained in this program was a pervasive racial arrogance, a sense of cultural superiority, and a touch of paternalism. For example, U.S. experts attempted to restructure Brazil's entire educational system, to overhaul its educational institutions and practices to reflect American concepts. They stressed practical education and the training of engineers, scientists, technicians, managers, and administrators. They believed that only with a "modern educational system" could Brazil move forward. By adopting the American system of education Brazil would benefit by increasing its much-needed skilled and managerial classes. Such an education system would, the Americans reasoned, also make the Brazilians more amenable to U.S. products and life-style. It would make them "more like us."

In a massive information program, U.S. officials attempted to influence Brazilian newspapers, journals, radio, and television stations in order to get the American message across to the masses. All was to be done, of course, without the United States appearing to influence the Brazilian public in any way.

In their efforts to persuade the Brazilians to follow the lead of the United States in opposing communism and to counter Communist propaganda with "American truth," U.S. planners also tried to displace traditional European influence in Brazil. U.S. culture, values, and ideas were the wave of the future.

As the official U.S. presence in Brazil continued to grow, so too did unofficial U.S. influence. It had profound effects on the social, economic, and political order of Brazil. Automobiles, electric appliances, skyscrapers, asphalt highways, soft drinks, modern department stores, rock music, movies, mass marketing techniques, and American slang invaded Brazil and influenced its development in ways officials from both countries never envisioned.

The Brazilians often depicted themselves as mistreated supplicants who were entitled to more from the colossus of the north. They believed that they were being treated unfairly compared to other, especially European, allies of the United States. At the same time, the Brazilians promoted themselves as equal partners with the United States. They did not want to be thought of as part of the Third World. The Brazilians constantly pressed the Truman and Eisenhower administrations for vast government-to-government development loans. They accepted U.S. advice, but what they really wanted was financial aid to fuel Brazilian development. Internal security and domestic economic development, especially industrialization, were far and away their major concerns, not the U.S. Cold War objectives of Communist containment and the creation of a vast worldwide U.S.-dominated trading system. The Brazilians wanted to make their nation into a capitalist industrial power, and they saw the United States as the only nation with sufficient resources to assist them in their efforts. Thus, although Brazilian leaders often disagreed with their American counterparts on specific issues, they remained solidly in the mainstream of capitalist development theories and solidly supported the United States in the international arena.

In the final analysis, the United States in Brazil during the late 1940s and early 1950s had great power and influence, both formally and informally. Although it is impossible to measure this influence quantitatively, this study shows the intensity of the American effort and illustrates its overall success.

Given the huge disparity of power and influence between Brazil and the United States, the vaunted "special relationship" between the two nations could never really exist. Instead, their relationship was essentially one of Brazilian subordination to the United States. It was a granter-grantee relationship, not a partnership. The plain fact was the U.S. government did not aid Brazilian development simply to help Brazil but to ensure that certain basic U.S. goals and objectives were implemented. Brazilian desires were secondary. Adamant in their beliefs, U.S. officials pushed the Brazilians hard to accept the U.S. position. The Brazilians had little choice about this if they wanted U.S. financing.

Both the Truman and Eisenhower administrations attempted to mold Brazilian development within a pro-U.S., anti-Communist, pro-capitalist framework.[2] Both administrations, however, despite their constant rhetoric of commitment to private capital, private initiative, and private interests, steadily increased the role of the U.S. government in attempting to influence all aspects of Brazilian political, economic, and cultural development. In spite of setbacks, an insensitivity to the rising tide of nationalism, and Cold War blinders, in general U.S. policy with regard to Brazil was a real American success story. Although Brazil followed a mixed development policy, it remained a close ally of the United States and staunchly anti-Communist. It experienced impressive economic growth based solidly on capitalism and emerged as a growing industrial power.[3] Today Brazil has a major stake in the U.S.-led capitalist world trading system.

This is not to say that Brazil simply followed American direction. Its development process was, despite heavy U.S. influence and a tendency to copy the financial and economic practices of the industrial countries, especially the United States, uniquely Brazilian. The import substitution process that occurred in Brazil, making industrialization possible, was not simply a repeat of the U.S. experience or the European industrial revolution. Nevertheless, the Brazilians relied heavily on U.S. advice and borrowed much from its developmental concepts.

By design and by accident, the United States had a major impact on Brazilian development. By the mid-1950s, American policymakers could legitimately claim that, at least in Brazil, their policies were working. Despite differing over their country's development goals, Brazilian leaders in general accepted the basic tenets of U.S. policy concerning anticommunism, private enterprise, private investment, and a capitalist worldwide trading system as part of their overall economic development and modernization plans. Even today Brazil remains solidly in the U.S.-led capitalist system. Although Brazil competes in the world market to sell agricultural products such as soybeans, citrus, poultry, and even high-tech weapons, Brazilian manufacturers have also become strong competitors in the U.S. market with shoes, textiles, and steel, and the United States remains Brazil's largest trading partner. U.S. corporations retain a large share of the Brazilian market, the United States continues to be the major provider of military and economic aid, and Brazil remains closely tied to U.S. financial centers.[4]

Notes

1. On this point see Hilton, "The United States, Brazil, and the Cold War," 69:3, 599–624. See also Rabe, *Eisenhower and Latin America*, p. 24.

2. See Rabe, *Eisenhower and Latin America*, p. 173, for a somewhat different view. Rabe argues that by the time Eisenhower retired from office in January 1961 he had instituted an entirely new U.S. approach to Latin America. Using political, military, economic, and cultural policies, it was designed to build Communist-proof societies in Latin America. Rabe claims that the tactics employed by the Eisenhower administration clearly differed from those used by the Truman government and that there was both continuity and change in Eisenhower/Truman policies toward Latin America. This study clearly shows that the two administrations were far closer to each other in terms of policy goals and objectives than they would have liked to admit and that the change of focus of the Eisenhower administration in the late 1950s had its origins in the Truman administration.

3. Stanley Hilton argues that Washington alienated Brazil during this period and that the Eisenhower administration's neglect of the region's largest and most important nation brought about an eclipse in the "special relationship." As a

result, by the late 1950s the Brazilian leadership began to replace dependence on and cooperation with the United States with a far more independent policy. While Hilton is certainly correct about Brazilian policy in the late 1950s, it is not unusual for an emerging state to seek a more independent position in the international arena. Brazil, nevertheless, remained solidly in the Western camp and committed to a capitalist economy. See Hilton, "The United States, Brazil, and the Cold War," pp. 599–624.

4. See Asencio, "Brazil and the United States, Friendly Competitors"; and Andre G. Frank, *Capitalism and Underdevelopment in Latin America: Historical Studies of Chile and Brazil* (New York: Monthly Review Press, 1967), pp. 213–18. See also Rabe, *Eisenhower and Latin America*, pp. 175–76. Rabe argues that, by the 1960s, officials in the Eisenhower administration saw their Latin American policy as unsuccessful.

Bibliography

Manuscript Collections

Dwight D. Eisenhower Presidential Library, Abilene, Kansas
    Dwight D. Eisenhower Diaries
    White House Central Files
    Ann Whitman File
    Papers of
        John Foster Dulles
        Milton S. Eisenhower
        Clarence B. Randall
Harry S. Truman Presidential Library, Independence, Missouri
    White House Central Files
    Papers of
        Dean Acheson
        Stanley Andrews
        Mervin Bohan
        Clark Clifford
        George Elsey
        Inter-American Economic and Social Council
        Herschel Johnson
        Edward G. Miller
        Presidential Committee on Foreign Aid
        Sidney Souers

Government Documents

Export-Import Bank of Washington. *Sixteenth Semiannual Report to Congress for the Period January–June 1953*. Washington, DC: Government Printing Office, 1953.

Institute of Inter-American Affairs. *Brazilian Technical Report Prepared for the Joint Brazil-United States Economic Development Commission Studies*. Washington, DC: Government Printing Office, 1955.

International Bank for Reconstruction and Development. *Eighth Annual Report to the Board of Governors, 1952–1953*. Washington, DC: Government Printing Office, 1953.

Joint Brazil-United States Economic Development Commission. *The Development of Brazil*. Washington, DC: Government Printing Office, 1954.

National Archives, Washington, DC

    Record Group 16. Records of the Office of the Secretary of Agriculture.

    Record Group 40. General Records of the Department of Commerce.

    Record Group 43. Records of International Conferences, Commissions, and Expositions.

        Records of the U.S. Section of the Joint Brazil-U.S. Technical Commission 1947–1949. Lot File 52-145.

    Record Group 56. General Records of the Department of the Treasury.

    Record Group 59. General Records of the Department of State.

        Central Decimal File, 1945–1954.

        Records of the Division of Research for the American Republics, Intelligence and Research Reports.

        Records of the Division of American Republics.

        Records of the Officer in Charge of Brazilian Affairs (Sterling J. Cottrell) 1953–1955. Lot File 58D-42.

        Records of the Assistant Secretary of State for Inter-American Affairs (Henry F. Holland) 1953–1956. Lot File 57D-295.

        Records of the Assistant Secretary of State for Inter-American Affairs (John M. Cabot) 1953–54. Lot File 55D-13.

        Records of the Assistant Secretary of State for Inter-American Affairs (Edward G. Miller) 1949–1953. Lot File 53D-26.

    Record Group 84. Records of the Foreign Service Posts of the Department of State.

    Record Group 151. Records of the Bureau of Foreign and Domestic Commerce, Office of International Trade.

    Record Group 165. Records of the War Department General and Special Staffs.

    Record Group 197. Records of the Civil Aeronautics Board.

    Record Group 218. Records of the United States Joint Chiefs of Staff.

Record Group 262. Records of the Foreign Broadcast Intelligence
Service.
Record Group 273. Records of the National Security Council.
Record Group 275. Records of the Export-Import Bank of Washington.
Record Group 306. Records of the U.S. Information Agency.
Record Group 330. Records of the Office of the Secretary of Defense.
Record Group 333. Records of the International Military Agencies,
Records of the U.S. Section, Joint Brazil-United States Military
Commission, Rio de Janeiro, Brazil, 1943–1947.
Record Group 353. Records of Interdepartmental and Intradepartmental
Committees (Department of State).
Randall Commission. *Report to the President and Congress*. Washington,
DC: Government Printing Office, 1954.
Truman, Harry S. *Public Papers of Harry S. Truman*. Washington, DC:
Government Printing Office, 1963.
U.S. Congress. House Foreign Affairs Committee. *Hearings on Inter-
American Military Cooperation Act, 1947*. 80th Cong., 1st sess.
Washington, DC: Government Printing Office, 1947.
———. House. *Hearings on HR 3342, U.S. Information and Educational
Exchange Act of 1947*. 80th Cong., 1st sess. Washington, DC:
Government Printing Office, 1947.
———. Senate Committee on Foreign Relations. *Hearings on Senate
Resolution 243, Expanded International Information and Education
Program*. 81st Cong., 2d sess. Washington, DC: Government Printing
Office, 1950.
———. Senate Committee on Foreign Relations. *Multinational
Corporations in Brazil and Mexico: Structural Sources of Economic
and Non-Economic Power*. 94th Cong., 1st sess. Washington, DC:
Government Printing Office, 1975.
———. Senate Committee on Foreign Relations. *Report of the Secretary
of State to the Committee*. 83d Cong., 1st sess. Washington, DC:
Government Printing Office, 1953.
———. Senate Committee on Foreign Relations. U.S.-Latin American
Study No. 4, "U.S. Business and Labor in Latin America," January 22,
1960. Senate Document 1656. 86th Cong., 2d sess. Washington, DC:
Government Printing Office, 1960.
U.S. Department of Commerce. *United States Investments in the Latin
American Economy*. Washington, DC: Government Printing Office,
1957.
U.S. Department of State. *Foreign Relations of the United States 1942*.
Vol. 5. *The American Republics*. Washington, DC: Government
Printing Office, 1962.
———. *Foreign Relations of the United States 1943*. Vol. 5. *The
American Republics*. 1965.

————. *Foreign Relations of the United States 1944.* Vol. 7. *The American Republics.* 1967.

————. *Foreign Relations of the United States 1945.* Vol. 9. *The American Republics.* 1969.

————. *Foreign Relations of the United States 1946.* Vol. 1. *General: The United Nations.* 1972.

————. *Foreign Relations of the United States 1946.* Vol. 11. *The American Republics.* 1972.

————. *Foreign Relations of the United States 1947.* Vol. 1. *General: The United Nations.* 1973.

————. *Foreign Relations of the United States 1947.* Vol. 8. *The American Republics.* 1972.

————. *Foreign Relations of the United States 1948.* Vol. 9. *The Western Hemisphere.* 1972.

————. *Foreign Relations of the United States 1949.* Vol. 2. *The United Nations: The Western Hemisphere.* 1975.

————. *Foreign Relations of the United States 1950.* Vol. 1. *National Security Affairs: Foreign Economic Policy.* 1977.

————. *Foreign Relations of the United States 1950.* Vol. 2. *The United Nations: The Western Hemisphere.* 1976.

————. *Foreign Relations of the United States 1951.* Vol. 1. *National Security Affairs: Foreign Economic Policy.* 1979.

————. *Foreign Relations of the United States 1951.* Vol. 2. *The United Nations: The Western Hemisphere.* 1979.

————. *Foreign Relations of the United States 1952–1954.* Vol. 2, Parts 1 and 2. *National Security Affairs.* 1984.

————. *Foreign Relations of the United States 1952–1954.* Vol. 4. *The American Republics.* 1983.

————. *Inter-American Conference on Problems of War and Peace February 23–March 3, 1945 Final Act of Chapultepec.* Washington, DC: Government Printing Office, 1945.

————. Office of Intelligence and Research. *Communist Offenses against the Integrity of Education, Sciences, and Culture.* Washington, DC: Government Printing Office, 1951.

————. *Private Enterprise in the Development of the Americas.* Inter-American Series No. 32. Washington, DC: Government Printing Office, 1956.

————. *Report of the Joint Brazil-United States Technical Commission.* Publication 3487. Washington, DC: Government Printing Office, 1949.

————. *Report of the U.S. Delegation to the Tenth Inter-American Conference, Caracas, Venezuela, March 26 thru March 30, 1954.* Washington, DC: Government Printing Office, 1954.

————. *Technical Cooperation: The Dramatic Story of Helping Others to Help Themselves.* Washington, DC: Government Printing Office, 1959.

————. *Your Child from One to Six.* Washington, DC: Government Printing Office, 1950.

U.S. Treaties and Other International Agreements, 1951. Vol. 2, pt. 2. Washington, DC: Government Printing Office, 1952.

U.S. Treaties and Other International Agreements, 1953. Vol. 4, pt. 1. Washington, DC: Government Printing Office, 1955.

U.S. Treaties and Other International Agreements, 1953. Vol. 9. Washington, DC: Government Printing Office, 1957.

U.S. Treaties and Other International Agreements, 1955. Vol. 6, pt. 3. Washington, DC: Government Printing Office, 1956.

Unpublished Documents

Barros, Alexandre de. "The Brazilian Military: Professional Socialization, Political Performance, and State Building." Ph.D. diss., University of Chicago, 1978.

Cardoso-Silva, Vera Alice. "Foreign Policy and National Development: The Brazilian Experiment under Vargas, 1951–1954." Ph.D. diss., University of Illinois, 1984.

Carvalho, José Murilo de. "Armed Forces and Politics in Brazil, 1930–1945." Paper presented at July 14, 1981, colloquium on Latin America by the Woodrow Wilson International Center for Scholars, Washington, DC.

Daugherty, Charles H. "Foreign Policy Decision Making in Brazil: Case Studies in Brazilian Policy towards the Soviet Union, 1945–1961." 2 vols. Ph.D. diss., Georgetown University, 1974.

Ekerman, Raul Jose. "Industrial Growth Unemployment and the Inflationary Process in Brazil during 1950–1966." Ph.D. diss., Cornell University, 1970.

Lanoue, Kenneth Callis. "An Alliance Shaken: Brazil and the United States, 1945–1950." Ph.D. diss., Louisiana State University, 1978.

Pancake, Frank. "Military Assistance as an Element of U.S. Foreign Policy in Latin America, 1950–1968." Ph.D. diss., University of Virginia, 1969.

Sa Almeida, Jorge. "The Political Influence of the Brazilian Middle Class, 1930–1964." M.A. thesis, Georgetown University, 1965.

Smith, Gordon W. "Agricultural Marketing and Economic Development: A Brazilian Case Study." Ph.D. diss., Harvard University, 1965.

Stephan, Alfred. "Patterns of Civil-Military Relations: The Brazilian Political System." Ph.D. diss., Columbia University, 1968.

Books

Alexander, Robert J. *Communism in Latin America*. New Brunswick, NJ: Rutgers University Press, 1957.
————. *The Perón Era*. New York: Columbia University Press, 1951.
Alfono, Juan Pablo Pérez. *Petróleo y dependencia* (Petroleum and dependency). Caracas: Síntesis Dos Mil, 1971.
Alves, Maria Helena Moreira. *The State and Opposition in Military Brazil*. Austin: University of Texas Press, 1985.
Ambrose, Stephen E. *Eisenhower: The President*. Vol. II. New York: Simon and Schuster, 1984.
————. *Rise to Globalism: American Foreign Policy, 1938–1980*. Baltimore: Penguin, 1980.
Andrade, Manuel Correia de Oliveira. *História econômica e administrativa do Brasil* (Economic and administrative history of Brazil). São Paulo: Editôra Atlas, 1976.
Appleton, Sheldon. *Eternal Triangle? Communist China, the United States and the United Nations*. East Lansing: Michigan State University Press, 1961.
Avila, Fernando Bostos de. *Economic Impact of Immigration: The Brazilian Immigration Problem*. The Hague: M. Nijhoff, 1956.
Baer, Werner. *The Brazilian Economy: Growth and Development*. 2d ed. New York: Praeger, 1983.
————. *Industrialization and Economic Development in Brazil*. Homewood, IL: Richard D. Irwin, 1965.
Baily, Samuel L. *Labor, Nationalism, and Politics in Argentina*. New Brunswick, NJ: Rutgers University Press, 1967.
————. *The United States and the Development of South America, 1945–1975*. New York: New Viewpoints, 1976.
Baklanoff, Eric N., ed. *New Perspectives of Brazil*. Nashville: Vanderbilt University Press, 1966.
————, ed. *The Shaping of Modern Brazil*. Baton Rouge: Louisiana State University Press, 1969.
Barber, Willard F., and Ronning C. Neale. *Internal Security and Military Power: Counterinsurgency and Civic Action in Latin America*. Columbus: Ohio State University Press, 1966.
Barraclough, Geoffrey. *Introduction to Contemporary History*. Baltimore: Penguin, 1968.
Barrett, Edward. *Truth Is Our Weapon*. New York: Funk and Wagnalls, 1953.
Bello, José Maria. *A History of Modern Brazil, 1888–1964*. Translated by James L. Taylor. Stanford: Stanford University Press, 1966.
Beloch, Israel, and Alzira Alves de Abreu, eds. *Dicionário Histórico-Biográfico Brasileiro, 1930–1983* (Brazilian historical-biographical

dictionary, 1930–1983). 4 vols. Rio de Janeiro: Fundacão Getúlio Vargas, 1984.

Benevides, Maria Victoria de Masquita. *O Governo Kubitschek, Desenvolvimento econômico e establilidade politica* (The Kubitschek government: Economic development and political stability). Rio de Janeiro: Defel, 1976.

Berle, Beatrice Bishop, and Travis Beal Jacobs, eds. *Navigating the Rapids, 1918–1971.* New York: Harcourt Brace Jovanovich, 1973.

Bermúdez, Antonio J. *La Política Petrolera Mexicana* (The politics of Mexican oil). Mexico City: D. F. Editoral J. Mortig, 1976.

————. *The Mexican Petroleum Industry: A Case Study in Nationalism.* Stanford: Institute of Hispanic American and Luso-Brazilian Studies, 1963.

Bernstein, Barton J., ed. *Politics and Policies of the Truman Administration.* Chicago: Quadrangle Press, 1970.

Betancourt, Rómulo. *Venezuela: Oil and Politics.* Translated by Everett Bauman. Boston: Houghton Mifflin, 1979.

Bingham, Jonathan B. *Shirt-Sleeve Diplomacy.* New York: Ayer Co., 1954.

Black, Jan Knippers. *United States Penetration of Brazil.* Philadelphia: University of Pennsylvania Press, 1977.

Blasier, Cole. *The Giant's Rival: The USSR and Latin America.* Pittsburgh: University of Pittsburgh Press, 1983.

Bogart, Leo. *The Age of Television: A Study of Viewing Habits and the Impact of Television on American Life.* New York: F. Ungar, 1972.

————. *Premises for Propaganda.* New York: Free Press, 1976.

Bourne, Richard. *Getúlio Vargas of Brazil, 1883–1954.* London: Charles Knight, 1974.

Brandi, Paulo. *Vargas, da vida para a história* (Vargas, his life in history). Rio de Janeiro: Zahar Editôres, 1985.

Bresser Pereira, Luiz Carlos. *Development and Crisis in Brazil, 1930–1982.* Boulder, CO: Westview Press, 1984.

Brown, William A., Jr. *American Foreign Assistance.* Washington, DC: Brookings Institution, 1953.

Burns, E. Bradford. *A History of Brazil.* 2d ed. New York: Columbia University Press, 1980.

————. *Nationalism in Brazil: A Historical Survey.* New York: Praeger, 1968.

Café Filho, João. *Do sindicato ao catete: Memórias politícas e confissões humanas* (From the labor movement to Catete Palace: Political memories and human confessions). Rio de Janeiro, Livraria José Olympia Editôra, S/A, 1966.

Camacho, Jorge A. *Brazil: An Interim Assessment.* Westport, CT: Greenwood, 1972.

Campbell, Gordon. *Brazil Struggles for Development.* London: Charles Knight and Company, 1972.

Cáo, José. *Dutra.* São Paulo: Instituto Progresso Editorial, S/A, 1949.

Carone, Edgard. *O Estado Novo, 1937–1945.* Rio de Janeiro: Defel, 1976.

Carvalho, Afonso de Raul. *Fernandes: Um Servidor do Brasil* (Fernandes: A servant of Brazil). Rio de Janeiro: Livraria Editôra Coelho Branco, 1956.

Carvalho, Fernando de. *O Communismo no Brasil.* Rio de Janeiro: Biblioteca do Exército, 1966–67.

Castro, José Viriato de. *Liber Petri Espada x vassoura: Marechal Lott* (Liberating the country, the sword against the broom: Marshal Lott). São Paulo: Distribuidores, Palácio do Livro, 1959.

Chacel, Julian M., et al., eds. *Brazil's Economic and Political Future.* Boulder, CO: Westview Press, 1988.

Chilcote, Ronald H. *The Brazilian Communist Party: Conflict and Integration, 1922–1972.* New York: Oxford University Press, 1974.

Clissold, Stephen. *Soviet Relations with Latin America, 1918–1968, A Documentary Survey.* London: Oxford University Press, 1970.

Coes, Donald V. *The Impact of Price Uncertainty: A Study of Brazilian Exchange Rate Policy.* New York: Garland Publishing, 1979.

Conn, Stetson, Rose C. Engleman, and Byron Fairchild. *Guarding the United States and Its Outposts: The United States Army in World War II.* Washington, DC: Government Printing Office, 1964.

―――. *The Western Hemisphere: The United States Army in World War II.* Washington, DC: Government Printing Office, 1965.

Connell-Smith, Gordon. *The United States and Latin America.* New York: John Wiley, 1974.

Cooke, Morris Llewellyn. *Brazil on the March, A Study in International Cooperation: Reflections on the Report of the American Technical Mission to Brazil.* New York: Whittlesey House, 1944.

Coutinho, Lourival. *O General Góes depõe* (General Góes speaks). 2d ed. Rio de Janeiro: Livraria Editôra Coelho Branco, 1956.

Daland, Robert T. *Brazilian Planning: Development, Politics and Administration.* Chapel Hill: University of North Carolina Press, 1967.

D'Araujo, Maria Celina Soares. *O Segundo Governo Vargas, 1951–1954 Democracia, Partidos e Crise Política* (The second Vargas government, 1951–1954, democracy, parties, and political crises). Rio de Janeiro: Zahar Editôres, 1982.

Davis, Shelton H. *Victims of the Miracle: Development and the Indians of Brazil.* Cambridge: Cambridge University Press, 1977.

Divine, Robert A. *Eisenhower and the Cold War.* New York: Oxford University Press, 1981.

Dizard, Wilson P. *The Strategy of Truth: The Story of the United States Information Service.* Washington, DC: Public Affairs Press, 1961.

Doyle, Michael. *Empires.* Ithaca: Cornell University Press, 1986.

Dulles, John W. *Unrest in Brazil: Political Military Crises, 1955–1964.* Austin: University of Texas Press, 1970.

————. *Vargas of Brazil: A Political Biography.* Austin: University of Texas Press, 1967.

Dutra, Eurico Gaspar. *O govêrno Dutra: Algumas realizacões, diretrizes doutrinárias um período de paz* (The Dutra government: Some lessons learned, leadership principles in a period of peace). Rio de Janeiro: Editôra Civilizacão Brasileira, 1956.

Eckes, Alfred E., Jr. *The United States and the Global Struggle for Minerals.* Austin: University of Texas Press, 1979.

Einaudi, Luigi R., and Alfred C. Stepan. *Latin American Institutional Development: Changing Military Perspectives in Peru and Brazil.* California: RAND Corporation, 1974.

Eisenhower, Milton. *The Wine Is Bitter: The United States and Latin America.* New York: Doubleday, 1963.

————. *U.S.-Latin American Relations, Report to the President.* Department of State Publication 5290. Washington, DC: Government Printing Office, 1953.

Elder, Robert E. *Information Machine: The United States Information Agency and American Foreign Policy.* Syracuse, NY: Syracuse University Press, 1968.

Espinosa, Manuel J. *Inter-American Beginnings of U.S. Cultural Diplomacy 1936–1948.* Department of State Publication 8854, International Information and Cultural Series 110. Washington, DC: Government Printing Office, 1976.

Esquenazi-Mayo, Roberto, and Michael C. Meyer, eds. *Latin American Scholarship since World War II: Trends in History, Political Science, Literature, Geography, and Economics.* Lincoln: University of Nebraska Press, 1976.

Ferreira, Heitor. *História Político-Econômica e Industricial do Brasil* (A political-economic and industrial history of Brazil). São Paulo: Companhia Editôra Nacional, 1970.

Ferrell, Robert H., ed. *The Eisenhower Diaries.* New York: W. W. Norton, 1981.

Feuer, Lewis Samuel. *Imperialism and the Anti-Imperialist Mind.* New York: Prometheus Books, 1986.

Figueiredo, Osmar Salles de. *Brasil, Passado e Presente* (Brazil, past and present). São Paulo: Editôra Pedagógica e Universitária, 1979.

Fitzgibbon, Russell H., ed. *Brazil: A Chronology and Fact Book.* New York: Oceana Publications, 1974.

Flynn, Peter. *Brazil: A Political Analysis*. Boulder, CO: Westview Press, 1979.

Franco, Afonso Arinos de Melo. *A escalada: Memórias* (Memoirs: The ladder). Rio de Janeiro: Livraria José Olympia Editôra, 1965.

———. *Planalto: Memórias* (Memoirs: The uplands). Rio de Janeiro: Livraria José Olympia Editôra, 1968.

Frank, Andre G. *Capitalism and Underdevelopment in Latin America: Historical Studies of Chile and Brazil*. New York: Monthly Review Press, 1967.

Furtado, Celso. *Análise do "modelo" brasileiro* (Analysis of the Brazilian model). 4th ed. Rio de Janeiro: Companhia Editora Nacional, 1973.

———. *A economià brasileiro* (The Brazilian economy). Rio de Janeiro: Editôra A Noite, 1954.

———. *The Economic Growth of Brazil: A Survey from Colonial to Modern Times*. Translated by Ricardo W. de Aguiar and Eric Charles Drysdale. Berkeley: University of California Press, 1963.

———. *A hegemónia dos Estados Unidos e o subdesenvolvimento da America Latina* (The hegemony of the United States and the underdevelopment of Latin America). Rio de Janeiro: Editôra Civilizacão Brasileira, 1973.

———. *Obstacles to Development in Latin America*. Translated by Charles Ekker. Garden City: Anchor Books, 1970.

Gaddis, John Lewis. *Strategies of Containment: A Critical Appraisal of Postwar American National Security Policy*. New York: Oxford University Press, 1982.

Gardner, Richard N. *Sterling-Dollar Diplomacy in Current Perspective: The Origins and Prospects of Our International Economic Order*. Rev. ed. New York: McGraw-Hill, 1969.

Gastaldi, J. Petrelli. *A Economia Brasileira e Os Problemas do Desenvolvimento* (The Brazilian economy and problems of development). São Paulo: Edicão Saraiva, 1968.

Goldhamer, Herbert. *The Foreign Powers in Latin America*. Princeton: Princeton University Press, 1972.

Gordon, Lincoln, and Engelbert L. Grammers. *United States Manufacturing Investment in Brazil: The Impact of Brazilian Government Policies, 1946–1960*. Boston: Harvard University Press, 1962.

Green, David. *The Containment of Latin America: A History of the Myths and Realities of the Good Neighbor Policy*. Chicago: Quadrangle Press, 1971.

Greene, Dorothy. *Cultural Centers in the Other American Republics*. Department of State Publication 2503. Washington, DC: Government Printing Office, 1946.

Grunwald, Joseph, and Philip Musgrove. *Natural Resources in Latin American Development.* Baltimore: Johns Hopkins University Press, 1970.

Gunther, John. *Inside Latin America.* New York: Harper, 1947.

Haines, Gerald K., and J. Samuel Walker, eds. *American Foreign Relations: A Historiographical Review.* Westport, CT: Greenwood Press, 1981.

Halle, Louis. *Cold War as History.* New York: Harper and Row, 1967.

Harmon, Ronald M., and Bobby J. Chamberlain. *Brazil: A Working Bibliography in Literature, Linguistics, Humanities, and the Social Sciences.* Tempe: Arizona State University Press, 1975.

Havighurst, Robert J., and J. Roberto Moreira. *Society and Education in Brazil.* Pittsburgh: University of Pittsburgh Press, 1965.

Headrick, Daniel R. *The Tentacles of Progress: Technology Transfer in the Age of Imperialism, 1850–1940.* New York: Oxford University Press, 1988.

Heald, Morrell, and Lawrence S. Kaplan. *Culture and Diplomacy: The American Experience.* Westport, CT: Greenwood Press, 1977.

Henriques, Affonso. *Ascensão e Queda de Getúlio Vargas* (The rise and fall of Getúlio Vargas). 3 vols. Rio de Janeiro: Distribuidora Record, 1966.

Herring, Hubert. *A History of Latin America from the Beginnings to the Present.* New York: Alfred A. Knopf, 1963.

Hewlett, Sylvia Ann. *Cruel Dilemmas of Development: Twentieth-Century Brazil.* New York: Basic Books, 1980.

Hilton, Ronald, ed. *Who's Who in Latin America: A Bibliographical Dictionary of Latin American Notable Men and Women of Latin America.* 3d ed., 7 vols. Stanford: Stanford University Press, 1945–1951.

Hilton, Stanley E. *Brazil and the Great Powers, 1930–1939: The Politics of Trade Rivalry.* Austin: University of Texas Press, 1975.

Hirschman, Albert O. *Journeys toward Progress: Studies of Economic Policy-Making in Latin America.* New York: Twentieth Century Fund, 1963.

Houston, John A. *Latin America in the United Nations.* New York: Carnegie Endowment for International Peace, 1956.

Hovey, Harold. *United States Military Assistance: A Study of Policies and Practices.* New York: Praeger, 1965.

Huntington, Samuel P. *The Soldier and the State: The Theory and Politics of Civil-Military Relations.* Cambridge, MA: Harvard University Press, 1957.

Ianni, Octávio. *Crisis in Brazil.* Translated by Phyllis R. Eveleth. New York: Columbia University Press, 1970.

Immerman, Richard H. *The CIA in Guatemala: The Foreign Policy of Intervention.* Austin: University of Texas Press, 1983.

Jaguaribe, Hélio. *Economic and Political Development: A Theoretical Approach and a Brazilian Case Study.* Cambridge, MA: Harvard University Press, 1968.

James, Preston. *Brazil.* New York: Odyssey Press, 1946.

————. *Latin America.* New York: Odyssey Press, 1959.

Kahil, Raouf. *Inflation and Economic Development in Brazil, 1946–1963.* Oxford: Clarendon Press, 1973.

Kaplan, Stephen S. *U.S. Military Aid to Brazil and the Dominican Republic: Its Nature, Objectives, and Impact.* Department of State Foreign Affairs Research Series 16217. Washington, DC: Government Printing Office, 1972.

Kaufman, Burton I. *Trade and Aid: Eisenhower's Foreign Economic Policy, 1953–1961.* Baltimore: Johns Hopkins University Press, 1982.

Kennan, George F. *Memoirs: 1925–1950.* Boston: Little, Brown and Co., 1967.

Kolko, Gabriel. *The Roots of American Foreign Policy: An Analysis of Power and Purpose.* Boston: Beacon, 1969.

Kuznets, Simon, Wilbert E. Moore, and Joseph J. Spengler, eds. *Economic Growth: Brazil, India, Japan.* Durham, NC: Duke University Press, 1955.

LaFeber, Walter. *America, Russia, and the Cold War, 1945–1975.* New York: Wiley, 1967.

Lafer, Celso, and Felia Pena. *Argentina y Brasil en el sistema de relaciones internacionales* (Argentina and Brazil in the system of international relations). Buenos Aires: Ediciones Nueva Vision, 1973.

Leff, Nathaniel H. *Economic Policy Making and Development in Brazil, 1947–1964.* New York: Wiley, 1968.

————. *Underdevelopment and Development in Brazil.* 2 vols. Boston: Allen and Unwin, 1982.

Leite, Mauro Renault and Novelli Junior. *Morechae Eurico Gaspar Dutra, O deves da verdade* (Morechae Eurico Gaspar Dutra, the duties of truth). Rio de Janeiro: Nova Fronteira, S/A, 1983.

Levine, Robert M. *The Vargas Regime.* New York: Columbia University Press, 1970.

Lieuwen, Edwin. *Arms and Politics in Latin America.* 2d ed. New York: Praeger, 1963.

Lieuwen, Edwin, and Miguel Jarrin. *Post-World War II Political Development in Latin America.* Study prepared at the request of the Subcommittee on American Republic Affairs of the Senate Foreign Relations Committee. November 19, 1959. Washington, DC: Government Printing Office, 1959.

Lima, Heitor Ferreira. *História político-econômica e industrial do Brasil* (A political-economic and industrial history of Brazil). 2d ed. São Paulo: Companhia Editôra Nacional, 1976.

Linz, Juan, and Alfred Stephan, eds. *The Breakdown of Democratic Regimes*. 4 vols. Baltimore: Johns Hopkins University Press, 1978.

Loeb, Gustaaf Frits. *Industrialization and Balanced Growth with Special Reference to Brazil*. Gronengen: J. B. Wolters, 1957.

Loewenstein, Karl. *Brazil under Vargas*. New York: Russell and Russell, 1973.

Lopes, Theodórico. *Minístros da guerra do Brasil, 1808–1950* (Brazilian ministers of war, 1808–1950). 4th ed. Rio de Janeiro: Editôra Civilizacão Brasileiro, 1957.

McCann, Frank D., Jr. *The Brazilian-American Alliance, 1937–1945*. Princeton: Princeton University Press, 1973.

Magalhães, Raymundo. *Getúlio*. São Paulo: Edicoes Mehocamentos, 1976.

Mainwaring, Scott. *The Catholic Church and Politics in Brazil, 1916–1985*. Stanford: Stanford University Press, 1986.

Martinez, José F. *Economic Developments in Brazil, 1949–1950*. Washington, DC: Pan American Union, 1950.

Martz, John D., ed. *The Dynamics of Change in Latin America*. Englewood Cliffs, NJ: Prentice-Hall, 1965.

Merrick, Thomas W., and Douglas H. Graham. *Population and Economic Development in Brazil: 1800 to the Present*. Baltimore: Johns Hopkins University Press, 1979.

Meyer, Michael C., ed. *Supplement to a Bibliography of United States-Latin American Relations since 1810*. Lincoln: University of Nebraska Press, 1979.

Moran, Emilio F., ed. *The Dilemma of Amazonian Development*. Boulder, CO: Westview Press, 1982.

Mourão, Milciades. *Dutra, História de um Govêrno* (Dutra, history of a government). Rio de Janeiro: Editôra Civilizacão Brasileira, 1955.

Ninkovich, Frank A. *The Diplomacy of Ideas: United States Foreign Policy and Cultural Relations, 1938–1950*. New York: Cambridge University Press, 1981.

Oliver, Robert W. *International Economic Cooperation and the World Bank*. London: Holmes and Meier, 1975.

Oliveria, Jose Teixeira. *O governo Dutra* (The Dutra government). Rio de Janeiro: Editôra Civilizacão Brasileira, 1956.

Owen, Roger, and Robert Sutcliffe, eds. *Studies in the Theory of Imperialism*. London: Longman, 1977.

Pan American Union. *The Constitution of the United States of Brazil, 1946*. As amended. Washington, DC: Pan American Union, 1963.

Petrelli-Gastaldi, J. *A Economia Brasileira e Os Problemas do Desenvolvimento* (The Brazilian economy and the problems of development). São Paulo: Edicão Saraíva, 1968.

Pinelo, Adalberto J. *The Multinational Corporation as a Force in Latin American Politics: A Case Study of the International Petroleum Company in Peru.* New York: Praeger, 1973.

Pinto, Rogerio. *The Political Ecology of the Brazilian National Bank for Development (BNDE).* Washington, DC: Organization of American States, 1969.

Potash, Robert A. *The Army and Politics in Argentina 1928–1945: Yrigoyen to Peron.* Stanford: Stanford University Press, 1969.

Prado, Caio. *História econômica do Brasil* (The economic history of Brazil). 12th ed. São Paulo: Editôra Brasiliense, 1970.

Price, Harry B. *The Marshall Plan and Its Meaning.* New York: Cornell University Press, 1955.

Rabe, Stephen G. *Eisenhower and Latin America: The Foreign Policy of Anticommunism.* Chapel Hill: University of North Carolina Press, 1988.

———. *The Road to OPEC: United States Relations with Venezuela, 1919–1976.* Austin: University of Texas Press, 1982.

Randall, Clarence R. *A Foreign Economic Policy for the United States.* Chicago: University of Chicago Press, 1954.

Roett, Riordan. *Brazil: Politics in a Patrimonial Society.* Boston: Allyn and Baca, 1972.

Rosenberg, Emily. *Spreading the American Dream: American Economic and Cultural Expansion 1890–1945.* New York: Hill and Wang, 1982.

Rostow, Walt W. *The United States in the World Arena: An Essay in Recent History.* New York: Harper, 1960.

Rowland, Donald W. *History of the Office of the Coordinator of Inter-American Affairs.* Washington, DC: Government Printing Office, 1947.

Schnabel, James F. *The History of the Joint Chiefs of Staff: The Joint Chiefs of Staff and National Policy.* Washington, DC: Government Printing Office, 1982.

Schuh, G. Edward. *The Agricultural Development of Brazil.* New York: Praeger, 1970.

Schwartzman, Simon. *Science and Higher Education in Brazil: An Historical View.* Washington, DC: Woodrow Wilson International Center for Scholars, 1979.

Selcher, Wayne A., ed. *Brazil in the International System: The Rise of a Middle Power.* Boulder, CO: Westview Press, 1981.

Shalom, Stephen R. *The United States and the Philippines: A Study of Neocolonialism.* Philadelphia: Institute for the Study of Human Issues, 1981.

Siegel, Gilbert B. *The Vicissitudes of Governmental Reform in Brazil: A Study of the Departmento Administrativo Do Servico Público (DASP).* Washington, DC: University Press of America, 1978.

Silva, Hélio. *O Ciclo de Vargas* (The Vargas cycle). Rio de Janeiro: Editôra Civilizacão Brasileira, 1964.

Silva, Hélio, and Maria Cecília Ribass Carneiro. *Café Filho, A Crise Institucional, 1954–1955* (Café Filho and the institutional crisis, 1954–1955). São Paulo: Grupo de Communicacão Tres, 1983.

————. *Eurico Gaspar Dutra: A Espada Sob a Lei, 1946–1951* (Eurico Gaspar Dutra: The sword under the law, 1946–1951). São Paulo: Grupo de Communicacão Tres, 1983.

Silvert, Kalman H. *The Conflict Society: Reaction and Revolution in Latin America.* New York: American Universities Field Staff, 1966.

————, ed. *Expectant Peoples: Nationalism and Development.* New York: Random House, 1966.

Skidmore, Thomas E. *Black into White, Race and Nationality in Brazilian Thought.* New York: Oxford University Press, 1974.

————. *Politics in Brazil, 1930–1964: An Experiment in Democracy.* New York: Oxford University Press, 1967.

Smith, Peter S. *Oil and Politics in Modern Brazil.* Toronto: Macmillan of Canada, 1976.

————. *Politics and Beef in Argentina: Patterns of Conflict and Change.* New York: Columbia University Press, 1969.

Soares, Orlando. *Desenvolvimento econômico-social do Brasil e Eua* (Socioeconomic development of Brazil and the United States). São Paulo: Colecâo Nôvos Tempes, 1976.

Sodré, Nelson Werneck. *História Militar do Brasil* (A military history of Brazil). Rio de Janeiro: Editôra Civilizacão Brasileiro, 1965.

Souza, Herbert de. *The World Capitalist System and Militarism in Latin America: A Comparative Analysis of the Brazilian and Peruvian Models.* Translated by Barbara Shepard. Toronto: University of Toronto Press, 1974.

Stephan, Alfred. *The Military in Politics: Changing Patterns in Brazil.* Princeton: Princeton University Press, 1971.

Stephens, Oren. *Facts to a Candid World: America's Overseas Information Program.* Stanford: Stanford University Press, 1955.

Stoessinger, John G. *The Might of Nations: World Politics in Our Times.* Rev. ed. New York: Random House, 1965.

Swanberg, W. A. *Luce and His Empire.* New York: Charles Scribner and Sons, 1972.

Távora, Juarez. *O Petróleo do Brasil* (The oil of Brazil). São Paulo: Editôra Fulgor, 1947.

Tendler, Judith. *Electric Power in Brazil: Entrepreneurship in the Public Sector.* Cambridge, MA: Harvard University Press, 1968.

————. *Inside Foreign Aid.* Baltimore: Johns Hopkins University Press, 1977.

————. *Rural Projects through Urban Eyes: An Interpretation of the World Bank's New-Style Rural Development Projects.* Washington, DC: World Bank, 1982.

Thompson, Charles A., and Walter H. C. Laves. *Cultural Relations and U.S. Foreign Policy.* Bloomington: Indiana University Press, 1971.

Tourenho, Eduardo. *Breve história da formacão econômica do Brasil* (A brief history of the developing economy of Brazil). Rio de Janeiro: Iramos Pongetti, 1962.

Trask, David F., Michael C. Meyer, and Roger R. Trask, eds. *A Bibliography of United States-Latin American Relations since 1810: A Selected List of Eleven Thousand Published References.* Lincoln: University of Nebraska Press, 1968.

Truman, Harry S. *Memoirs.* 2 vols. Garden City, NJ: Doubleday, 1955–56.

Tugwell, Franklin. *The Politics of Oil in Venezuela.* Stanford: Stanford University Press, 1975.

Tunstall, Jeremy. *The Media Are American.* New York: Columbia University Press, 1977.

Vargas, Getúlio. *A nova política do Brasil* (The new politics of Brazil). 11 vols. Rio de Janeiro: José Olympio, 1938–1947.

————. *A politica nacionalista do petróleo no Brasil* (The national politics of oil in Brazil). Rio de Janeiro: Tempo Brasileiro, 1964.

Vergara, Luiz. *Fui secretário de Getúlio Vargas: Memórias dos anos de 1926–1956* (I was the secretary to Getúlio Vargas: Memoirs of the years 1926–1956). Rio de Janeiro: Editôra Globo, 1960.

Wagner, Harrison R. *United States Policy toward Latin America.* Stanford: Stanford University Press, 1970.

Waterston, Albert. *Development Planning: Lessons of Experience.* Baltimore: Johns Hopkins University Press, 1979.

Wesson, Robert. *The United States and Brazil: Limits of Influence.* New York: Praeger, 1981.

Whitaker, Arthur P. *Nationalism in Latin America, Past and Present.* Gainesville: University of Florida Press, 1962.

————. *The United States and Argentina.* Cambridge, MA: Harvard University Press, 1954.

Williams, William A. *The Tragedy of American Diplomacy.* Rev. 2d ed. New York: Dell, 1972.

Wilson, Theodore A. *The Marshall Plan, 1947–1951.* New York: Foreign
  Policy Association, 1977.
Wirth, John D. *The Politics of Brazilian Development, 1930–1954.*
  Stanford: Stanford University Press, 1970.
Wood, Bryce. *The Making of the Good Neighbor Policy.* New York:
  Columbia University Press, 1961.
World Bank. *Brazil: Human Resources Special Report.* Washington, DC:
  World Bank, 1979.
Young, Jordan M., ed. *Brazil, 1954–1964: End of a Civilian Cycle.* New
  York: Facts on File, 1972.
————. *The Brazilian Revolution of 1930 and the Aftermath.* New
  Brunswick, NJ: Rutgers University Press, 1967.

Articles

Acheson, Dean. "Waging Peace in the Americas." Department of State
  Bulletin 21 (September 26, 1949): 462–66.
Asencio, Diego C. "Brazil and the United States: Friendly Competitors." In
  Julian M. Chacel et al., eds., *Economic and Political Future*, 247–51.
  Boulder, CO: Westview Press, 1988.
Baer, Werner. "Socio-Economic Imbalances in Brazil." In Eric N. Baklanoff,
  ed., *The Shaping of Modern Brazil*, 137–54. Baton Rouge: Louisiana
  State University Press, 1969.
Baklanoff, Eric N. "Foreign Private Investment and Industrialization in
  Brazil." In Baklanoff, ed., *The Shaping of Modern Brazil*, 101–36.
  Baton Rouge: Louisiana State University Press, 1969.
Bento, Claudio Moreira. "Getúlio Vargas e a Evolucão Da Doutrina Do
  Exercito (Getúlio Vargas and the evolution of army doctrine)." *Revista
  do Instituto Historico e Geográfico Brasileiro* (Brazilian institute of
  history and geography review) 339 (1983): 63–71.
Bernstein, Barton J. "Truman and the Cold War." In Barton J. Bernstein, ed.,
  Politics and Policies of the Truman Administration, 15–77. Chicago:
  Quadrangle Press, 1970.
Bloomfield, Lincoln P. "China, the United States, and the United Nations."
  International Organization 20:4 (1966): 653–76.
Boldenheimer, Susanne. "Dependency and Imperialism: The Roots of Latin
  American Underdevelopment." *Policy and Society* 1:3 (1971): 327–57.
Bonilla, Frank. "A National Ideology for Development: Brazil." In
  Kalman H. Silvert, ed., *Expectant Peoples: Nationalism and
  Development*, 232–64. New York: Random House, 1966.
Bose, Tarum C. "The Point Four Programme: A Critical Study."
  International Studies 7:1 (1965): 66–97.

"Brazil: The Crisis and the Promise." *Fortune* 50 (November 1954): 119–25.

Dos Santos, Theotónio. "The Structure of Dependence." *American Economic Review* 60:2 (1970): 231–36.

Dulles, John W. F. "The Contribution of Getúlio Vargas to the Modernization of Brazil." In Eric N. Baklanoff, ed., *The Shaping of Modern Brazil*, 36–46. Baton Rouge: Louisiana State University Press, 1969.

————. "Post-Dictatorship Brazil, 1945–1964." In Eric N. Baklanoff, ed., *New Perspectives of Brazil*, 3–58. Nashville: Vanderbilt University Press, 1966.

Erb, Claude C. "Prelude to Point Four: The Institute of Inter-American Affairs." *Diplomatic History* 9 (Summer 1985): 249–60.

Farer, Tom J. "Reagan Country." *New York Review of Books* 27:20 (December 8, 1980): 9–10.

Figueres, Jose. "The Problems of Democracy in Latin America." *Journal of International Affairs* 9 (May 1955): 11–21.

Francis, Michael J. "Military Aid to Latin America in the U.S. Congress." *Journal of Inter-American Studies* 6 (July 1964): 389–404.

Furtado, Celso. "Political Obstacles to Economic Growth in Brazil." *International Affairs* 41 (April 1965): 253–55.

"Germany Invests Overseas." *Economist* 24 (September 26, 1953): 119–32.

Green, David. "The Cold War Comes to Latin America." In Barton Bernstein, ed., *Politics and Policies of the Truman Administration*, 149–95. Chicago: Quadrangle Press, 1970.

Haines, Gerald K. "Under the Eagle's Wing: The Franklin D. Roosevelt Administration Forges an American Hemisphere." *Diplomatic History* 1:4 (Fall 1977): 373–88.

Halle, Louis [Y, pseud.]. "On a Certain Impatience with Latin America." *Foreign Affairs* 18 (July 1950): 565–79.

Haring, Clarence H. "Vargas Returns in Brazil." *Foreign Affairs* 29 (January 1951): 308–14.

Hilton, Stanley. "Military Influence on Brazilian Economic Policy 1930–1945: A Different View." *Hispanic American Historical Review* 53 (February 1973): 71–94.

————. "The United States, Brazil, and the Cold War, 1945–1960: End of the Special Relationship." *Journal of American History* 68:3 (December 1981): 599–624.

Hoff-Wilson, Joan. "Economic Foreign Policy." In Alexander DeConde, ed., *Encyclopedia of American Foreign Policy*, 1:281–91. New York: Scribner's, 1978.

Holmes, Oliver. "Brazil: Rising Power in the Americas." *Foreign Policy Reports* 27 (October 15, 1945): 210–19.

Immerman, Richard H. "Guatemala as Cold War History." *Political Science Quarterly* 94 (Winter 1979–80): 575–99.

Iriye, Akira. "Culture and Power: International Relations as Intercultural Relations." *Diplomatic History* 3:2 (1979): 115–28.

Leontief, Wassily. "The Situation Is Desperate but Not Critical." *New York Review of Books* 27:19 (December 4, 1980): 45–46.

"Letter from Brazil." *Fortune* 35 (February 1947): 207–8.

Luce, Henry. Editorial. *Life* 10:61 (February 17, 1941): 3.

Magdoff, Harry. "Imperialism without Colonies." In Roger Owen and Robert Sutcliffe, eds., *Studies in the Theory of Imperialism*, 144–70. London: Longman, 1977.

McCann, Frank D. "Brazilian Foreign Relations in the Twentieth Century." In Wayne A. Selcher, ed., *Brazil in the International System: The Rise of a Middle Power*, 1–24. Boulder, CO: Westview Press, 1981.

McMahon, Robert J. "The Eisenhower Administration and Third World Nationalism: A Review Essay, Critique of the Revisionists." *Political Science Quarterly* 101:3 (1986): 453–73.

Maier, Charles S. "The Politics of Productivity: Foundations of American International Economic Policy after World War II." *International Organization* 31:4 (1977): 607–33.

Nash, Ray. "God, Coffee and Conversation." *U.N. World* 4 (October 1950): 36.

Nichols, Jeanette P. "Hazards of American Private Investment in Underdeveloped Countries." *Orbis* 4 (Summer 1960): 174–91.

Nunn, Frederick M. "Effects of European Military Training in Latin America: The Origins and Nature of Professional Militarism in Argentina, Brazil, Chile, and Peru, 1870–1940." *Military Affairs* 39:1 (February 1975): 1–7.

———. "Military Professionalism and Professional Militarism in Brazil, 1870–1940: Historical Perspectives and Political Implications." *Journal of Latin American Studies* 4:1 (May 1972): 29–54.

Paterson, Thomas G. "Foreign Aid under Wraps: The Point Four Program." *Wisconsin Magazine of History* 56:2 (1972–73): 119–26.

———. "The Quest for Peace and Prosperity: International Trade, Communism, and the Marshall Plan." In Barton J. Bernstein, ed., *Politics and Policies of the Truman Administration*, 78–112. Chicago: Quadrangle Press, 1970.

Rabe, Stephen G. "The Elusive Conference: United States Economic Relations with Latin America, 1945–1952." *Diplomatic History* 2:3 (Summer 1978): 279–94.

Rose, Tarum C. "The Point Four Programme: A Critical Study." *International Studies* 7:1 (1965): 66–97.

Rosen, Bernard C. "The Achievement Syndrome and Economic Growth in Brazil." *Social Forces* 42 (March 1964): 341–54.

Rowe, Edward T. "The United States, the United Nations, and the Cold War." *International Organization* 25:1 (1971): 59–78.

Santos, Eduardo. "Latin American Realities." *Foreign Affairs* 34 (January 1956): 245–57.

Santos, John F. "A Psychologist Reflects on Brazil and Brazilians." In Eric N. Baklanoff, ed., *New Perspectives of Brazil*, 233–63. Nashville: Vanderbilt University Press, 1966.

Sargeant, Howland. "Helping the World to Know Us Better." Department of State *Bulletin* 19 (November 28, 1948): 672.

Saunders, John V. D. "Education and Modernization in Brazil." In Eric N. Baklanoff, ed., *New Perspectives of Brazil*, 109–41. Nashville: Vanderbilt University Press, 1966.

"Sears, Roebuck in Rio." *Fortune* 41 (February 1950): 78.

Swansbrough, Robert H. "The Mineral Crisis and U.S. Interest in Latin America." *Journal of Politics* 38:1 (1976): 2–24.

"There Is Money to be Made in Brazil." *Business Week* (December 29, 1951): 97–98.

Thomas, Earl. "Emerging Patterns of the Brazilian Language." In Eric N. Baklanoff, ed., *The Shaping of Modern Brazil*, 264–300. Baton Rouge: Louisiana State University Press, 1969.

Trask, Roger. "George F. Kennan's Report on Latin America." *Diplomatic History* 2:3 (Summer 1978): 307–12.

————. "The Impact of the Cold War on United States-Latin American Relations 1945–1949." *Diplomatic History* 1:3 (1977): 271–84.

————. "Inter-American Relations." In Roberto Esquenazi-Mayo and Michael C. Meyers, *Latin American Scholarship since World War II: Trends in History, Political Science, Literature, Geography, and Economics*, 42–60. Lincoln: University of Nebraska Press, 1976.

Walker, J. Samuel. "The Cold War." In Gerald K. Haines and J. Samuel Walker, eds., *American Foreign Relations: A Historiographical Review*, 187–98. Westport, CT: Greenwood Press, 1981.

"What's Wrong in Brazil?" *U.S. News & World Report* 37 (September 3, 1954): 2.

Williams, William A. "The Age of Mercantilism: An Interpretation of the American Political Economy 1763–1828." *William and Mary Quarterly* 15:4 (1958): 419–37.

Newspaper Articles

"Brazil Begins Campaign to Lure Investments by U.S. Food Industry." *Wall Street Journal*, July 7, 1953.

Brooke, Jim. "Industrial Pollution Sears Brazil's 'Valley of Death.' " *Washington Post*, May 10, 1981.

Diehl, Jackson. "Brazilian Stresses Austerity." *Washington Post*, March 27, 1985.

"Goodbye to All That." *Washington Post*, February 8, 1981.

Lowenthal, Abraham F. "Manana Land No More." *Washington Post*, January 20, 1981.

Sculz, Tad. "Pioneers Carve a New Frontier." *Washington Post*, September 4, 1983.

Index